DATA
COMPRESSION

TECHNIQUES AND
APPLICATIONS

THOMAS J. LYNCH, Ph.D.

DATA
COMPRESSION
TECHNIQUES AND
APPLICATIONS

VNR VAN NOSTRAND REINHOLD COMPANY
New York

Production Service: Bernie Scheier & Associates
Designer: Adriane Bosworth
Copy Editor: Carol Dondrea
Illustrator: John Foster
Compositor: Syntax International

Printed in the United States of America

2 3 4 5 6 7 8 9 10—88 87 86

Library of Congress Cataloging in Publication Data

Lynch, Thomas J., 1932–
    Data compression techniques and applications.

    Includes bibliographies and index.
    1. Data compression (Computer science)   I. Title.
QA76.9.D33L96 1984   001.64   85-5756
ISBN 0-534-03418-7

Contents

Preface

Data compression is no longer a theoretical curiosity—it is now a practical requirement in many data systems. With the advances in electronic technology, it is now possible to implement in hardware many data compression techniques that formerly were executed only on large-scale general-purpose digital computers.

In the last few years there has been a growing interest in applying data compression techniques to actual data and communication systems in the commercial sector (compression of newspaper page masters for transmission), in the military (video compression for remotely piloted vehicles), and in many government agencies, such as NASA (image compression from spacecraft). In each potential application there is a need to learn what compression techniques are available, how they operate, and what the implementation considerations are for each technique.

This book is intended to provide this information and serve as a reference source for practicing communication engineers, computer scientists, information scientists, and data systems managers.

No experience in data compression is necessary in order to use this book since each compression technique is described separately and fully, and the necessary theoretical background is developed so that outside references are not needed.

The book is organized into three parts: Theoretical Background, Techniques, and Applications. Under *Theoretical Background*, the necessary theory is presented that allows the reader to understand the concepts and terminology used in later chapters. In addition, the fundamental data compression techniques of quantization and optimum source coding (e.g., the Huffman code) are described. Under *Techniques*, transform coding, predictive coding, nonredundant sample coding, and binary source coding are covered. Included also under *Techniques* are the practical implementation considerations of time coding, buffer control, error control, and system design. Under *Applications*, the use of data compression in the real world of speech transmission, telemetry, television, pictures, and data bases is described. The examples of specific applications are meant to be typical and illustrative, but certainly not exhaustive.

Examples and exercises have been included under *Theoretical Background* and *Techniques* for study and self-practice by the reader. Annotated references are given at the end of each chapter that guide the reader to more theoretical developments and examples of practical implementations. These references have been carefully chosen so that they reinforce the presentation in the individual chapter, but as such they do not constitute a complete bibliography on data compression.

The material in this book has been used in a course of the same name given by the author as part of the George Washington University Continuing Engineering Education Program.

Thomas J. Lynch

To my family:
Corinne, Maura and Brian

DATA
COMPRESSION

TECHNIQUES AND
APPLICATIONS

PART I

Theoretical
Background

CHAPTER 1

Introduction to Data Compression Theory

1.1 WHAT IS DATA COMPRESSION?

The idea of data compression is not new. There has always been an interest in economical communication, whether it be oral, written, electromagnetic, or digital. There is still today a widespread use of abbreviations and acronyms in both oral and written material. The Morse code, which speeded up telegraphy, is an example of an early data compression technique. In 1939 Dudley invented the VOCODER (VOice CODER), which made possible the transmission of voice over a very narrow telephone channel bandwidth. Digital communication is now replacing almost all forms of analog communication, and the need for digital data compression is growing. So now we return to the question: What is data compression?

Data compression is the reduction in the amount of signal space that must be allocated to a given message set or data sample set. This signal space may be in a physical *volume*, such as a data storage medium like magnetic tape; an interval of *time*, such as the time required to transmit a given message set; or in a portion of the electromagnetic spectrum, such as the *bandwidth* required to transmit the given message set. All these forms of the signal space—volume, time, and bandwidth—are interrelated:

$$\text{Volume} = f(\text{time} \times \text{bandwidth}) \tag{1.1.1}$$

Thus, a reduction in volume can be translated into a reduction in transmission time or bandwidth. The parameter to be reduced or compressed usually determines *where* the data compression operation will be performed in the system.

The importance of these parameters has varied over the years. At first there was—and, in fact, there still is—a great interest in reducing the bandwidth required to transmit analog signals, such as in telephony. Later, in systems such as facsimile, increasing the speed of transmission became important. And finally today the volume of the data is the critical parameter in need of reduction or compression in many systems, especially digital systems.

An obvious question is: Why data compression? Simply stated, one compresses data (1) to meet an operational requirement under an existing system performance constraint, such as limited bandwidth, or (2) to realize a cost saving in the design of a new system. As higher rate digital systems have been developed into the gigabit range, the data storage and secondary retrieval and dissemination requirements have increased the cost of data bases and communication links to remote terminals. So in spite of the availability of greater bandwidth in one part of the data system, data compression is still a desirable, if not necessary, operation in other parts of the system.

Data compression has been called other names in the literature; the two most common are data compaction and source coding. The name *source coding* is an information-theoretic term and is used to distinguish this type of coding from *channel coding*. In this book, the terms *data compression* and *source coding* are used interchangeably.

1.2 CLASSES OF DATA COMPRESSION

There have been many attempts to group data compression techniques into various classes but, to date, there is no agreed-upon classification. This is not too surprising since data compression, or source coding, is still a relatively new area in communication theory. There does seem to be agreement among most authors, however, that data compression techniques are either to some extent *reversible* or indeed *irreversible*. This dichotomy has been represented by many different names, including the following:

REVERSIBLE	IRREVERSIBLE
Noiseless coding	Fidelity-reducing coding
Redundancy reduction	Entropy reduction

Often, in attempting to classify a variety of techniques into only two classes, some techniques will be seen to fall into both classes—and this is the case with the classification of data compression techniques. Although no one classification system is perfect, we will nevertheless use in this book the second set of labels: *redundancy reduction* and *entropy reduction*. These names were first used for data compression classification by Blasbalg and Van Blerkom in 1962, and they can be described briefly as follows (the terms *entropy* and *redundancy* will be defined mathematically in Chapters 2 and 3, respectively):

An *entropy reduction* operation results in a reduction of information, since entropy is defined as the average information. The information lost can never be recovered, so an entropy reduction operation is irreversible.

A simple example of entropy reduction is the use of a threshold in monitoring sample values. In such a system, the only data transmitted is the time at which a sample value exceeds the preassigned threshold. If this event occurs infrequently then a large compression of signal space is achieved, but the original actual sample values cannot be reconstructed and thus information is lost.

We can think of data as a combination of information and redundancy (Shannon 1948). A *redundancy-reduction* operation removes, or at least reduces, the redundancy in such a way that it can be subsequently reinserted into the data. Thus, redundancy reduction is always a reversible process, and because of this property, there has always been a strong interest in redundancy-reduction techniques.

A simple example of redundancy reduction is the elimination of repetitive data. If one is sending data that does not change for a long period of time, then many consecutive data samples will be repetitive. An obvious technique for avoiding this is to count the number of repetitions between changes in the sample values and send only the changes along with the intervening repetition counts. Clearly the original data structure can always be reconstructed from this compressed data—no information is lost.

In Figure 1.1 we have classified the data compression techniques covered in this book under entropy reduction and redundancy reduction. The chapters in which the general techniques are discussed have been noted in various blocks in the figure; the chapters in which the specialized techniques can be found are noted in the blocks labeled "Other." The rationale behind this classification should become clear, as each technique is described in later chapters.

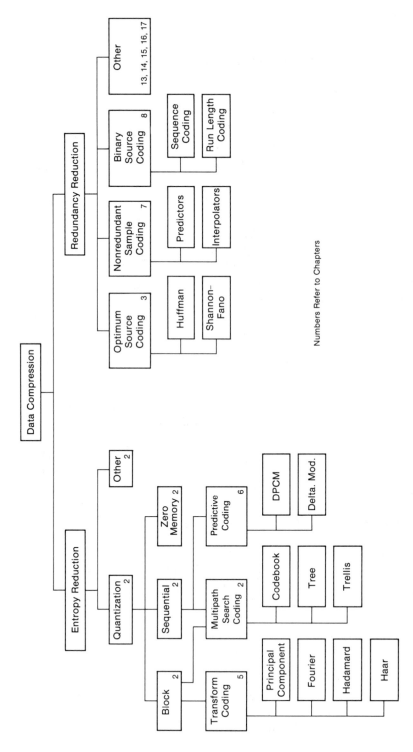

Figure 1.1 *A Classification of Data Compression Techniques*

1.3 APPROACH OF PART I

The title of Part I, Theoretical Background, is not meant to imply that all theoretical views of data compression will be described and rigorously derived. Since this book concentrates on the techniques and applications of data compression, only enough theoretical background will be given to enable the reader to understand the basis of the material in the rest of the book. Many of the topics in Part I, such as quantization and Huffman coding, are discussed throughout the book.

Chapter 2, Entropy Reduction, introduces the concept of compression with distortion, or irreversible compression. Rate distortion theory is introduced because it gives us a theoretical bound on the performance of a compression system under the constraint of a specified amount of average distortion. Irreversible techniques such as sampling, filtering, limiting, and statistical parameter extraction are examples of entropy reduction, but the basic technique of quantization is described most fully since it is the most used entropy-reduction technique if not the most used of all data compression techniques.

As can be seen in Figure 1.1, entropy reduction has been classified into two major classes: Quantization and Other. Many techniques other than quantization can be classified as entropy reduction—for example, the irreversible techniques mentioned above—but since these various techniques are typically very specially designed to preserve only some of the information content of the source, depending on the particular application, any attempt to describe these techniques would have very little use as a general reference for other design requirements. It would also be necessary to describe in detail the actual data of interest from the source, as well as the actual use of the particular information extracted from this data. Quantization, on the other hand, is more general in its application. If we can model the data source from a statistical standpoint, we can design efficient quantizers, as will be shown in Chapter 2.

In Figure 1.1, under quantization, there are three categories: block, sequential, and zero memory (or scalar). The zero memory type was studied and implemented first. In this type of quantization, each sample is quantized independently of all others with the same quantizer, hence the name zero memory quantization. The other two categories of quantization, block and sequential, take advantage of dependency between samples, and it has been shown that they can provide better performance than the scalar variety. The most common form of block quantization is transform coding, in which a transformation is first applied to a block of source samples, and then a fixed number of bits is allocated among the various transformed samples for their quantization in some optimal fashion. The techniques of transform coding are covered in Chapter 5. Under sequential quantization, there are two types: predictive coding and multipath search coding. Predictive coding has been in use for a number of years in the forms of differential pulse code modulation and delta modulation. In these techniques, the next sample is predicted and the difference between the predicted value and the actual value is quantized. These techniques are covered in Chapter 6. Multipath search coding is the newest form of quantization to be studied and the motivation behind this study is the performance bounds predicted by the rate distoration function for sources with memory. It is felt that this type of quantization, which is of the block type, has the potential for approaching the rate distortion bound with the least amount of design complexity (see Chapter 2).

Chapter 3, Redundancy Reduction, introduces the concept of reversible compression with zero distortion, or in some cases, limited minimal distortion. In the case of entropy reduction, we need models for continuous sources, but for redundancy reduction, we need models for discrete sources. The two models that have been used in the literature are the statistically independent model, and the Markov model. An important mathematical property of any data source is its entropy, defined as the average information available from the source. This entropy parameter has proven to be a valuable performance bound for redundancy-reduction compression techniques, and it can be computed for each of the above source models. Its units are bits per sample, so we can compare it to the average sample word length in bits per sample resulting from an actual compression scheme. When the average word length equals the entropy, we have reached the maximum compression ratio possible with no distortion. Obviously, we can use the entropy to compare and evaluate various compression techniques.

In Figure 1.1, redundancy reduction is divided into four classes: optimum coding, nonredundant sample coding, binary source coding, and other. The optimum coding techniques, the Shannon-Fano code and the Huffman code, are both designed for the statistically independent source. Nonredundant sample coders transmit only those samples that are designated nonredundant by a prespecified algorithm. These coders are covered in Chapter 7. Binary source codes compress blocks or strings of binary symbols, and these codes are covered in Chapter 8. There are other redundancy-reduction techniques, and examples of these may be found in Chapters 13 through 17. These chapters, which comprise Part III, cover the data compression application areas of speech, telemetry, television, pictures, and data bases. It should be noted that some of the compression techniques described in Part III are also of the entropy-reduction type, for example the VOCODER, which synthesizes speech at the receiver from transmitted speech parameters.

SUGGESTIONS FOR FURTHER READING

The following items are suggested for further reading and study:

Blasbalg, H., and Van Blerkom, R. "Message Compression." *IRE Trans. on Space Electronics and Telemetry*, vol. SET-8, no. 3, 1962, pp. 228–238.

Blasbalg and Van Blerkom distinguish between entropy reduction (ER) and redundancy reduction (RR) and give some examples of each type—e.g., ER: statistical monitoring, and RR: prediction, run-length coding and the Shannon–Fano code.

Davisson, L. D., and Gray, R. M. *Data Compression.* Vol. 14 of *Benchmark Papers in Electrical Engineering and Computer Science.* Stroudsburg, Pa.: Dowden, Hutchinson and Ross, Inc., 1976.

This book is actually a collection of papers in the field of data compression compiled by Davisson and Gray. The papers have been grouped into the following categories: noiseless source coding, distortion-rate theory, quantization, block data compression and nonblock data compression. At the beginning of each group, the editors comment briefly on the papers that follow.

Shannon, C. E. "A Mathematical Theory of Communication," *Bell System Technical Journal*, vol. 27, 1948, pp. 379–423, 623–656.

In this frequently referenced paper, Shannon lays the theoretical groundwork for data compression (source coding) as well as channel coding. The concepts of information, entropy, and redundancy are defined for the discrete as well as the continuous case.

CHAPTER 2

Entropy Reduction

2.1 INTRODUCTION

In any system in which information from a data source must be transmitted, there are two fundamental questions:

1. What information should be transmitted?
2. How should it be transmitted?

These questions are based on the rather obvious goals of transmitting only that information which is required and of having it received with minimum or zero distortion.

In the past, the second question was addressed first, and the answer was formalized by Shannon in 1948 in his famous paper. In this paper, Shannon defines a quantity C, called the *capacity* of the communications channel, and proves that symbols can be transmitted over this channel at an arbitrarily small error rate as long as the symbol rate does not exceed the channel capacity C. The encoding of the source information into the channel symbols has been called the channel coding problem, and it has received considerable attention over the last 35 years. (See Appendix A for a brief review of channel coding techniques.)

The first question, however, did not receive theoretical attention until 1959, when Shannon defined and developed the *rate distortion function* as the minimum average source rate $R(D)$, in bits per sample, that would guarantee a distortion no greater than a specified distortion D at the receiver as long as $R(D) \le C$. The rate distortion concept is inherently different from the channel coding concept. Whereas in the channel coding problem we are trying to achieve or approach error-free transmission, in the rate distortion concept we are seeking to find a minimum source rate that will keep the end-to-end average distortion in the system less than or equal to a specified distortion. This is typically what one must do in designing a data compression system, and for this reason Berger, in his book on rate distortion theory (1971), called the theory a "mathematical basis for data compression."

The source rate, of course, depends on the way in which the original data are encoded. This encoding is the main problem of data compression, and it typically involves the transformation from a continuous data source to a discrete set of time samples with discrete amplitude values. In order to understand this continuous-to-discrete transformation we need a measure of the average information of the source. This measure is called the *entropy*, and when we code the source in such a way that some information is lost we call this an *entropy-reduction* compression operation.

In this chapter we define and describe information entropy, and rate distortion. In addition, we describe the continuous-to-discrete transformations of sampling and quantization, with a particular emphasis on quantization since it is often an integral part of many data compression techniques (such as differential pulse code modulation, or DPCM.)

2.2 CONTINUOUS AND DISCRETE DATA SOURCES

Many data sources, such as speech and images, are usually in continuous form, both in time and amplitude, at the input to the data encoding and transmission system. At this point in the system the original signals may be sampled or not, depending on how they are modulated onto the carrier frequency for transmission. There are two types of modulation systems: continuous wave and pulse. Continuous wave modulation is, in turn, of two basic types: amplitude modulation (AM) and angle modulation [this latter including phase modulation (PM) and frequency modulation (FM)]. In continuous wave modulation systems, the original signal is modulated onto the carrier in continuous or analog form. In pulse modulation systems, however, the original signal is sampled and each sample value is used to control some characteristic of a transmitted pulse, as is obvious from the names of these various schemes: pulse amplitude modulation (PAM), pulse duration modulation (PDM), and pulse position modulation (PPM). In these three pulse modulation systems, the original continuous signal is converted to a discrete time-sampled signal, but each sample is still continuous in amplitude. In the pulse modulation scheme called pulse code modulation (PCM), the discrete time samples are converted to discrete amplitude values by the process of quantization. The two operations of time sampling and amplitude quantization are closely coupled to data compression.

Time sampling has a theoretical basis: *the sampling theorem.* This theorem states that if a bandlimited time signal (bandlimit = B Hz) is sampled instantaneously at a constant rate at least twice the highest frequency component of the signal ($2B$), then the resulting samples contain all the information in the original signal. If the signal interval is T seconds, then $2BT$ samples will completely specify it. This sampling rate of twice the highest spectral component is also called the Nyquist rate or the Nyquist frequency. If the sampling rate exceeds this Nyquist rate, then the samples contain not only all the original information but some redundancy as well. Herein lies a potential for data compression—removing the redundancy from these samples. The concept of redundancy and redundancy reduction is covered in Chapter 3.

In order to have a usable received signal, it is necessary to reconstruct the original signal from the sample values. Theoretically, this is accomplished in the time domain by adding up the amplitudes of sin t/t-type time functions centered on the samples and weighted by their amplitudes. Mathematically, for n samples spaced $1/2B$ seconds apart, the reconstructed signal is given by:

$$f(t) = 2B \sum_{j=1}^{n} a_j \frac{\sin \pi(2Bt - j)}{\pi(2Bt - j)} \tag{2.2.1}$$

where a_j is the amplitude of the jth sample. In actual practice, this reconstruction operation is done in the frequency domain by passing the samples through a low-pass filter with a bandwidth equal to B. It can be shown that the response of such an idealized filter to a series of impulses weighted by a_j is exactly the expression in (2.2.1).

Sampling of an actual signal usually results in some small information loss since actual signals do not have sharply defined frequency spectra, and thus have low-energy spectral components extending beyond one-half a practical sampling frequency. But even more information is lost in an operation that takes place before sampling, namely filtering. This is usually in the form of a low-pass or band-pass filtering operation in which frequency components of the original signal are eliminated.

In PCM, amplitude quantization is the second step, after sampling, that is used to convert a continuous, or analog, signal into a time-discrete, or digital, signal. Quantization is not only an integral part of PCM, but also an integral part of some data compression schemes, such as transform coding (Chapter 5) and DPCM (Chapter 6).

From a philosophical viewpoint, quantization is the most fundamental form of entropy reduction, since once we quantize the amplitude values, we can never reconstruct them exactly. By contrast, the sampling theorem tells us that time sampling at or above the Nyquist rate preserves all the information in $2BT$ samples. Thus, time sampling could be considered the most fundamental form of redundancy reduction, provided it's at the Nyquist rate.

2.3 THE CONCEPT OF INFORMATION AND ENTROPY

2.3.1 Discrete Source Entropy

Information is defined in terms of a measure of uncertainty. The less likely a message, the larger its information, and the more likely a message, the smaller its information. Mathematically, we would say that the information content of a message or an event to be transmitted is a monotonically decreasing function of its probability of occurrence. The *negative logarithm* of the probability is such a function, and it exhibits an interesting feature: When the probability is equal to one, it equals zero. This is intuitively satisfying since it says you receive no information when you know, beyond any doubt, what event is going to occur.

Thus, the information content of the *i*th event of a discrete memoryless source (that is, a source with no dependence between successive events) is called the *self-information* and is given by:

$$I_i = -\log_2 P_i \quad \text{in bits} \tag{2.3.1}$$

where P_i is the probability of the *i*th event, $0 \leq P_i \leq 1$. The logarithm function can be to any base, but the base 2 will be used in this book since it is easier to relate to binary coding schemes and also base 2 is widely used in the literature. The function of (2.3.1) is shown in Figure 2.1 for some discrete values of P_i.

If we average the information content of all possible events from a source, we have what is known as the *entropy* of the source. For the case of a discrete

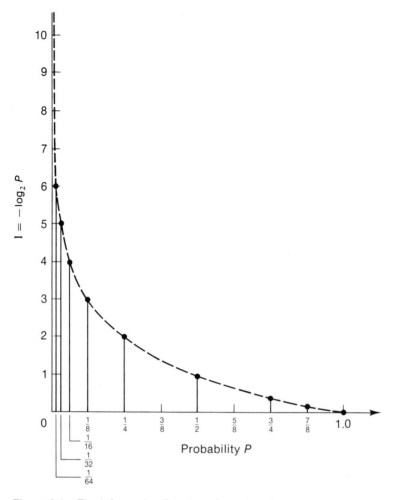

Figure 2.1 *The Information Function, $I = -log_2 P$.*

memoryless source, the entropy is simply the average information as defined in (2.3.1) or

$$H = -\sum_{i=1}^{M} P_i \log P_i \tag{2.3.2}$$

where M is the total number of discrete values.

A memoryless source is actually a special case of a more generally defined source with memory. For the more general source we allow successive events to have some dependence on one another, which of course is more typical of real sources. In order to define the entropy of a general discrete source we must use a limit as follows.

Consider a random vector $\mathbf{X}$ made up of n successive discrete-valued events generated by a random stationary source.* Let $P(x)$ be the probability that the vector $\mathbf{X}$ takes the value x (a specific n-event sequence). Then the entropy on a vector basis is:

$$H(\mathbf{X}) = -\sum_{\text{all } x} P(x)\log_2 P(x) \tag{2.3.3}$$

The entropy per event is simply the limit of the per event vector entropy or:

$$H = \lim_{n \to \infty} \{n^{-1} H(\mathbf{X})\} \tag{2.3.4}$$

The entropy H as defined by (2.3.4) is actually called the *entropy rate* since it is computed on a per sample basis in bits per sample or bits per symbol.

2.3.2 Continuous Source Entropy

So far we have defined information and entropy for a discrete source only. What about a continuous source? If we go back to the original definition of self-information in Equation (2.3.1), we see that as we go from a discrete source to a continuous source, we increase the number of values of the index i. As $i \to \infty$, then $P_i \to 0$, and $-\log P_i \to \infty$, so we say that a continuous source has events with infinite information. Likewise the entropy, which is the average information, will also be infinite. There are two ways out of this dilemma: a practical way and a mathematical way. The practical way simply recognizes the fact that any physical process has to be observed by an instrument or by a human sense, such as vision, each of which has a finite resolving power and dynamic range. Thus, the measurements and observations of physical processes will always have a finite, but possibly quite large, entropy. A mathematical approach is to use the probability density, $p(x)$, of a continuous source in the expression for entropy as follows:

$$h(x) = -\int_{-\infty}^{\infty} p(x)\log p(x)dx \tag{2.3.5}$$

---

* A stationary source is defined as follows: Let $t = (t_1, t_2, \ldots, t_n)$ be a time index vector, and, for all integers k, $(t + k) = (t_1 + k, t_2 + k, \ldots, t_n + k)$. Then if $P_{t+k}(x) = P_t(x)$, the source is stationary.

where

$$\int_{-\infty}^{\infty} p(x)dx = 1 \qquad (2.3.6)$$

The entropy defined by (2.3.5) is actually called the *differential entropy* and can be used to characterize continuous sources. Most of the properties of discrete entropy apply to differential entropy, except for one important difference: Differential entropy is not an absolute measure of uncertainty as is discrete entropy. A simple example will illustrate this: If

$$p(x) = \begin{cases} \dfrac{1}{k}, & 0 \le x \le k \\ 0, & \text{elsewhere} \end{cases}$$

then

$$h(x) = \log k$$

If $k < 1$, $h(x) < 0$ or the differential entropy is negative for certain values of k. But the discrete entropy $H(x) \ge 0$ as can be seen from equation (2.3.2).

2.4 THE CONCEPT OF RATE DISTORTION

As was stated in Section 2.1, the rate distortion function is the minimum average source rate, $R(D)$, in bits per event, that guarantees that the average distortion will be no greater than the value D as long as $R(D) \le C$, the channel capacity. It should be understood that $R(D)$ and C have the same equivalent units here: bits per event, bits per sample, or bits per word. In this context C is sometimes called the code rate. In the literature, channel capacity is also defined in terms of the channel bandwidth, which leads to the units of bits per second for C. One can relate these two systems of units by the simple formula:

$$C(\text{bits/sample}) \times \text{Sample rate(samples/sec)} = C(\text{bits/sec}) \qquad (2.4.1)$$

The sample rate is used here since we are dealing with sampled data sources. Thus for source coding, the terms entropy rate, source rate, rate distortion, and channel capacity all have the same units: bits per sample.

The rate distortion function is mathematically defined as the minimum average mutual information between the source and receiver subject to the constraint of a fixed average distortion D. This average distortion is a function of a distortion measure (sometimes called a fidelity criterion), $d(x, y)$, which defines the "cost" of not reproducing the value of the original source sample x exactly in the output sample y.

The following formulas are the basic definitions in rate distortion theory. For a continuous amplitude source:

$$R(D) = \min_{(\text{all } p(y/x))} I(x; y) = \min \iint dx\, dy\, p(x)p(y/x)\frac{\log p(y/x)}{q(y)} \qquad (2.4.2)$$

where

$$q(y) = \int dx\, p(x)p(y/x)$$

satisfying:

$$\text{Average distortion} = \iint dx\, dy\, p(x)p(y/x)d(x, y) \le D \qquad (2.4.3)$$

For a discrete amplitude source:

$$R(D) = \min_{(\text{all } P(Y/X))} I(X; Y) = \min \sum_X \sum_Y P(X)P(Y/X)\frac{\log P(Y/X)}{Q(Y)} \qquad (2.4.4)$$

where

$$Q(Y) = \sum_X P(X)P(Y/X)$$

satisfying:

$$\text{Average distortion} = \sum_X \sum_Y P(X)P(Y/X)D(X, Y) \le D \qquad (2.4.5)$$

At first glance, the minimization of the mutual information in these equations seems to be just the opposite of what one would normally want to do. In most communication systems, we want to maximize the transfer of useful information—or, in other words, maximize the mutual information between source and receiver. But in the case of the rate distortion function, we are trying to find the minimum rate at which information about the source can be sent to the receiver and yet have the average distortion not exceed a specified amount D. The explanation for this apparent anomaly is easy to understand when we keep in mind what we're *given* in each case. In the case of the channel capacity, we are given the channel and must maximize the mutual information over all possible sources. In the case of the rate distortion function, we are given the source and must minimize the mutual information over all possible channels, subject to the distortion constraint.

The minimization of the mutual information over all possible channels in the $R(D)$ case is really in terms of all possible $p(y/x)$ or $P(Y/X)$ in (2.4.2) and (2.4.4), respectively. These conditional probability functions define a different channel in each case, and it is possible that this minimization process might result in a probability function that would correspond to an unrealizable channel. For this reason, the rate distortion function is used primarily as a theoretical lower bound against which the actual source rate is compared in a real system.

Another way of using the $R(D)$ function is as follows. If the maximum average distortion is given, then one can theoretically determine if it is possible to stay within this distortion limit by computing the rate distortion function, $R(D)$, and comparing it to C. Only if $C \geq R(D)$ can the distortion specification be met. A rigorous proof of this theorem can be found in Berger's book on rate distortion theory (1971), but the following nonrigorous explanation from the same book is very useful.

The noisy coding theorem of Shannon (1948) tells us that if we are given a discrete stationary source with entropy rate H and a discrete memoryless channel with capacity C, then if $H \leq C$, the output of the source can be encoded for transmission over the channel with an arbitrarily small frequency of errors (or equivocation). If $H > C$, then it is possible to encode the source so that the equivocation is less than $H - C + \varepsilon$, where ε is arbitrarily small, but there is no method of encoding that gives an equivocation less than $H - C$.

Now we can use this theorem with the rate distortion function as follows. If $H > C$, then an average of at least $H - C$ bits of information per source sample are lost in traversing the channel. If we are to encode the source to meet the distortion requirement D with $R(D)$ bits per source sample, then $H - R(D)$ bits are lost in transmission. But if $H > C$, no less than $H - C$ bits per source sample can be lost, or

$$H - R(D) \geq H - C \tag{2.4.6}$$

giving

$$R(D) \leq C \tag{2.4.7}$$

The rate distortion function $R(D)$ is a monotonically nonincreasing function of D and is only defined for $0 \leq D \leq D_{\max}$. Also

$$R(D) = 0 \quad \text{for } D \geq D_{\max} \tag{2.4.8}$$

and for the discrete memoryless source with $d(x, y) = 0$ when $x = y$, and $d(x, y) = 1$ when $x \neq y$:

$$R(0) = H, \text{ the entropy} \tag{2.4.9}$$

An example of a rate distortion function for a continuous source is as follows: For the Gaussian memoryless source of mean μ and variance σ^2,

$$p(x) = (2\pi\sigma^2)^{-1/2} \exp\left[-\frac{(x-\mu)^2}{2\sigma^2}\right]$$ (2.4.10)

the rate distortion function for the squared error distortion measure,

$$d(x, y) = (x - y)^2$$ (2.4.11)

is found to be (see Berger 1971, p. 99):

$$R(D) = \frac{1}{2} \log_2 \frac{\sigma^2}{D}, \qquad 0 \le D \le \sigma^2$$ (2.4.12)

A plot of (2.4.12) is shown in Figure 2.2. In this figure we have plotted $R(D)$ as a function of (D/σ^2) for convenience, but the shape of the curve is still typical of $R(D)$ functions for continuous sources as follows:

1. It vanishes for $D \ge D_{max}$.
2. It approaches ∞ as $D \to 0$.
3. It has a concave upward shape.

An example of a rate distortion function for a discrete source is as follows. For a discrete, memoryless binary source, with output A or B:

$$P(A) = p$$
$$P(B) = 1 - p$$ (2.4.13)

From (2.4.9), we have that $R(0) = H(p)$ where

$$H(p) = -p \log_2 p - (1 - p) \log_2(1 - p)$$ (2.4.14)

Now for a distortion measure of

$$d(x, y) = 0 \qquad (x = y)$$
$$d(x, y) = 1 \qquad (x \ne y)$$ (2.4.15)

the rate distortion function is found to be:

$$R(D) = H(p) - H(D), \qquad 0 \le D \le p$$ (2.4.16)

and this is plotted in Figure 2.3 for different values of p. If we look at the case where $p = 0.5$ (A and B are equally likely to occur), we see that $R(0) = 1 = H$.

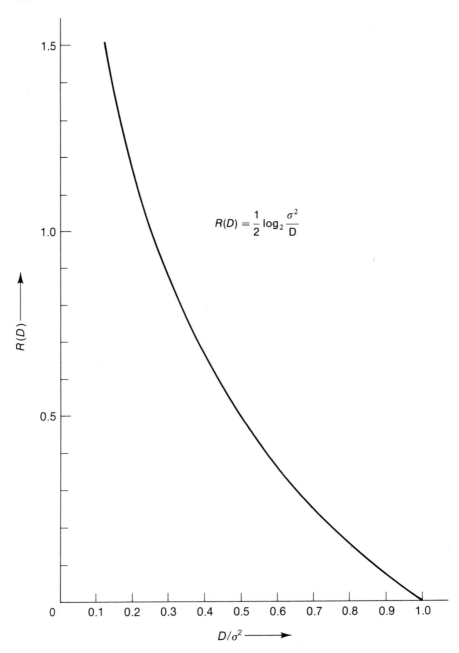

Figure 2.2 *Rate Distortion Function for a Gaussian Memoryless Source with Squared Error Distortion.*

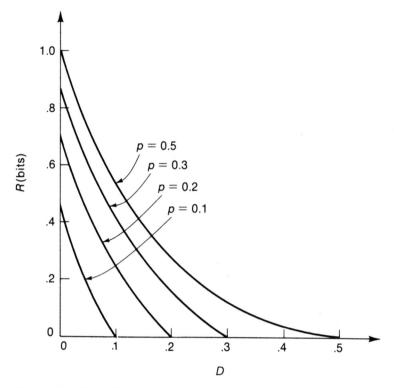

Figure 2.3 *Rate Distortion Function for a Memoryless Binary Source with P(A) = p and P(B) = 1 − p. From: Toby Berger, Rate Distortion Theory: A Mathematical Basis for Data Compression, © 1971, p. 48. Reprinted by permission of Prentice-Hall Inc., Englewood Cliffs, N.J.*

When the average distortion $D = p$, we see that $R(D) = 0$. As we lower the probability, p, of output A we see that the $R(D)$ curve descends, which means we can use a smaller number of bits per symbol for coding purposes. At this point, a legitimate question might be: From a practical standpoint, how can we use less than one bit per symbol to encode a binary source? The answer is through *block coding*, wherein we code a sequence of symbols at one time in such a way as to approach the rate distortion bound. This type of coding is discussed in Section 2.5.

2.5 QUANTIZATION

It has been stated that *quantization* is the most common form of data compression. This is true, not only from the standpoint of analog-to-digital conversion (for PCM, for example) but also because of the fact that quantization is an integral part of many other data compression techniques, such as transform coding (see Chapter 5) and DPCM (see Chapter 6). In the quantization of data samples, we can look at the design approach in two ways: (1) We are given a fixed number of quantization levels and we wish to minimize the "quantization noise." This noise, or distortion, is due to the fact that a whole range of amplitude values within a quantization *interval* is being represented by only one amplitude value (called the quantization *level*) within that interval. (2) We are given a fixed quantization nosie or distortion, and we wish to minimize the average number of bits per sample that will meet the distortion specification. The latter approach is related to the rate distortion function and, in fact, the rate distortion function can be used as a theoretical lower bound for the source rate for certain source models.

There are basically three forms of quantization:

1. Zero-memory quantization
2. Block quantization
3. Sequential quantization

Zero-memory quantization is the quantization of one analog sample at a time. *Block quantization* is the representation of a block of input analog samples by a block of output values chosen from a discrete set of possible output blocks. *Sequential quantization* is the quantization of a sample sequence using information from neighboring samples on a block or nonblock basis.

2.5.1 Zero-Memory Quantization

In this type of quantization, we are trying to minimize the quantizing noise, given a fixed number of quantizing levels. We quantize one sample at a time and use the same quantizer characteristic for all samples. This type of quantization is sometimes called *scalar* as well as *zero memory*.

INPUT-OUTPUT CHARACTERISTICS

A zero-memory quantizer input-output characteristic takes the form of a staircase function, as shown in Figure 2.4. Two types of quantizer characteristics are shown, the difference between them being the way in which the zero region is handled. In part (a), the zero input interval produces a zero output level, and this is called a *midtread quantizer*. In part (b) there are two input intervals around zero: the positive interval produces a positive level, and the negative interval, a negative level. Because of this there is no zero level in the output and this is called a *midriser quantizer*.

A quantizer is usually characterized by the number of output levels, M.

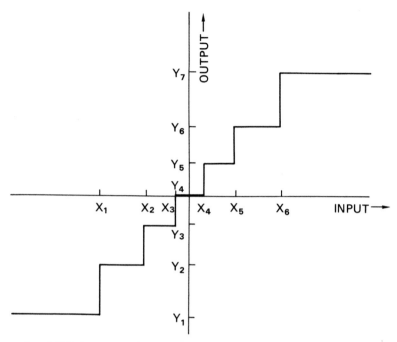

A. MIDTREAD QUANTIZER CHARACTERISTIC

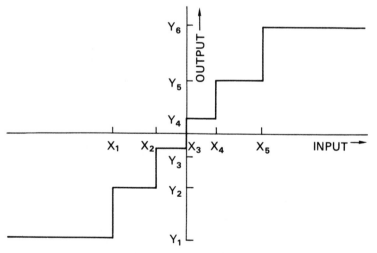

B. MIDRISER QUANTIZER CHARACTERISTIC

Figure 2.4 *Quantizer Characteristics.*

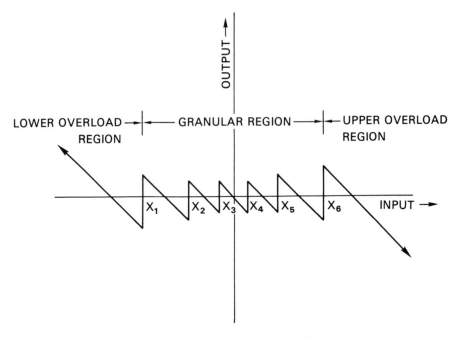

Figure 2.5 *Quantizing Error for Midtread Quantizer of Fig. 2.4(a).*

The quantizing error is simply the difference between the input analog value and the corresponding discrete output level. In Figure 2.5 the quantizing error for the *midtread quantizer* of Figure 2.4(a) is shown. As can be seen from Figure 2.4, the upper and lower input intervals are left unbounded, so that a large positive or negative value results in an overload condition corresponding to a large quantizing error, as shown in Figure 2.5. The quantizing error function is normally divided into the upper and lower overload regions and the granular noise region, as shown in Figure 2.5.

Exercise 2.1

Sketch the quantizing error for the *midriser quantizer* shown in Figure 2.4(b) and compare with Figure 2.5.

The instantaneous quantizing error between the input x and the output

$y(x)$ is defined as

$$Q_E = y(x) - x \qquad (2.5.1)$$

The average distortion in terms of a mean-square distortion measure is given by

$$D = \int_{-\infty}^{\infty} [y(x) - x]^2 p(x) dx \qquad (2.5.2)$$

If the variance σ^2 of the input x is known, then a signal-to-noise ratio can be written as:

$$\text{SNR} = 10 \log_{10}\left(\frac{\sigma^2}{D}\right) \qquad \text{in dB} \qquad (2.5.3)$$

UNIFORM QUANTIZER

The uniform quantizer is of special interest because of its simplicity. If one assumes that $p(x)$ is constant within each input interval (e.g., the input probability density is uniform over the quantizer's range), then an approximation to its mean-square average distortion is obtained as follows.

Consider the uniform quantizer characteristic shown in Figure 2.6. Let the output level y_i always be in the midpoint of the input interval $\Delta = x_i - x_{i-1}$. Also, assume that the probability density $p(x)$ is constant in the interval $\Delta = x_i - x_{i-1}$ and equal to $p(x_i)$. Then the distortion can be written in terms of a summation of distortions in each Δ interval. The intervals are classified into three regions as follows (see Figure 2.5):

Lower overload region: $\Delta = x_1 - x_0,$ $x_1 \gg x_0$
Granular region: $\Delta = x_i - x_{i-1},$ $2 \le i \le M - 1$
Upper overload region: $\Delta = x_M - x_{M-1},$ $x_M \gg x_{M-1}$

Then

$$D = \sum_{i=1}^{M} \int_{x_{i-1}}^{x_i} [y_i(x) - x]^2 p(x_i) dx \qquad (2.5.4)$$

For simplicity, assume that the contribution of the overload region is negligible, so that $p(x_1) = p(x_M) = 0$, or

$$D = -\sum_{i=2}^{M-1} p(x_i) \left\{ \frac{[y_i(x) - x]^3}{3} \right\}\Bigg|_{x_{i-1}}^{x_i} \qquad (2.5.5)$$

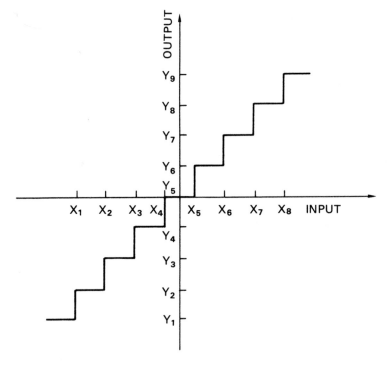

Figure 2.6 *Uniform Quantizer With M = 9.*

But

$$x_i = y_i(x) + \frac{\Delta}{2}$$

$$x_{i-1} = y_i(x) - \frac{\Delta}{2}$$

Substituting

$$D = \frac{1}{12} \sum_{i=2}^{M-1} p(x_i)\Delta^3 \qquad (2.5.6)$$

But

$$\sum_{i=2}^{M-1} p(x_i)\Delta \approx 1$$

Thus,

$$D = \frac{\Delta^2}{12} \tag{2.5.7}$$

If the probability density function (pdf) is:

$$p(x) = \frac{1}{2V} \quad (-V \le x \le V) \tag{2.5.8}$$

then the variance of the input signal is

$$\sigma^2 = \int_{-\infty}^{\infty} x^2 p(x) dx$$

Using (2.5.8),

$$\sigma^2 = \frac{V^2}{3} \tag{2.5.9}$$

Then

$$\text{SNR} = 10 \log_{10} \left(\frac{V^2}{3} \right) \left(\frac{12}{\Delta^2} \right) \tag{2.5.10}$$

But

$$\Delta = \frac{2V}{M}, \quad \text{for } M \gg 2 \tag{2.5.11}$$

Then

$$\text{SNR} = 10 \log_{10} M^2 = 20 \log_{10} M \tag{2.5.12}$$

If we use a binary code for M, then $M = 2^n$ and

$$\text{SNR} = 20n \log_{10} 2 = 6n \quad (\text{in dB}) \tag{2.5.13}$$

Although (2.5.13) was derived with simplifying assumptions, this linear relationship between SNR and n, the quantization bits, indeed holds for other memoryless sources and quantizers. This is shown in Table 2.1 where n has been replaced by r. See Section 2.5.5 for the development of Table 2.1.

Table 2.1   *SNR Comparisons for Zero-Memory Quantizers*

Source	Distortion Measure	Quantization	SNR (in dB) (r = bits/sample)
Gaussian Memoryless	$(x - y)^2$	Rate distortion bound	$6r$
Gaussian Memoryless	$(x - y)^2$	Uniform quantizer with entropy coding	$6r - 1.5$
Gaussian Memoryless	$(x - y)^2$	Optimum nonuniform quantizer with entropy coding	$6r - 2.45$
Gaussian Memoryless	$(x - y)^2$	Optimum nonuniform quantizer	$6r - 4.35$
Continuous Memoryless	$(x - y)^2$	Uniform quantizer	$6r - 7.27$

NONUNIFORM QUANTIZERS

A data source with a uniform probability density function is not very common, so the obvious question is how should one arrange the sizes of the input intervals in the case of a nonuniform pdf—or in other words, what is the optimum quantization?

In 1948, Bennett modeled a quantizer for a nonuniform probability density with a monotonically increasing nonlinearity, $E(x)$, followed by a uniform quantizer of M levels. From this model, he developed an approximate formula for the mean-square distortion as follows:

$$D = \frac{1}{12M^2} \int_{L_1}^{L_2} \frac{p(x)}{[\lambda(x)]^2} \, dx \qquad (2.5.14)$$

where: $p(x)$ is the input probability density

$\lambda(x) = E'(x)/(L_2 - L_1)$

$L_2 - L_1$ is the quantizer range

$E'(x)$ is the slope of the nonlinear function

In 1951 Panter and Dite also analyzed quantization noise by using the mean-square error between input and output of the quantizer as the distortion measure. By assuming that the input probability density function is constant over a given quantization interval, they set the derivative of the distortion with respect to the level equal to zero and obtained the following results:

1. The quantization level should be at the midpoint of the quantization interval.

2. The total distortion is at a minimum when the mean-square distortion over an interval is independent of the interval. This minimum distortion

is given by:

$$D_{min} = \frac{1}{12M^2} \left[\int_{-V}^{V} p^{1/3}(x)dx \right]^3 \tag{2.5.15}$$

where M is the number of levels, $p(x)$ is the symmetrical input density function, and V is one-half the amplitude range. Panter and Dite also indicated an approximate technique for choosing quantization levels, given the input probability density function.

Lloyd (1982)* and Max (1960) also analyzed quantization noise using the same distortion measure, the mean-square error. However, Lloyd and Max did not assume a constant input probability density over an interval, and by setting the derivative of the distortion with respect to the level y_i and the interval limit x_i equal to zero, they obtained the following results:

1. Each interval limit should be midway between the neighboring levels, that is,

$$x_i = \frac{(y_i + y_{i+1})}{2} \tag{2.5.16}$$

2. Each level should be at the centroid of the input probability density function over the interval for that level, that is,

$$\int_{x_{i-1}}^{x_i} (x - y_i)p(x)dx = 0 \tag{2.5.17}$$

Lloyd and Max defined an iterative procedure for finding the levels given the input probability density function, and computed the interval limits and levels for an input signal with a normally distributed amplitude probability density.
    A comparison of the Panter–Dite and Lloyd–Max procedures for quantization is shown in Figure 2.7. The iterative procedure of Lloyd–Max is as follows for M even and a symmetric distribution, as shown in Figure 2.7(b):

1. Pick y_1.
2. Compute x_1 from

$$\int_{x_0}^{x_1} (x - y_1)p(x)dx = 0$$

3. Compute $y_2 = 2x_1 - y_1$.

---

* It should be noted that this procedure was developed by S.P. Lloyd in 1957 in an unpublished Bell Labs memorandum, and was later published in 1982.

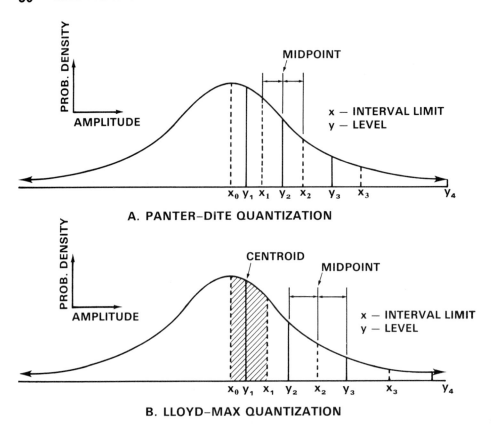

Figure 2.7 *Quantization by the Methods of Panter-Dite and Lloyd-Max.*

4. Continue the process until $y_{M/2}$.
5. Check if $y_{M/2}$ is the centroid of the area of $p(x)$ between $x_{M/2-1}$ and ∞, namely,

$$\int_{x_{M/2-1}}^{\infty} (x - y_{M/2})p(x)dx = 0$$

6. If not, go back to step 1 and pick another y_1. Repeat entire procedure.

COMPANDING

Another way of looking at a nonuniform quantizer is by way of a nonlinear function followed by a uniform quantizer. This arrangement has been called *companding*, and it is entirely equivalent to nonlinear quantization.

In some applications, such as speech, it is not practical to use different nonuniform quantizers for different source probability distributions. Instead, one would prefer a quantizing characteristics that would be relatively insensitive to changes in the input signal probability distribution. It has been found that a logarithmic function provides this insensitivity or "robustness," as it is sometimes called.

Two logarithmic functions have been in use: the μ-law curve and the A-law curve (see Gersho 1977). The μ-law curve is used for PCM speech companding in the United States, Canada, and Japan and it looks as follows:

$$y(x) = \frac{V \log(1 + \mu x/V)}{\log(1 + \mu)} \tag{2.5.18}$$

The A-law curve is used for speech companding in PCM speech systems in Europe, and it looks as follows:

$$y(x) = \begin{cases} \dfrac{Ax}{1 + \log A}, & 0 \le x \le \dfrac{V}{A} \\[2ex] \dfrac{V + V \log(Ax/V)}{1 + \log A}, & \dfrac{V}{A} \le x \le V \end{cases} \tag{2.5.19}$$

Because companding involves logarithmic nonlinear functions, it is also referred to as "log PCM" in the literature.

2.5.2 Block Quantization

Instead of quantizing each sample individually with the same quantizing function, we can, in general, approximate a sequence or block of n samples by a sequence selected from a codebook of S sequences that most closely matches the input sequence. More specifically, this optimum match is based on the minimization of the distortion between the two sequences. This is the general definition of *block quantization*, which is sometimes called *vector quantization* in the literature. Clearly, there is an opportunity for compression here over the zero-memory (or scalar) approach since we can identify which one of the S sequences we are using with $\log_2 S$ bits to give a code rate, r, of:

$$\text{Average number of bits per sample, } r = \frac{\log_2 S}{n} \tag{2.5.20}$$

If, in the zero-memory case, we quantize the entire n-sample sequence, wherein each sample has M levels, we have:

$$\text{Average number of bits per sample, } r = \frac{\log_2 M^n}{n} = \log_2 M \tag{2.5.21}$$

Now, rate distortion theory tells us that the expression in (2.5.20) approaches $R(D)$ as $n \to \infty$ (see Berger 1971). Thus we have:

$$\frac{\log_2 S}{n} \to R(D) \leq H \leq \log_2 M \qquad (D > 0)$$

$$(n \to \infty)$$

(2.5.22)

Having established a theoretical motivation for block quantization, the next question is: How do we do it? The method that has received a lot of attention and use was first published by Huang & Schultheiss (1963). It is really a two-step process. We first apply an orthogonal transformation to the samples in the sequence, and then quantize each resulting transformed sample with a different quantizer in order to minimize the average distortion for a given code rate. This given code rate is usually in the form of a fixed number of bits that are available for encoding the entire transformed block. Of course, this restricted number of bits is less than the total number of bits required to encode the original block, a sample at a time, resulting in a compression. The way in which the limited number of bits is used to encode the transformed samples is called the "bit allocation" procedure, and it is driven by the fact that the transformed samples have different variances. As a matter of fact, these transformed samples can be ordered in terms of decreasing variance, and typically the variance drops off quickly as we go through these ordered components. A common interpretation of this rapid decrease in variance is that the orthogonal transformation "packs" more information into the lower ordered transformed samples, or components, and thus allows for a more efficient quantization, resulting in an appreciable data compression.

This method of block quantization by transformation and bit allocation is called *transform coding* and it will be described in more detail in Chapter 5. For a general, theoretical treatment of block quantization, see Gersho (1979). Another more recent approach to block quantization is called *multipath search coding* and it will be described in the next section.

2.5.3 Sequential Quantization

In block quantization we optimize the source coding of only the samples in the given block, independent of the samples in the previous or subsequent blocks. In sequential quantization we remove this restriction and allow a coding system based on overlapping blocks of data that can code one sample at a time instead of one block at a time. There are basically two types of sequential quantizers: predictive coders and multipath search coders.

Predictive coders include the well-known techniques of delta modulation and differential pulse code modulation (DPCM). Both of these techniques predict the next sample value and then quantize the difference between the predicted value and the actual value. The prediction is based on a weighted combination of previously predicted values. Delta modulation uses a 1-bit quantizer, whereas DPCM uses a k-bit quantizer. Both techniques are covered in detail in Chapter 6.

Multipath search coders (MSC) use future as well as previous sample values in order to select a quantized version of a given input sample. Because of this property, they are sometimes called delayed-decision coders, look-ahead coders, or tree or trellis encoders. Compression is obtained by virtue of the fact that the selected quantized version of the input sample sequence is coded into a binary channel sequence wherein each sample is represented by one binary digit. Unlike delta modulation we are not limited by the amplitude quantization of one bit per sample for sample reconstruction at the receiving end since we have the quantized-sequence-to-binary-sequence mapping function available at the receiver. There are three types of MSC techniques in use at the present time (Fehn and Noll 1982): codebook coding, tree coding, and trellis coding.

Codebook coding (sometimes called *list coding*) involves the use of a codebook of 2^n highly probable n-sample sequences. From the codebook, one sequence is selected each time that minimizes the distortion between itself and the actual input sequence. The index of the selected sequence is coded as an n-bit word and sent to the receiver, where the same codebook is stored. If each sample has M levels, then there are M^n possible sequences but only 2^n "typical" sequences, giving a compression ratio of

$$R = \frac{\log_2 M^n}{\log_2 2^n} = \log_2 M \qquad (2.5.23)$$

The techniques of *tree and trellis coding* make use of geometric structures that are normally used in convolutional coding for the purpose of error control. The main difference is the fact that the structures that are normally used for *decoding* in convolutional coding are used for *encoding* in quantization. (See Appendix A for a brief description of convolutional coding techniques.) Instead of storing the 2^n "typical" sequences as a list, as in the case of codebook coding, each typical sample sequence is stored as a sequence of branches in a tree structure. When a sequence is selected, its corresponding tree path is transmitted as a binary sequence, with each bit corresponding to a direction at each sequential node of the tree. An intuitive justification for this approach could be stated as follows: As we move away from the first sample in the sequence, the subsequent samples are usually less correlated to the first sample and thus have more possible values—like a tree structure. A similar procedure is used in trellis coding since the trellis structure is really a truncated tree structure. Unlike codebook coding, tree and trellis coding can be done on an incremental basis (one sample at a time) instead of on a block basis. This is very similar to maximum-likelihood or Viterbi decoding of convolutional channel codes (see Appendix A).

There is a growing interest in tree/trellis coding since, theoretically, the $R(D)$ performance bound can be approached arbitrarily closely by means of these codes with less complexity than with block codes. The key task is to specify the tree or trellis that will provide the near optimum rate. A generic tree structure for source coding is shown in Figure 2.8. It is easy to show that a tree code of depth l with α branches per node and β letters per branch contains α^l code words, each of length $l\beta$. The code rate on a sample (or branch) basis is:

$$r = \frac{\log_2 \alpha^l}{l} = \log_2 \alpha \text{ in bits per sample} \tag{2.5.24}$$

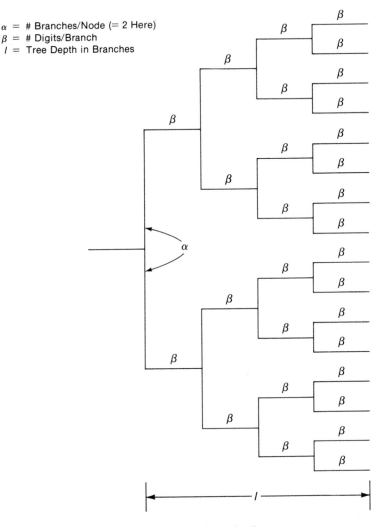

α = # Branches/Node (= 2 Here)
β = # Digits/Branch
l = Tree Depth in Branches

Figure 2.8   *Schematic Tree Code for Quantization*

which is independent of the tree depth l, and for $\alpha = 2$ is equal to one bit per sample.

In tree coding there are three design tasks:

1. Population of the tree branches
2. Encoding by tree searching
3. Decoding by generation of the branches from the transmitted tree path

Tasks 1 and 2 are the most difficult, and task 3 is the most straight-forward. In fact, task 3 can be implemented by means of a shift register with appropriate taps and modulo 2 adders. (See Figures A.2 and A.3 in Appendix A).

Task 1, the population of the branches, is the most challenging task since here one is trying to predict what "typical" sequences will look like from a given source. There are various techniques for choosing these "typical" sequences, some using random coding techniques. [See Fehn and Noll (1982) and Stewart et al. (1982) for a description of these techniques.]

Task 2, tree searching, can be expedited by an algorithm called the (M, L) algorithm (see Berger 1971). This algorithm sequentially searches only M paths at a time as it moves into the tree an additional node at a time, and stops when it reaches node level L. Not surprisingly, this algorithm is very similar to the Viterbi algorithm for convolutional code decoding. (See Appendix A.)

2.5.4 Quantizers and Rate Distortion Bounds

Since a quantizer is an entropy-reduction type of data compression, it naturally produces distortion, and this distortion is inversely related to the number of quantization levels (see equation (2.5.15), for example). Now, the greater the number of quantization levels, M, the higher the code rate, r, in bits per sample, and thus we have a trade-off between rate and distortion. For this reason, it is useful to compare the performance of various quantization schemes to the rate distortion bound for the same source.

We saw in Section 2.4 that a Gaussian memoryless source with a squared-error distortion measure has a rate distortion function given by equation (2.4.12):

$$R(D) = \frac{1}{2} \log_2 \frac{\sigma^2}{D}, \qquad 0 \le D \le \sigma^2$$

This function is shown in Figure 2.2 and also in Figure 2.9. If we were to quantize such a continuous source, the function of equation (2.4.12) would establish the lower bound for the code rate versus distortion for a squared-error distortion measure. The next question is: How close can we come to this curve with an ideal quantizer? We define an ideal quantizer in this case to be one

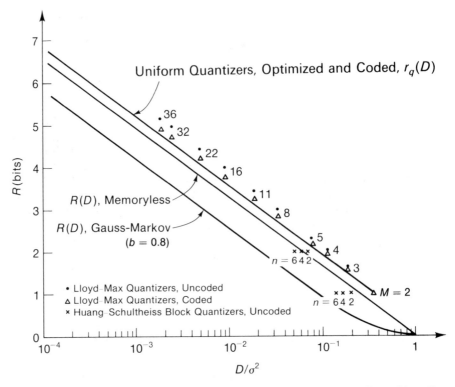

Figure 2.9 *Comparisons of Various Quantization Schemes and Rate Distortion Functions. From: Toby Berger, Rate Distortion Theory: A Mathematical Basis for Data Compression, © 1971, p. 149. Reprinted by permission of Prentice-Hall Inc., Englewood Cliffs, N.J.*

that is designed for minimum code rate (bits per sample) given a fixed distortion, D. It should be noted that most quantizer optimizations [such as those due to Lloyd (1982) and Max (1960)] involve the minimization of the error or distortion, given a fixed number of quantization levels (or, in other words, a fixed code rate).

The minimum rate quantizer has been defined by Goblick and Holsinger (1967) for the Gaussian memoryless source, and the resulting rate as a function of distortion is given by

$$r_q(D) = \frac{1}{4} + \frac{1}{2} \log_2 \frac{\sigma^2}{D} \qquad (2.5.25)$$

(see Figure 2.9).

We can achieve this optimum quantizer rate by a combination of uniform quantization followed by a so-called optimum block-to-variable-length code. This latter type of coding is also called "entropy coding" (since it approaches the entropy of the source) and it is typically one of two types: Shannon–Fano or Huffman. Both types will be described in detail in Chapter 3. The important result here is that one can approach to within one-quarter bit per sample the rate distortion bound for a Gaussian memoryless source by using uniform quantization followed by optimum block-to-variable-length coding. This two-step approach to quantization is not only a theoretical means of optimization but is actually used as an alternative to one-step nonuniform quantization in some systems, such as DPCM (see Chapter 6).

Having established an ideal zero-memory quantizer rate versus distortion function, we now ask how well some actual zero-memory quantizers compare to this function. The Lloyd–Max nonuniform quantizer for the Gaussian memoryless source and the squared-error distortion measure performs within one-half bit per sample of the ideal quantizer r_q and within 1 bit per sample of the rate distortion bound [$R(D)$ memoryless], as can be seen by the round dots in Figure 2.9. Here each round dot corresponds to a different number, M, of quantization levels. If in each of these cases we were to apply entropy coding, we would approach even closer to the ideal quantizer function—and these rates are represented by the triangles in Figure 2.9.

What about block quantization? Before we can look at the rate versus distortion performance of block quantizers, we need a rate distortion bound for a source that is appropriate for block quantization. Since block quantizers take advantage of the sample-to-sample correlation in a block, we need a model of a source with memory. Such a source is the stationary Gauss–Markov source, where the probability of each sample amplitude is given by equation (2.4.10), and the correlation function for a shift of k samples is given by:

$$\varphi(k) = \sigma^2 |b|^k, \qquad -1 < b < 1 \tag{2.5.26}$$

The resulting rate distortion function for the squared-error criterion is (see Berger 1971):

$$R(D) = \frac{1}{2} \log_2 \left(\frac{1 - b^2}{D} \right) \qquad D \leq \frac{1 - b}{1 + b} \tag{2.5.27}$$

This $R(D)$ function is plotted in Figure 2.9 for $b = 0.8$ and it is appreciably lower (by about three-quarters of a bit) than the $R(D)$ function for the Gaussian memoryless source. Using the method of orthogonal transformation followed by optimum bit allocation, as developed by Huang and Schultheiss (1963), we can plot some r versus D results for block lengths, n, of two, four, and six samples (see Figure 2.9). These results shown on Figure 2.9 are for two coding rates: 1 bit per sample and 2 bits per sample. As can be seen from the plotted points, the longer the block, the closer to the $R(D)$ lower bound. More details on this technique are given in Chapter 5.

For sequential quantization, the tree code approach has the potential of approaching the rate distortion bound for a time-sampled, memoryless source (see Berger (1971), p. 209). This theoretical result has inspired much research into finding practical tree or trellis codes that will allow a code rate of 1 bit per sample at a reasonably low distortion. Recently, Pearlman (1982) has shown through simulations that nearly optimum rate distortion function performance can be obtained by quantizing a memoryless source with a variation on the trellis code approach called the *sliding-block code*. In fact, Pearlman's coder shows a code rate less than that predicted by the ideal quantizer [see equation (2.5.25)].

2.5.5 Quantizer Comparison by SNR for Memoryless Sources

These comparisons of the theoretical performance of quantizers are often given in the literature in terms of signal-to-quantizing-noise-ratio (SNR). We can summarize the preceding results in terms of SNR as follows:

FOR THE GAUSSIAN MEMORYLESS SOURCE

1. The $R(D)$ lower bound in bits per sample is:

$$R(D) = r = \frac{1}{2} \log_2 \frac{\sigma^2}{D}, \qquad 0 \le D \le \sigma^2 \qquad \text{[equation (2.4.12)]}$$

$$\text{SNR} = 10 \log_{10} \frac{\sigma^2}{D} = 10 \log_{10} 2^{2r}$$

$$\text{SNR} = 6r \quad \text{in dB} \tag{2.5.28}$$

2. The ideal quantizer rate is given by:

$$r_q = \frac{1}{4} + \frac{1}{2} \log_2 \frac{\sigma^2}{D} \qquad \text{[equation (2.5.25)]}$$

In order to compare different quantization schemes consistently, we keep the code rate constant. Then for the ideal quantizer:

$$r_q = r = \frac{1}{4} + \frac{1}{2} \log_2 \frac{\sigma^2}{D}$$

$$\text{SNR} = 10 \log_{10} \frac{\sigma^2}{D} = 10 \log_{10} 2^{2(r - 1/4)}$$

$$\text{SNR} = 6r - 1.5 \quad \text{in dB} \tag{2.5.29}$$

The constant in (2.5.29) is sometimes referred to as the "1.5 dB gap" in the literature.

3. For the optimum nonuniform quantizer with entropy coding, Gersho (1977) has empirically found the following expression to fit the data

tabulated by Max (1960) for quantizers with more than eight levels:

$$SNR = 6r - 2.45 \qquad \text{in dB} \tag{2.5.30}$$

4. For optimum nonuniform quantization without entropy coding, using equation (2.5.15), Gersho (1977) assumed a large M and neglected overload noise to obtain:

$$SNR = 6r - 4.35 \qquad \text{in dB} \tag{2.5.31}$$

FOR ANY CONTINUOUS MEMORYLESS SOURCE

5. For the uniform quantizer, assume an overload of 4σ, $(V = 4\sigma)$. Then

$$\Delta = \frac{8\sigma}{M - 2} \tag{2.5.32}$$

for a midtread quantizer (see Figure 2.6). For $M \gg 2$,

$$\Delta = \frac{8\sigma}{M} \tag{2.5.33}$$

But

$$D = \frac{\Delta^2}{12} \tag{2.5.7}$$

Then

$$D = \frac{16\sigma^2}{3M^2}$$

$$SNR = 10 \log_{10} \frac{\sigma^2}{D}$$

$$SNR = 10 \log_{10} \left(\frac{3M^2}{16} \right)$$

If $M = 2^n$

$$SNR = 6n - 7.27 \tag{2.5.34}$$

For comparison purposes, let $n = r$; then

$$SNR = 6r - 7.27 \qquad \text{in dB} \tag{2.5.35}$$

These results are summarized in Table 2.1 on page 28.

2.6 OTHER ENTROPY-REDUCTION TECHNIQUES

There are many other types of entropy-reduction techniques besides quantization. Quantization is certainly the most widely used and, in conjunction with sampling, it is the basis of all analog-to-digital conversion schemes. There are other schemes, however, in which we intentionally reduce or lose information, and many of these depend to a large extent on the particular application of the received data.

Simple operations such as *pulse counting, zero-crossing detection,* and *limiting* are some typical examples of techniques in which a large portion of the signal information is lost in order to preserve only that information which is directly useful to the particular application. More complex techniques actually process the raw data and extract useful parameters. An example of such a technique is statistical parameter extraction, which is defined as follows.

In the transmission of data from signal sources, such as scientific experiments on board spacecraft, it is often necessary to send information only about the statistics of the data. These statistics may be defined in terms of *statistical parameters*, and hence we have the entropy-reduction process of *statistical parameter extraction*. Such statistical parameters as mean and variance require computation, so the question is : What measurements should be made in order to allow the computation of these statistical parameters? An example of such measurement techniques is the method of *quantiles* used on histograms.

A quantile is defined as follows: For a cumulative probability distribution $F(x)$, the pth quantile z_p is the lower limit of all x such that $F(x) > p$, where $0 \leq p \leq 1$. For example, for $p = 1/2$, the quantile is called the *median*; for $p = 1/4$, the quantile is called the *quartile*, and so on.

Quantiles have been studied for use in parameter estimation for spacecraft telemetry and it has been found that as few as four quantiles will given reasonably good estimates of the mean and standard deviation of a given histogram (Posner 1964).

HIGHLIGHTS

- The efficient encoding of data in order to preserve useful information is the main purpose of data compression, typically involving the transformation from a continuous data source to a discrete set of time samples with discrete amplitude values, and in some cases, subsequent compression of these discrete values.

- The continuous to discrete transformation is accomplished by time sampling and quantization. Time sampling, if done at the Nyquist rate, is a reversible process, but quantization is irreversible, and hence a fundamental form of entropy reduction.

- The distortion due to quantization is inversely proportional to the number of quantizing levels, and thus there is a basic trade-off between distortion and rate, in bits per sample.

- A very useful theoretical performance bound for quantization is the rate distortion function, which is the minimum rate, in bits per sample, that can be used, at the same time keeping the average distortion less than a specified amount.

- For a Gaussian memoryless source, the rate distortion bound can be approached to within one-quarter bit per sample with a combination of uniform quantization and entropy coding.

- For a source with memory, such as the Gauss–Markov source, block quantization or sequential quantization will approach the rate distortion bound more closely than zero-memory quantization.

- At the present time there is increasing interest in a form of sequential quantization called tree/trellis coding, which has the potential of approaching the rate distortion bound for a source with memory with less complexity than block quantization.

SUGGESTIONS FOR FURTHER READING

The following items are suggested for further reading and study:

Andrews, H. C. "Bibliography on Rate Distortion Theory." *IEEE Trans. on Info. Theory*, vol. IT-17, no. 2, March 1971, pp. 198–199.

Bennett, W. R. "Spectra of Quantized Signals." *Bell Sys. Tech. J.* vol. 27, July 1948, pp. 446–472.

In this paper, a zero-memory quantizer is modeled with a monotonically increasing nonlinearity followed by a uniform N-level quantizer, and an approximate expression for the mean-square quantizing error is obtained.

Berger, T. *Rate Distortion Theory*. Englewood Cliffs, N.J.: Prentice-Hall, 1971.

This book gives a thorough treatment of rate distortion theory as well as some applications to data compression.

Cattermole, K. W. *Principles of Pulse Code Modulation*. London: Elsevier, 1969.

In this book, the basic characteristics of PCM are covered and the A-law method of companding is explained.

Fehn, H. G., and Noll, P. "Multipath Search Coding of Stationary Signals With Applications to Speech." *IEEE Trans. on Comm.*, vol. COM-30, no. 4, April 1982, pp. 687–701.

This is a good survey of multipath search coding including: codebook coding, tree coding, and trellis coding. Applications to speech waveforms are also given.

Gersho, A. "Asymptotically Optimal Block Quantization." *IEEE Trans. on Info. Theory*, vol. IT-25, no. 4, July 1979, pp. 373–380.

In this article, the earlier work of Bennett (1948) on quantization modeling for a mean-square error criterion is generalized for block quantization.

Gersho, A. "Quantization." *IEEE Communication Society Magazine*, September 1977, pp. 16–29.

In this survey article, Gersho briefly covers the development of quantization techniques, optimum quantization, and companding.

Goblick, T. J., and Holsinger, J. L. "Analog Source Digitization: A Comparison of Theory and Practice." *IEEE Trans. on Info. Theory*, vol. IT-13, April 1967, pp. 323–326.

In this paper, the authors compare the ideal quantizer for the Gaussian memoryless source to the rate distortion bound for the same source and find that there is difference of only one-quarter bit/sample in code rate or 1.5 dB in SNR between the two.

Huang, J. J. Y., and Schultheiss, P. M. "Block Quantization of Correlated Gaussian Random Variables." *IEEE Trans. on Comm. Sys.*, vol. CS-11, no. 3, 1963, pp. 289–296.

Block quantization is achieved by first transforming the correlated samples into uncorrelated samples by an orthogonal matrix multiplication and then assigning a different number of quantizing bits to each uncorrelated sample under the constraint of a fixed total number of bits per block.

IEEE Trans. on Info. Theory, vol. IT-28, no. 2, March 1982 (Special issue on quantization).

This special issue contains 14 papers and two correspondence items on quantization, covering such topics as: vector quantizers, Lloyd–Max quantizers, two-dimensional quantizers, and feedback quantizers.

Jayant, N. S., ed. *Waveform Quantization and Coding*. New York: IEEE Press, 1976.

This book is a collection of 69 papers on quantization, grouped under such topics as: speech, pictures, implementation, and noise effects. An extensive bibliography on quantization is also included.

Lloyd, S. P. "Least Squares Quantization in PCM." *IEEE Trans. on Info. Theory*, vol. IT-28, no. 2, March 1982, pp. 129–137.

This is the same material that appeared in the unpublished 1957 Bell Labs report by Lloyd and that preceded similar work by Max in 1960. The technique involved is an iterative procedure for optimum scalar quantization and has been called the Lloyd–Max quantization technique.

Max, J. "Quantizing for Minimum Distortion." *IRE Trans. on Info. Theory*, vol. IT-6, no. 1, March 1960, pp. 7–12.

Max develops an iterative procedure for optimum quantization without the constant probability density assumption made by Panter and Dite.

Nyquist, H. "Certain Topics in Telegraph–Transmission Theory." *AIEE Transactions on Comm. and Electronics*, vol. 47, 1928, pp. 617–644.

In this paper, Nyquist defines the minimum sampling rate of twice the upper bandlimit, now called the *Nyquist rate*.

Oliver, B. M., Pierce, J. R., and Shannon, C. E. "The Philosophy of PCM." *Proceedings of IRE*, vol. 36, November 1948, pp. 1324–1331.

This historic paper describes the basic characteristics of PCM and discusses its advantages over FM.

Panter, P. F., and Dite, W. "Quantization Distortion in Pulse Count Modulation with Non-Uniform Spacing of Levels." *Proceedings of IRE*, vol. 49, January 1951, pp. 44–48.

In this paper, Panter and Dite develop a scheme for optimum quantization based on the assumption of constant probability density within an input interval.

Papoulis, A. "Error Analysis in Sampling Theory." *Proc. IEEE*, vol. 54, July 1966, pp. 947–955.

In this paper, Papoulis examines the errors introduced in reconstructing a sampled bandlimited time function.

Pearlman, W. A. "Sliding Block and Random Source Coding with Constraint Size Reproduction Alphabets." *IEEE Trans. on Comm.*, vol. COM-30, no. 8, August 1982, pp. 1859–1867.

Simulations using a trellis-type quantization code for both a Gaussian source and a Laplacian source show performances (in bits/sample) better than that obtained by uniform quantizing followed by entropy coding.

Posner, E. C. "The Use of Quantiles for Space Telemetry Data Compression." *National Telemetering Conf. 1964*, Los Angeles, Calif., Proc. No. 1–3.

In this paper, the use of four quantiles for estimating the mean and variance of a large data set is discussed.

Shannon, C. E. See Chapter 1, Suggestions for Further Reading.

Shannon, C. E. "Coding Theorems for a Discrete Source with a Fidelity Criterion." *IRE National Convention Record—1959*, Part 4, pp. 142–163.

In this paper, Shannon further develops the concept of the source rate, given a fidelity criterion, and defines the rate distortion function.

Stewart, L. C., Gray, R. M., and Yinde, Y. "The Design of Trellis Waveform Coders." *IEEE Trans on Comm.*, vol. COM-30, no. 4, April 1982, pp. 702–710.

A new approach to the design of trellis waveform coders uses a training sequence of actual data from the source to improve the trellis decoder.

Wintz, P. A., and Kurtenbach, A. J. "Waveform Error Control in PCM Telemetry." *IEEE Trans. on Info. Theory*, vol. IT-14, 1968, no. 5, pp. 650–661.

In this paper, the authors consider the errors due to sampling, quantization, and channel noise in optimizing the communication system.

CHAPTER 3

Redundancy Reduction

3.1 INTRODUCTION

Redundancy-reduction techniques remove or reduce that portion of the data which can be reinserted or reconstituted at the receiving end of the system with little or no residual distortion. For this reason, redundancy reduction has been called reversible coding, transparent coding, and noiseless coding in the literature.

In Chapter 2, we examined entropy reduction in relation to the rate distortion bound on the code rate in bits per sample. The source was continuous, and after time sampling, the main operation on the data was quantization into discrete amplitude levels. In this chapter we look at the application of redundancy reduction to this resulting discrete source with the goal of reducing the number of bits required to encode a block of data with zero or minimal distortion. We review the entropy of a discrete source and, in particular, a source with memory—the Markov source. From this we define redundancy and the compression ratio. The optimum noise-less coding techniques of Huffman and Shannon–Fano are described in detail with illustrative examples. These techniques are introduced early in the book because of their importance as components in many data compression systems. This will be seen later both in Part II and Part III.

3.2 THE SOURCE MODEL

An information source typically produces an output which is an amplitude that is a function of one or more variables. The two most common independent variables are time and position. However, position may be made equivalent to time in many systems (e.g., when the data are scanned picture elements). As was explained in Section 2.2, the time variable may be discrete or continuous and the source may produce an output that is discrete or continuous in amplitude. In this chapter, we consider the discrete time and amplitude case only. The discrete time variable is obtained by time sampling, and the discrete amplitude function is obtained by quantization. We now examine the concept of discrete source models with two different outputs: statistically independent samples and Markov-dependent samples.

3.2.1 Statistically Independent Samples

If we consider only the case of time dependence, then the output amplitude may be written as:

$$m_k = f_q(t_k) \tag{3.2.1}$$

where the function f_q includes the amplitude quantization and t_k represents the sampling intervals with $k = 1, 2, 3, \ldots$. The sample m_k can take any one of M levels ($q = 1, 2, 3, \ldots, M$). If the samples are statistically independent, then

$$P(m_k, m_{k-1}) = P(m_k)P(m_{k-1}) \tag{3.2.2}$$

In other words, there is no dependence between samples.

This source is a useful reference source as well as the appropriate source for the optimum noiseless codes: the Huffman code and the Shannon–Fano code. These codes operate on one sample at a time and utilize no intersample dependence.

3.2.2 Markov-dependent Samples

When there is dependence between samples, the value of a given sample depends on the values of contiguous previous samples. This dependence can be modeled by a Markov process. In general, a Markov process of order v is defined by the conditional probability

$$P(m_k/m_{k-1}, m_{k-2}, m_{k-3}, \ldots, m_{k-v})$$

Thus, the intersample dependency stretches over a sequence of v samples. Many analysts have used the first-order Markov ($v = 1$) model, which is defined by the conditional probability:

$$P(m_k/m_{k-1})$$

For the first-order model, if we let $m_{k-1} = i$ and $m_k = j$, then the joint probability of values i and j occurring is:

$$P(i, j) = P(i)P(j/i) \tag{3.2.3}$$

This is in contrast to the statistically independent model, where

$$P(i, j) = P(i)P(j)$$

[see (3.2.2)].

Both the statistically independent and the Markov-dependent source models are used in analyzing and designing data compression schemes for discrete sources. Neither model, however, is very realistic. A source with statistically independent samples is not very common, nor is a source in which intersample dependence is over only one previous sample. But what these models lack in realism, they make up for in simplicity.

A situation often arises in which we have insufficient information about the source to enable us to choose an appropriate model for it. In this case we design a compression scheme that is independent of the source statistics in its performance. Such a code is called a *universal* code (Davisson 1973) and more will be said about this type of coding in Chapter 8.

3.3 INFORMATION, ENTROPY, AND REDUNDANCY

Since the purpose of redundancy reduction is to reduce the *redundancy* of a source of information, we must first define what is meant by information and redundancy for the general source.

3.3.1 Information and Entropy

We restrict our attention to the source that is discrete in time and amplitude, and, accordingly, define the information content of an individual sample from such a source as:

$$I_{m_k} = -\log P(m_k/m_{k-1}, m_{k-2}, \ldots, m_{k-v}) \qquad (3.3.1)$$

for the Markov model, (with all logarithms to base 2) and

$$I_{m_k} = -\log P(m_k) \qquad (3.3.2)$$

for the statistically independent model. We write the entropy of a source as the average information content, or in the case of the Markov model:

$$H_M = - \sum_{A_k A_{k-1} A_{k-2}, \ldots, A_{k-v}} P(m_k, m_{k-1}, m_{k-2}, \ldots, m_{k-v})$$
$$\times \log P(m_k/m_{k-1}, m_{k-2}, \ldots, m_{k-v}) \qquad (3.3.3)$$

where A_k represents the set of possible values of the sample m_k, and the summation is evaluated over the product ensemble formed by the $v + 1$ samples. In particular, for the first-order Markov process:

$$H(y/x) = - \sum_{i=1}^{M} \sum_{j=1}^{M} P(i, j) \log P(j/i) \qquad (3.3.4)$$

where $P(i, j) = P(i)P(j/i)$. For the statistically independent model, we have

$$H_{SI} = - \sum_{i=1}^{M} P(m_i) \log P(m_i) \qquad (3.3.5)$$

This corresponds to the memoryless source defined in Chapter 2 [equation (2.3.2)]. In the special case where $P(m_i) = 1/M$, then: $H_{SI} = \log M$. This value of entropy, $\log M$, is the *maximum* entropy value for a source with M messages.

Exercise 3.1

Given an independent source with the following message probabilities:

MESSAGE	PROBABILITY
A	1/2
B	1/4
C	1/8

D	1/16
E	1/32
F	1/64
G	1/128
H	1/128

a. Compute the information of each message.

b. Compute the entropy of the source.

c. If the message probabilities were changed to maximize the entropy, what would these probabilities be and what would be the maximum entropy?

Example 3.1

Consider the source described by the following probabilties:

i	$P(i)$
A	1/4
B	1/4
C	1/4
D	1/4

$P(j/i)$ $\overset{i}{\underset{j}{\diagdown}}$	A	B	C	D
A	1/2	1/2	0	0
B	1/4	1/2	1/4	0
C	1/8	1/8	1/2	1/4
D	0	1/2	0	1/2

The entropy of this source is given by (3.3.4):

$$H(y/x) = -\sum_{i=1}^{M} \sum_{j=1}^{M} P(i,j) \log P(j/i)$$

where $P(i,j) = P(i)P(j/i)$. Using the given values of $P(i)$ and $P(j/i)$, we find:

$P(i,j)$ $\overset{i}{\underset{j}{\diagdown}}$	A	B	C	D
A	1/8	1/8	0	0
B	1/16	1/8	1/16	0
C	1/32	1/32	1/8	1/16
D	0	1/8	0	1/8

Then, multiplying the nonzero elements of $P(i, j)$ by the corresponding $\log_2$ values of $P(j/i)$ row by row, we get:

$$H(y/x) = -[1/8(-1) + 1/8(-1)$$
$$+ 1/16(-2) + 1/8(-1) + 1/16(-2)$$
$$+ 1/32(-3) + 1/32(-3) + 1/8(-1) + 1/16(-2)$$
$$+ 1/8(-1) + 1/8(-1)]$$
$$= 1\tfrac{5}{16}$$

This value should be compared to that of the same source with independent samples, where:

$$H(x) = -\sum_{i=1}^{M} P(i) \log P(i)$$

With $P(i) = 1/4$, $H(x) = 2$.

Exercise 3.2

a. Compute the entropy of the source given by:

i	$P(i)$
A	1/2
B	1/4
C	1/8
D	1/8

i j	A	B	C	D
A	1/2	1/2	0	0
B	1/4	1/2	1/4	0
C	1/8	1/8	1/2	1/4
D	0	1/2	0	1/2

b. If the source were statistically independent, what would be the entropy?

3.3.2 Redundancy

We can think of a data set as made up of information and redundancy. Information is the commodity we wish to preserve and thus we must transmit it.

Redundancy, however, is like extra baggage that we wish to avoid transporting. Of course, redundancy can be removed and reinserted at a later time and place. But why reinsert it if it is not information? Even though we don't normally transmit the redundancy in a data compression system, it is often necessary to reinsert it at the receiving end simply because we may not recognize the original data without it. An example of this is a scanned and digitized picture. In such a data set we have sequential scan lines, with each line containing quantized picture elements. In a picture that has large uniform regions there will be runs of nonchanging picture elements. These redundant picture elements, or pixels as they are called, can be easily compressed by counting and coding their run lengths (not surprisingly, this is called run-length coding). Each scan line then can be reduced to alternating pixel values and run-length codes. However, if we were to display these compressed lines in a raster format, the resulting picture would look very little like the original.

How does redundancy relate to the two source models we have discussed? For the case of the Markov model, each sample depends on some number of contiguous previous samples. If we knew this dependency, we could predict the next sample; all we would have to transmit then would be sufficient information about our prediction to allow the receiver to reconstruct the original sample sequence. The number of bits per sample would be less than the value for straight binary coding of each sample, and depending on how clever our prediction and coding scheme was, we would approach the entropy in terms of bits per sample.

For the case of the statistically independent model, we cannot predict and eliminate dependent samples—there aren't any. Instead, we take advantage of the typical nonuniform probability distribution of most data sources. If this distribution were uniform, then the entropy would be a maximum, equal to $\log_2 M$, where M is the number of levels. But real sources seldom have uniform probability distributions; thus, their entropy is always less than $\log_2 M$. Now straight binary coding of each sample would result in a sample code rate of $\log_2 M$ bits per sample, but we can use optimum variable-length coding techniques, such as Huffman and Shannon–Fano coding to make the sample code rate approach the entropy. These codes are described in Section 3.5.

Redundancy has been defined as follows:

$$\text{Redundancy} = \log_2 M - H \tag{3.3.6}$$

And a zero-redundancy source has $H = \log_2 M$. The term *relative redundancy* is defined as follows:

$$\text{Relative redundancy} = \frac{\text{Redundancy}}{\log_2 M} \tag{3.3.7}$$

Exercise 3.3

Compute the redundancy of the sources in Example 3.1 and in Exercise 3.2.

It should be emphasized that we are dealing with a discrete source here, and for this source the uniform source probability function maximizes the entropy. For the continuous source we have quite a different situation. Here, the Gaussian distribution maximizes the differential entropy (see Berger 1971, p. 108).

3.4 THE COMPRESSION RATIO

There are many ways of defining the *compression ratio*, and these different approaches are discussed in this section. In general, the compression ratio is simply the ratio of the bits per sample before compression to the bits per sample after compression. As will be seen, there is often a significant difference between the theoretical upper bound for the compression ratio that one might compute and the actual compression ratio that one would then measure for the same system.

3.4.1 The Upper Bound

The upper bound for the compression ratio is defined as follows:

$$R_{\max} = \frac{\log_2 M}{H} \qquad (3.4.1)$$

We may now show the relationship between maximum compression ratio and relative redundancy. The general expression for relative redundancy can be written as:

$$\text{Relative redundancy} = \frac{\text{Redundancy}}{\log_2 M} = 1 - \frac{H}{\log_2 M} \qquad (3.4.2)$$

Using the expression for maximum compression ratio in (3.4.1):

$$\text{Relative redundancy } (RR) = 1 - \frac{1}{R_{max}} \qquad (3.4.3)$$

or

$$R_{max} = \frac{1}{1 - (RR)} \qquad (3.4.4)$$

Thus, if a statement is made that a source is 75% redundant, an equivalent statement is that the maximum compression ratio is 4 to 1.

For any source, we reach the maximum compression ratio when the source coding results in a source rate equal to the entropy.

3.4.2 Approaching the Upper Bound

Many redundancy-reduction techniques take advantage of intersample dependence, so the question is: How does one approach the maximum compression ratio given by (3.4.1)? We may think of approaching the maximum compression ratio as a two-step process:

1. *Make samples statistically independent.* This involves changing the characteristics of the source from those of the Markov model to those of the statistically independent model, the latter having an entropy equal to or greater than the former. This results in a reduction of redundancy [equation (3.3.6)] and relative redundancy [equation (3.3.7)].

2. *Make the average word length equal, or nearly equal, to the entropy of the statistically independent sample source.* The coding that makes the average word length approach the entropy is often referred to as optimum source coding or entropy coding (see Section 3.5).

As can be seen from this development, the measurement or estimation of the entropy of a data source can be a useful way to estimate the maximum compression ratio that can be obtained without distortion. With this estimate in hand, one can then try out various compression schemes on the data source and compare the actual compression ratios. When a compression scheme is found that provides a compression ratio near the estimated maximum, then there is no need to search further for a "better" compressor—in terms of compression ratio.

3.5 OPTIMUM SOURCE ENCODING

Optimum source encoding is used here to mean the *second-step* reduction of redundancy, as expressed by equation (3.3.6). In this type of coding, we start with statistically independent samples and code them in such a way as to make the average word length equal to the sample entropy. This method of coding is also called *entropy coding* in the literature. The first method of implementing such coding was described by Shannon (1948) and Fano (1949), and an improved method was developed by Huffman (1952).

3.5.1 Shannon–Fano Code

The Shannon–Fano coding procedure provides a means of constructing reasonably efficient codes with instantaneous decodability. Efficiency is defined here as

$$\text{Efficiency} = \frac{H}{\bar{l}} \times 100 \tag{3.5.1}$$

where $\bar{l}$ is the average length of the code word. A code that is instantaneously decodable can be unambiguously decoded as soon as it is received; that is, the beginning of each variable-length code word can be found in the code word sequence.

Shannon–Fano code reaches an efficiency of 100% only when the source message probabilities are negative powers of 2. The coding procedure is as follows:

1. Arrange the source message probabilities in descending order.
2. Divide the message set into two subsets of equal, or almost equal, total probability and assign a *zero* as the first code digit in one subset, and a *one* as the first code digit in the second subset.
3. Continue this process until each subset contains only one message.

Example 3.2 illustrates the procedure.

Example 3.2

The following message set with probabilities is given:

m_i	1	2	3	4	5	6	7
P_i	0.4	0.1	0.1	0.1	0.1	0.1	0.1

By subdividing the messages according to the Shannon–Fano coding procedure we obtain the code shown in Figure 3.1. This code is instantaneously decodable since no code word is a prefix of any other code word. This porperty has given rise to the equivalent name: *prefix code*.

The average code word length is computed by the formula:

$$\bar{l} = \sum_i l_i P_i \tag{3.5.2}$$

and is found to be 2.700 bits for this Shannon–Fano code. By comparison, the entropy, given by:

$$H = -\sum_i P_i \log P_i \tag{3.5.3}$$

is computed to be 2.529 bits. Thus, the efficiency of this code is 93.8%

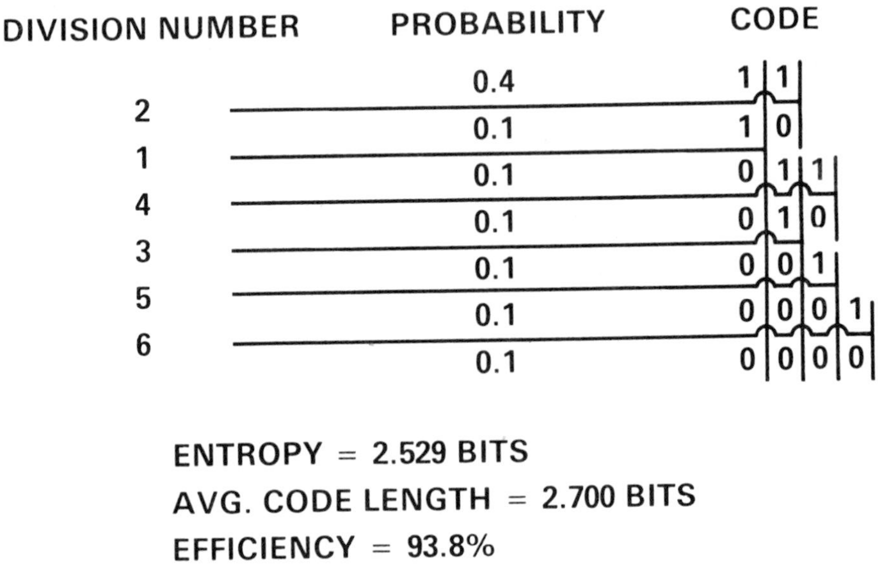

ENTROPY = 2.529 BITS

AVG. CODE LENGTH = 2.700 BITS

EFFICIENCY = 93.8%

Figure 3.1   *Example of a Shannon–Fano Code*

Shannon (1948) showed that the average code word length for statistically independent symbols produced by this coding procedure has the bounds:

$$H \leq \bar{l} < H + 1 \qquad\qquad (3.5.4)$$

3.5.2 The Huffman Code

Huffman (1952) developed a procedure for encoding a statistically independent source in such a way as to yield the minimum average word length, or in other words, the most efficient code. This code also has the property of instantaneous decodability, and makes use of the concept of a *coding tree*. The coding procedure is as follows:

1. Arrange the source probabilities in descending order.
2. Combine the two lowest probabilities and continue this procedure, always putting the higher probability branch on top until unity is reached.
3. Assign a *zero* to the upper member and a *one* to the lower member of each pair—or vice versa.
4. Trace the path from each message probability to the unity point, recording the ones and zeros along the path.
5. For each message write the one–zero sequence thus obtained from right to left.

Example 3.3 illustrates the procedure.

Example 3.3

We consider the same source described in Example 3.2 and proceed as shown in Figure 3.2. The code in Figure 3.2 has an average length of 2.600 bits or an efficiency of 97.4%. We compare this to 93.8% for the corresponding Shannon–Fano code.

As in the case of the Shannon–Fano code, the Huffman code reaches 100% efficiency when the source probabilities are negative powers of 2. In general, when the source probabilities are not negative powers of 2, the Huffman code always has a higher efficiency than the Shannon–Fano code.

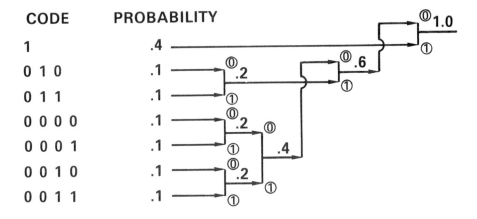

CODE   PROBABILITY

ENTROPY = 2.529 BITS
AVG. CODE LENGTH = 2.600 BITS
EFFICIENCY = 97.4%

Figure 3.2 *Example of a Huffman Code*

Exercise 3.5

For the source given, find the Shannon–Fano code and the Huffman code. For each code, what is the average word length and the efficiency?

i	A	B	C	D	E	F
$P(i)$	1/2	1/8	1/8	1/8	1/16	1/16

In practical situations, the source contains a large number of messages, and in many cases there is a large number of very low probability messages. If we were to follow the Huffman code procedure, long code words would result for these low probability messages, and this would add complexity and storage requirements to the design. An alternate approach that has been used is to lump all the very low probability messages into one category and assign a unique code word to signify that category. Then, for all messages belonging to this category, the unique code word will be sent followed by the actual message (Hankamer 1979).

3.5.3 The Morse Code

The Shannon–Fano and Huffman coding procedures result in a variable-length code in which the length of a code word varies approximately inversely with the probability of the message or sample value. It is not surprising then to find the same *general* relationship in one of the oldest variable-length codes, the Morse code. For example, the two most common letters in the English language are *e* and *t*, and these letters are Morse coded with a dot and a dash, respectively.

3.6 OTHER REDUNDANCY-REDUCTION TECHNIQUES

As was shown in Figure 1.1, the optimum noiseless codes are only one type of redundancy-reduction technique, albeit a very important one. Two other types shown in that same figure are: non-redundant sample codes and binary source codes. In addition, there are redundancy-reduction techniques that are clearly related to the type of data being compressed. For example, in data base compression there are special kinds of alphanumeric compression codes. These applications-oriented techniques are discussed in the appropriate chapters in Part III.

3.6.1 Nonredundant-Sample Codes

When one thinks of compressing discrete data, one of the first techniques that comes to mind is to eliminate repetitive samples. For example, if one were monitoring a battery voltage with time-sampled digital measurements, one could expect long periods of time during which no change in the measured voltage would be evident. There would be no need to record or transmit all these repetitive measurements. Indeed, all that need be transmitted would be the measurements that represented changes, along with the run lengths of the intervening unchanging measurements. This is called run-length coding. It has become customary to call the changing measurements *nonredundant*, and the unchanging measurements *redundant*. A more general form of this type of compression uses the simple rule of transmitting only the nonredundant samples, where a nonredundant sample is defined as one that cannot be predicted by some given prediction algorithm. This type of compression is described in Chapter 7. Two system requirements must be accounted for when one uses this kind of compression. One is time coding and the other is buffering.

Time coding is required since we must be able to reconstruct the original sample sequence of nonredundant and redundant samples from only the transmitted nonredundant samples. There are many different ways of coding the time information, and since these codes handle a two-symbol source (a sample is either redundant or nonredundant), they can be used for other binary data sources as well. This type of coding is discussed briefly in the next section and in detail in Chapter 8.

Buffering is required in the transmission of nonredundant samples in order to maintain a synchronous output from a nonsynchronous input. There are two main problems in the design of a buffer, and they are: the control of buffer overflow and the control of buffer underflow. Buffering is described in Chapter 9.

3.6.2 Binary Source Codes

A binary data source is simply one that produces only two symbols or levels. An example of this is a sampled and quantized two-level picture such as a typewritten page or a line drawing. One can use mathematical models, such as we did in Section 3.2, to compute the entropy of such a source. Then, in turn, one can design a redundancy-reduction scheme that will allow the output code rate to approach this entropy. There are a number of compression schemes for binary sources, and they are described in Chapter 8.

In Chapter 8 the source to be coded is actually the time information for a nonredundant-sample compression system. As was pointed out previously, this type of compression scheme labels samples either nonredundant or redundant, so the time information that must be sent along is that of a two-symbol source. The techniques of binary source coding described in Chapter 8 are broken down into three categories, according to what information is actually coded:

1. The entire two-symbol sequence

2. The time of occurrence of one type of symbol

3. The alternating runs of the two types of symbols

An interesting example of an application of some of these techniques is two-level facsimile, as described in Chapter 16.

3.6.3 Effect of Channel Noise

What happens when data compressed by a redundancy-reduction technique is corrupted by noise in the transmission channel? To put the answer very simply: Worse things happen than would normally happen had the data not been compressed. For example, in the case of the optimum noiseless codes, a single bit error can cause the loss of the self-synchronizing property of these codes, resulting in the loss of a large block of data. It should be noted that the term *noiseless coding* refers to a lack of noise or distortion due to the compression technique—not due to the channel. In nonredundant-sample coding, an error in a nonredundant sample value can cause an error propagation in the reconstructed data sequence. Likewise, in binary coding a single bit error can destroy a whole block of reconstructed data. Noise effects on compressed data as well as the trade-offs between data compression and data expansion (due to error-control coding) are treated in Chapter 10.

HIGHLIGHTS

- Redundancy reduction is a reversible process and, as such, must operate on a discrete data source. The two discrete sources commonly used for redundancy reduction are: the statistically independent source, and the Markov source.

- A very useful theoretical performance bound for redundancy-reduction techniques is the entropy, which is defined as the average information available from an information source.

- If one can compute the entropy, H, of a source, then the theoretical maximum compression ratio can be computed for an M-level source as

$$R_{max} = \frac{\log_2 M}{H}$$

- For the statistically independent source, the Shannon–Fano and Huffman codes provide the maximum compression ratio when the probability of each level is a negative power of 2. When these probabilities are not negative powers of 2, the Huffman code provides a higher compression ratio than the Shannon–Fano code.

SUGGESTIONS FOR FURTHER READING

The following items are suggested for further reading and study:

Berger, T. See Chapter 2, Suggestions for Further Reading.

Davisson, L. D. "Universal Noiseless Coding." *IEEE Trans. on Info. Theory*, vol. IT-19, 1973, pp. 783–795.

In this paper, Davisson defines the concept and extends the theory of universal coding. He also outlines the historical development of this approach to source coding.

Fano, R. M. *The Transmission of Information.* Technical Report No. 65, M. I. T., Research Lab. of Electronics, 1949.

In this report, Fano describes the Shannon–Fano code (see Chapter 1, Suggestions for Further Reading). This report was later expanded and published by Fano as the book *Transmission of Information* (New York: John Wiley and Sons, 1961). It is still useful as a basic reference for information theory.

Hankamer, M. "A Modified Huffman Procedure with Reduced Memory Requirement." *IEEE Trans. on Comm.,* vol. COM-27, no. 6, June 1979, pp. 930–932.

The source messages are partitioned into two disjoint sets: probable and least probable. When a least probable message appears at the input to the encoder, a unique code word is first transmitted followed by the actual message. This has the effect of greatly reducing the memory required for the coding scheme with only a slight decrease in code efficiency.

Huffman, D. A. "A method for the Construction of Minimum Redundancy Codes." *Proc, IRE.* vol. 40, September 1952, pp. 1098–1101.

In this classic paper, the Huffman code is developed and applied.

Shannon, C. E. See Chapter 1, Suggestions for Further Reading.

PART II

Techniques

CHAPTER 4

Introduction to Data Compression Techniques

4.1 INTRODUCTION

In Part I, theoretical background was given to help readers better understand the techniques of data compression. In addition, some data compression techniques were actually described—certain forms of quantization (Chapter 2) and two optimum source codes (Chapter 3.) These techniques were introduced early in the book not only because they are often integral components of many data compression systems, but also because their performance can be quantitatively compared to the theoretical bounds of the rate distortion function (Chapter 2) and the entropy function (Chapter 3).

In Part II we look at techniques of data compression that are widely used and frequently referenced in the literature. These techniques include the following (refer to Figure 1.1). Transform coding (Chapter 5) is a form of block quantization in which the original correlated analog samples are first decorrelated by a linear transformation and then optimally quantized. Predictive coding (Chapter 6) is a form of sequential quantization in which the difference between the next sample and its predicted value is quantized. Nonredundant sample coding (Chapter 7) is a technique that decides whether samples are redundant or nonredundant according to some preset algorithm, and then transmits the nonredundant samples with appropriate timing information. Binary coding (Chapter 8) is the coding of a binary source in such a way that the average code rate is less than one bit per sample. These techniques are sometimes used in combination with each other as well as in combination with the techniques described in Part I (see Chapter 11).

Of course, some compression techniques are specially designed and adapted to certain data applications, such as speech, telemetry, television, pictures, and data bases. Some of these techniques are actually special versions of the techniques described in Parts I and II; others are unique and thus do not relate to any of the more widely used techniques. These applications-oriented techniques are described in Part III.

4.2 FOUR BASIC TECHNIQUES

The four types of data compression techniques covered in Part II are: transform coding, predictive coding, nonredundant sample coding, and binary source coding. Let us look at each briefly by way of introduction.

4.2.1 Transform Coding

In Chapter 2, we saw that, from a theoretical standpoint, block quantization is an efficient way to quantize data samples, and it remains to find techniques that will implement it. One such technique is called *transform coding*; in this technique we actually transform the original samples in a block, before quantization, and then apply a different quantizer to each transformed sample, or coefficient, as it is sometimes called. The obvious goal is to quantize the entire block with fewer bits than would be needed to quantize the original block, one sample at a time, with the same quantizer. In transform coding, a fixed number of bits (smaller than would be necessary to quantize the original block) is allocated among the various coefficients according to some rule. The transformation that is normally used is a linear transformation, and we will look at these in Chapter 5: principal component, Fourier, Hadamard, and Haar.

An interesting property of transform coding is that the actual transformation that is used is usually reversible, which would make one think that transform coding is a redundancy-reduction technique. However, since the part of transform coding that actually performs the data compression is the quantization which, of course, is irreversible, transform coding is normally classified as an entropy-reduction technique.

Transform coding requires a buffer to store a block of samples, but this buffer is sized to the block and there are no overflow or underflow problems. Transmission errors that affect the transformed samples will have a reduced effect on the reconstructed (or inverse transformed) samples since the error effects tend to be spread out over these reconstructed samples.

4.2.2 Predictive Coding

Another variation on quantization is *predictive coding*; in this technique we quantize the difference between a predicted sample and its actual value. This approach is motivated by the fact that, for most data sources, the variance of the above difference will be less than the variance of the original data, thus making possible a smaller range quantizer and hence a compression. There are two well-known examples of predictive coding: delta modulation and differential pulse code modulation. As in the case of transform coding, the quantization operation, which is central to predictive coding, makes it an entropy-reduction technique.

Predictive coding usually works on one sample at a time, so a buffer is not required, unless we are applying predictive coding to blocks of data. Predictive coding exhibits a sensitivity to channel errors that can produce objectional effects in the reconstructed data (streaks in pictures, for example).

4.2.3 Nonredundant Sample Coding

The type of data compression that first comes to the mind of most individuals who are not familiar with the various techniques described in the literature is *nonredundant sample coding*. A popular concept of how to perform data compression is to "leave out repeating values," which is a special case of nonredundant sample coding.

Nonredundant sample coding is normally classified as a redundancy-reduction technique even though some algorithms use an aperture to test for redundancy, which aperture may, in fact, reduce the data precision. Nonredundant sample techniques require buffers with overflow and underflow control, time coding, and, like most compression techniques, some protection from channel errors.

4.2.4 Binary Source Coding

One may wonder why a binary data source requires special data compression techniques and why we deal with it separately, especially in the literature. One reason is that we can model a binary source in a more realistic way than a nonbinary source, with relatively simple models. With these models available, we can attempt to design optimum compression schemes for the binary source. In this case the measure of performance, and hence near-optimality, is how close the code rate approaches the source entropy. Another reason binary sources get special attention is actually just the opposite from the first reason. There has been growing interest in finding codes that will give uniformly good performance in spite of a lack of information about the source statistics. These codes are called *universal codes.*

Binary source codes are classified as redundancy-reduction techniques, and they typically require some buffering and some error protection. It is interesting to note that the time coding methods for nonredundant sample coding are readily applicable to binary source coding since the time information they are normally coding is a binary source in itself.

4.3 IMPLEMENTATION CONSIDERATIONS

We would like to conceptualize an ideal data compressor as a single-system component into which we feed original data and out of which comes compressed data. We could then transmit this compressed data to a receiver, which would contain another single component that would reconstruct the original data from the compressed data. All that would be required would be the design of the two components. Unfortunately, the integration of data compression into a data system is typically not so simple. Some data compression techniques, such as nonredundant sample coding, require that timing information be added to the compressed data in order to reconstruct the original data. Other techniques, such as optimum source coding and nonredundant sample coding, require a buffer between the data compressor and the transmission channel in order to convert the asynchronous output of the data compressor into a synchronous symbol stream for transmission. When data compression is added to any data system, the reconstructed data is more vulnerable to transmission errors, and in many cases some form of error control must be added to the system.

These three functions/components are also described in Part II. In Chapter 8, the requirement for sending timing information with some types of compressed data is analyzed, and different time coding schemes are described and compared on a performance basis. Since the timing information is produced by labeling the original data samples as either redundant or nonredundant, some of the time codes described in Chapter 8 can also be used to code and compress a *binary* data source. This type of binary coding has important applications to picture coding, especially two-level facsimile and graphics (see Chapter 16).

In Chapter 9 we look at the requirement for buffering the output of some data compressors and we examine the problems of buffer overflow and buffer underflow, along with the techniques of controlling buffer fullness.

In Chapter 10 we examine the effect of transmission errors on a data system employing compression and look at the basic trade-off between overall compression ratio and error control: More error control means a smaller compression ratio. (A short description of error-control coding is given in Appendix A, to introduce techniques that would be typically incorporated into a data compression system.)

4.4 SYSTEM DESIGN CONSIDERATIONS

System design, in general, attempts to ensure that the final system will meet system requirements and be cost effective. When we apply system design to a data compression system we find that the requirements are of two types: constraining and subject to trade-off.

The *constraining requirements*, in turn, are also of two types: *system operability* and *system cost*. System operability demands that data compression be used since no other design approach will be feasible (in a limited bandwidth situation, for example). If data compression will appreciably reduce system cost, this is often a sufficient justification for using it.

Having found a legitimate need for data compression, we next examine those requirements that may be subject to *trade-off*. These are: *compression ratio, distortion, and complexity*.

The required compression ratio usually indicates whether redundancy reduction or entropy reduction is needed. There is a trade-off here between compression ratio and distortion, and this is covered in Chapter 10. The complexity of a compression algorithm implementation not only depends on the algorithm itself but also on the ancillary requirements of timing information, buffering, and error control.

In Chapter 11, system requirements and trade-off issues are examined for three types of compression: transform coding, predictive coding, and non-redundant sample coding. In addition, a generalized procedure is given for algorithm selection and the combining of compressors in cascade.

CHAPTER 5

Transform Coding

5.1 INTRODUCTION

In this chapter, we examine the data compression technique called *transform coding*. Transform coding involves linear transformations in which the signal space is mapped into a transform space where the transformed samples are then compressed for transmission or storage. The reconstruction operation involves an inverse transformation of the compressed transformed samples. This sequence of operations is shown in Figure 5.1.

The sequence involves two operations on the *source* side of the channel: transformation and quantization; and two operations on the *receiver* side of the channel: decoding and inverse transformation. Each of these operations requires some amount of memory, and this need for memory—particularly at the source end of the system—is involved in one of the important system complexity considerations for compression by transform coding.

The choice of the transformation (and the inverse transformation as well) is often dictated by practical implementation considerations, even though it is possible to design an "optimum" transformation, the principal component (or Karhunen–Loève) transformation, described in Section 5.2.1. The function of the transformation operation is to make the transformed samples more independent than the original samples so that the subsequent operation of quantization may be done more efficiently.

In transform coding systems the total number of bits available for quantizing a block of transformed samples is fixed, and it is necessary to allocate these bits to the quantized transformed samples in such a way as to minimize to overall quantization distortion. Since the total number of bits available is always less than the number required to code all the transformed samples with a fixed-length uniform quantizer, a compression is obtained in the transformed samples. Because quantization is an integral part of transform coding, it is considered a form of block quantization (see Figure 1.1).

In this chapter we look at four linear transformations that are appropriate for transform coding: principal component, Fourier, Hadamard, and Haar. We also examine the methods of bit allocation in quantizing the transformed samples.

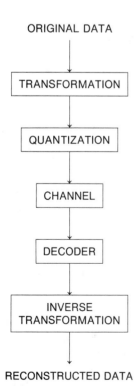

Figure 5.1 *Data Compression by Transform Coding*

5.2 FOUR TRANSFORMS

Four transforms have appeared in the transform coding literature many times, and have been implemented in actual compression systems. These are:

Principal component (Karhunen–Loève)

Fourier

Hadamard

Haar

It should be remembered in each case that the transformation *itself* is not providing the compression, but rather it is remapping the signal into another domain in which compression can be accomplished more easily. The subsequent operation of quantization with bit allocation compresses the transformed samples, which are then ready for transmission or storage. For this reason, it is important to understand the transformation operation from the standpoint of what it is intended to do, namely, make the transformed samples more independent and ordered (in terms of their variance) so that they may be more efficiently quantized. There is a large literature on most of the transformations covered here, and thus, their treatment in this section will be concise with some illustrative examples and appropriate references.

5.2.1 Principal Component Transform

The principal component transform has been considered an optimum transformation, and for this reason many other transformations have been compared to it for performance. Hotelling (1933) was the first to derive and publish this transformation under the name "principal component." This is a discrete transformation. Some years later, the corresponding continuous transformation was developed by both Karhunen and Loève (1947, 1948). In the literature the discrete transformation is referred to both ways: principal component and Karhunen–Loève (KL). In this book we use the designation principal component since we are assuming that the input will be data samples—not continuous in time.

In order to describe this transformation, we will show how it is used to transform an image of picture samples, or picture elements (*pixels*) as they as normally called. To simplify the description, we assume a raster-scanned picture that we will convert to a one-dimensional data set by forming a new long vector from the successive scan lines as follows: For an image with L lines and L pixels per line, let $f(x, y_j)$ represent all the L pixels in the jth line, where $j = 1, 2, \ldots, L$.

Then

$$[f(z)] \equiv [f(x, y_1), f(x, y_2), \ldots, f(x, y_L)] \tag{5.2.1}$$

is the L^2 vector composed of all the pixels taken in the normal raster pattern sequence, in other words, the whole image.

Then we define an $L^2 \times L^2$ matrix $[A]$ such that the transformed pixels are defined as:

$$[F(w)] = [A][f(z)] \tag{5.2.2}$$

Each component of $[F(w)]$ (sometimes called a *coefficient*) can be expressed as a linear combination of all the original pixels:

$$F(w_k) = \sum_{i=1}^{L^2} f(z_i)A_{ik}, \qquad k = 1, 2, \ldots, L^2 \tag{5.2.3}$$

The original pixels can be reconstructed from the transformed pixels by means of the inverse transformation

$$[f(z)] = [A]^t[F(w)] \tag{5.2.4}$$

and similarly, each original pixel can be expressed as a linear combination of all the coefficients, $F(w_k)$:

$$f(z_i) = \sum_{k=1}^{L^2} F(w_k)A_{ki}, \qquad i = 1, 2, \ldots, L^2 \tag{5.2.5}$$

The ideal would be for the transformation, $[A]$, to produce *independent* coefficients, $F(w_k)$. However, the closest we can come to this is with a transformation that produces *uncorrelated* coefficients. Such a transformation is a matrix whose columns are the normalized eigenvectors of the covariance matrix of the original pixels.

The covariance matrix is defined as

$$C_f = E\{([f(z)] - E\{[f(z)]\})([f(z)] - E\{[f(z)]\})^t\} \tag{5.2.6}$$

Writing this expression out for C_f with the simplifying assumption that $E\{[f(z)]\} = 0$ and the simplifying notation $f(z_i) = f_i$:

$$C_f = \begin{bmatrix} E(f_1^2) & E(f_1 f_2) & E(f_1 f_3) & \cdots & E(f_1 f_{L^2}) \\ E(f_2 f_1) & E(f_2^2) & E(f_2 f_3) & \cdots & E(f_2 f_{L^2}) \\ E(f_3 f_1) & E(f_3 f_2) & E(f_3^2) & \cdots & E(f_3 f_{L^2}) \\ \vdots & \vdots & \vdots & & \vdots \\ E(f_{L^2} f_1) & E(f_{L^2} f_2) & E(f_{L^2} f_3) & \cdots & E(f_{L^2}^2) \end{bmatrix} \tag{5.2.7}$$

Now the expected values of the various squares and cross-products in C_f are typically obtained by averaging products of pixels with the same spatial separation and relative location from a *larger* image of which the L^2 dimensional vector $[f(z)]$ is an $L \times L$ *subimage*.

The eigenvectors of C_f are the solutions ϕ to the matrix equation:

$$C_f \phi = \lambda \phi \tag{5.2.8}$$

where λ represents the eigenvalues. First we solve for the eigenvalues from the characteristic equation:

$$\det[C_f - \lambda I] = 0 \tag{5.2.9}$$

where I is the unit matrix. We then arrange the λ's in decreasing order such that $\lambda_1 \geq \lambda_2 \geq \lambda_3 \geq \ldots \geq \lambda_{L^2}$ and substitute into $(C_f - \lambda I)\phi = 0$ to solve for the eigenvectors.

When the matrix $[A]$ (whose columns are the ϕ solutions) is applied to $[f(z)]$, the covariance of the resulting coefficients $F(w_k)$ is a diagonal matrix with diagonal elements $\lambda_1, \lambda_2, \ldots, \lambda_{L^2}$. Thus, the coefficients, $F(w_k)$, are uncorrelated by definition.

Example 5.1

As a simple example, consider the two-pixel image

$$f(x_1)f(x_2)$$

which can be expressed as the vector

$$[f(z)] = [f(x_1), f(x_2)]$$

In order to compute the covariance matrix, assume that this two-pixel image is taken from a larger 4×4 image that has the following pixel values:

6	4	5	5
5	4	5	4
5	6	5	6
4	6	5	5

The mean pixel value is 5 and the covariance matrix of the original two-pixel image is then (letting $f(x_i) = f_i$ so that $f_1 = f(x_1)$, $f_2 = f(x_2)$):

$$C_f = \begin{bmatrix} E[(f_1 - 5)^2] & E[(f_1 - 5)(f_2 - 5)] \\ E[(f_2 - 5)(f_1 - 5)] & E[(f_2 - 5)^2] \end{bmatrix}$$

In order to simplify the computation of the elements of C_f we subtract the mean value (5) from each element in the 4×4 matrix, obtaining:

$$\begin{array}{cccc} 1 & -1 & 0 & 0 \\ 0 & -1 & 0 & -1 \\ 0 & 1 & 0 & 1 \\ -1 & 1 & 0 & 0 \end{array}$$

Then we compute the elements of C_f by averaging in each case over the 12 possible two-pixel subimages in the 4- $\times$ -4 image (one shown in the dashed box). Then

$$E[(f_1 - 5)^2] = \frac{6}{12} = \frac{1}{2}$$

$$E[(f_2 - 5)^2] = \frac{6}{12} = \frac{1}{2}$$

and

$$E[(f_1 - 5)(f_2 - 5)] = E[(f_2 - 5)(f_1 - 5)] = -\frac{2}{12} = -\frac{1}{6}$$

So

$$C_f = \begin{bmatrix} \dfrac{1}{2} & -\dfrac{1}{6} \\ -\dfrac{1}{6} & \dfrac{1}{2} \end{bmatrix} = \begin{bmatrix} 3 & -1 \\ -1 & 3 \end{bmatrix}$$

Solving the characteristic equation,

$$\det[C_f - \lambda I] = 0$$

$$\det\begin{bmatrix} (3-\lambda) & -1 \\ -1 & (3-\lambda) \end{bmatrix} = 0$$

$$(3-\lambda)^2 - 1 = 0$$

$$(\lambda - 2)(\lambda - 4) = 0$$

Thus, the eigenvalues are $\lambda_1 = 4$ and $\lambda_2 = 2$.
To find the eigenvectors, we substitute the eigenvalues in $[C_f - \lambda I]\phi = 0$

for $\lambda_1 = 4$

$$\begin{bmatrix} -1 & -1 \\ -1 & -1 \end{bmatrix}\begin{bmatrix} \phi_1 \\ \phi_2 \end{bmatrix} = 0$$

or $\qquad \phi_1 = -\phi_2 \Rightarrow \begin{bmatrix} \phi_1 \\ \phi_2 \end{bmatrix} = \begin{bmatrix} -1 \\ 1 \end{bmatrix}$

for $\lambda_2 = 2$

$$\begin{bmatrix} 1 & -1 \\ -1 & 1 \end{bmatrix}\begin{bmatrix} \phi_1 \\ \phi_2 \end{bmatrix} = 0$$

or $\qquad \phi_1 = \phi_2 \Rightarrow \begin{bmatrix} \phi_1 \\ \phi_2 \end{bmatrix} = \begin{bmatrix} 1 \\ 1 \end{bmatrix}$

The transformation is then

$$[A] = \begin{bmatrix} -1 & 1 \\ 1 & 1 \end{bmatrix}$$

If we compute the covariance matrix of the transformed pixels, we get the expected diagonal matrix:

$$C_F = [A]^t C_f [A] = \begin{bmatrix} -1 & 1 \\ 1 & 1 \end{bmatrix}\begin{bmatrix} 3 & -1 \\ -1 & 3 \end{bmatrix}\begin{bmatrix} -1 & 1 \\ 1 & 1 \end{bmatrix} = \begin{bmatrix} 8 & 0 \\ 0 & 4 \end{bmatrix} = \begin{bmatrix} 2 & 0 \\ 0 & 1 \end{bmatrix}$$

The development in Example 5.1 may seem to be extremely impractical for an image of only two pixels, and so it is. This example was presented to illustrate the steps involved in developing the principal component transformation. Obviously, in a real system, the image would be larger than two pixels, and herein lies a fundamental design choice: how large an image should be transformed. Typically, one would break up a larger image into smaller subimages, and this would produce a trade-off between the number of subimages and the complexity of the principal component transformation. To give an idea of a typical image, or block size, a 16- × -16 or 256-pixel image was used by Wintz (1972) in a nonadaptive principal component transformation.

Example 5.1 nevertheless shows some fundamental characteristics of the principal component transformation that are worth listing:

1. The principal component transformation decorrelates the data samples, as can be seen from the resulting diagonal covariance matrix.
2. A new transformation matrix has to be formed (from the eigenvectors of the covariance matrix) for each new data set.
3. For an L- × -L pixel image, the eigenvectors of an $L^2 \times L^2$ matrix have to be found.

Three other features of this transformation are not obvious from Example 5.1, and they are:

4. Given a block of N samples, the principal component transformation packs the maximum amount of variance into the first K coefficients (compared to any other transformation) where $K < N$. This permits higher ordered coefficients to be discarded to obtain a compression.
5. It minimizes the mean-squared error between the original block of samples and the corresponding block of reconstructed samples. This mean-squared error is equal to the sum of the variances of the discarded coefficients.
6. There is no "fast" principal component transformation in the same sense that there is a fast Fourier transformation (see Section 5.2.2).

5.2.2 Fourier Transform

The *Fourier transform* is probably the most familiar transformation. In many textbooks, it is explained in terms of analog, continuous signals as opposed to digital, sampled signals. But in the data compression systems we are considering here, as shown schematically in Figure 5.1, we are assuming sampled data, which leads to a special form of the Fourier transformation, namely, the *discrete Fourier transform* (DFT). Whereas in the case of continuous signals, there are suitably weighted infinite sine and cosine functions that, when added together, give a good approximation of the original continuous signal, in the case of the DFT there is a discrete set of orthogonal functions,

$$W_{k,m} = e^{-\frac{j2\pi km}{N}}, \qquad (j = \sqrt{-1}) \qquad (5.2.10)$$

that, when suitably weighted and summed, give a good approximation to the original input N-sample sequence. We express the transformed coefficients in the following way. If $X(m)$ is a sequence of N finite-valued real or complex sample values, where $m = 0, 1, 2, \ldots, N - 1$, the Fourier-transformed coefficients are given by (Ahmed and Rao 1975):

$$C_x(k) = \frac{1}{N} \sum_{m=0}^{N-1} X(m) e^{-\frac{j2\pi km}{N}} \qquad k = 0, 1, 2, \ldots, N - 1 \tag{5.2.11}$$

For example, for $k = 0$,

$$C_x(0) = \frac{1}{N} \sum_{m=0}^{N-1} X(m)$$

sometimes called the average value. Likewise, for $k = 1$,

$$C_x(1) = \frac{1}{N} \sum_{m=0}^{N-1} X(m) e^{-\frac{j2\pi m}{N}}$$

As can be seen from this formulation, each transformed coefficient, $C_x(k)$, is a weighted sum of the original samples divided by the number of samples, N. In matrix form, the DFT looks like:

$$[C] = \frac{1}{N} [W][X], \left(W_{k,m} = e^{-\frac{j2\pi km}{N}} \right) \tag{5.2.12}$$

or

$$\begin{bmatrix} C(0) \\ C(1) \\ \vdots \\ C(N-1) \end{bmatrix} = \frac{1}{N} \begin{bmatrix} W_{0,0} & W_{0,1} & \cdots & W_{0,N-1} \\ W_{1,0} & & & \\ \vdots & & & \vdots \\ W_{N-1,0} & & \cdots & W_{N-1,N-1} \end{bmatrix} \begin{bmatrix} X(0) \\ X(1) \\ \vdots \\ X(N-1) \end{bmatrix} \tag{5.2.13}$$

The corresponding inverse DFT is given by:

$$X(m) = \sum_{k=0}^{N-1} C_x(k) e^{j\frac{2\pi km}{N}} \tag{5.2.14}$$

The inverse DFT can also be expressed in matrix form. This is illustrated in Example 5.2.

Example 5.2

Given: The sequence $X = 1, 2, 3, 4$
Find: The DFT and inverse DFT
The DFT is given by:

$$\begin{bmatrix} C(0) \\ C(1) \\ C(2) \\ C(3) \end{bmatrix} = \frac{1}{4} \begin{bmatrix} 1 & 1 & 1 & 1 \\ 1 & -j & -1 & j \\ 1 & -1 & 1 & -1 \\ 1 & j & -1 & -j \end{bmatrix} \begin{bmatrix} 1 \\ 2 \\ 3 \\ 4 \end{bmatrix}$$

$$C(0) = \frac{5}{2}$$

$$C(1) = -\frac{1}{2} + \frac{j}{2}$$

$$C(2) = -\frac{1}{2}$$

$$C(3) = -\frac{1}{2} - \frac{j}{2}$$

The inverse DFT is given by:

$$\begin{bmatrix} X(0) \\ X(1) \\ X(2) \\ X(3) \end{bmatrix} = \begin{bmatrix} 1 & 1 & 1 & 1 \\ 1 & j & -1 & -j \\ 1 & -1 & 1 & -1 \\ 1 & -j & -1 & j \end{bmatrix} \begin{bmatrix} \frac{5}{2} \\ -\frac{1}{2}(1 - j) \\ -\frac{1}{2} \\ -\frac{1}{2}(1 + j) \end{bmatrix}$$

$$X(0) = 1$$

$$X(1) = 2$$

$$X(2) = 3$$

$$X(3) = 4$$

In pictorial form, the X and C values look as shown in Figure 5.2.

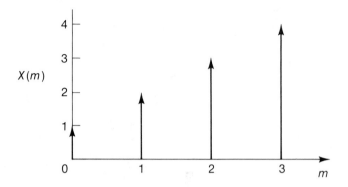

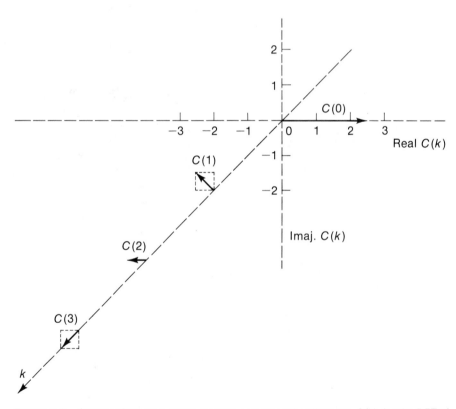

Figure 5.2 *Original Samples, X(m), and Transformed Coefficients, C(k), for the DFT of Example 5.2.*

In spite of the fact that the DFT is a fixed transformation, it has been shown that it can perform almost as well as the principal component transformation (Pearl 1973). A closely related version of the DFT is the *discrete cosine transform* (DCT), which was defined by Ahmed in 1974.

Both the DFT and DCT can be computed by a rapid algorithm, called the *fast Fourier transform* (FFT). The FFT was developed by Cooley and Tukey in 1965 and has been in wide use for speeding up transformation and inverse transformation processes that formerly took a long time. As will be seen in the next sections, the Hadamard and Haar transforms also lend themselves to computation by fast transforms. [See the book by Ahmed and Rao (1975).]

5.2.3 Hadamard Transform

The *Hadamard transform* uses a fixed transformation matrix that takes the form of a sampled two-level square wave. The two levels are $+1$ and -1, and the 2- $\times$ -2 matrix looks as follows:

$$H_2 = \begin{vmatrix} 1 & 1 \\ 1 & -1 \end{vmatrix} \tag{5.2.15}$$

The Hadamard transform has a convenient property: Higher order transformations that have a dimensionality that is a power of 2 can be generated from lower order transformations as follows:

$$H_{2N} = \begin{vmatrix} H_N & H_N \\ H_N & -H_N \end{vmatrix} \tag{5.2.16}$$

For example,

$$H_4 = \begin{vmatrix} 1 & 1 & 1 & 1 \\ 1 & -1 & 1 & -1 \\ 1 & 1 & -1 & -1 \\ 1 & -1 & -1 & 1 \end{vmatrix} \tag{5.2.17}$$

In order to understand how the Hadamard transform is used in practice today, we must review a little history. In 1893 Hadamard developed the matrix structure shown in (5.2.16). In 1922 Rademacher identified a set of rectangular functions of time, a sample of which is shown in Figure 5.3. These functions are orthonormal; that is, the integral of the product of any two different functions is zero and the integral of the square of any one function is equal to 1.

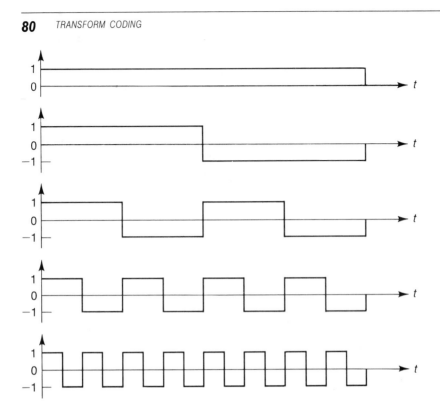

Figure 5.3   *The First Five Rademacher Functions*

In 1923, Walsh completed this set of functions by adding orthonormal functions in between the Rademacher functions, as shown in Figure 5.4a. If a subset of the Walsh functions (starting at the lowest) is sampled at a frequency high enough to detect all changes in level, then we have a matrix that looks very much like the Hadamard matrix, except for the ordering of the rows. That is, the Hadamard matrix can be used to represent the Walsh functions—reordered. The Walsh matrix for $N = 8$ is shown in Figure 5.4b. A term that has come into use in connection with these two-level matrices is the *sequency*, which is defined as the number of sign changes in a given row.

This historical development brings us to the present-day transformation called the *Walsh–Hadamard transform* (WHT). Although this is sometimes referred to in the literature as the Hadamard transform, the transformation matrix really represents sampled Walsh functions reordered by the Hadamard matrix form.

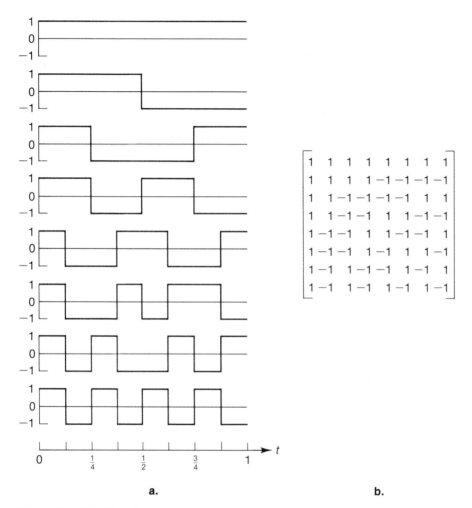

Figure 5.4 *The First Eight Walsh Functions*

Example 5.3

Given: The sequence $X = 1, 2, 3, 4$
Find: The WHT and the inverse WHT
For $X = 1, 2, 3, 4$

$$\text{WHT} = \frac{1}{4}\begin{bmatrix} 1 & 1 & 1 & 1 \\ 1 & -1 & 1 & -1 \\ 1 & 1 & -1 & -1 \\ 1 & -1 & -1 & 1 \end{bmatrix}\begin{bmatrix} 1 \\ 2 \\ 3 \\ 4 \end{bmatrix} = \begin{matrix} \frac{5}{2} \\ -\frac{1}{2} \\ -1 \\ 0 \end{matrix}$$

and

$$\text{WHT}^{-1} = \begin{bmatrix} 1 & 1 & 1 & 1 \\ 1 & -1 & 1 & -1 \\ 1 & 1 & -1 & -1 \\ 1 & -1 & -1 & 1 \end{bmatrix}\begin{bmatrix} \frac{5}{2} \\ -\frac{1}{2} \\ -1 \\ 0 \end{bmatrix} = \begin{matrix} 1 \\ 2 \\ 3 \\ 4 \end{matrix}$$

In the literature, the WHT has been referred to as the BIFORE (BInary FOurier REpresentation) transform (Ahmed and Rao 1975). As in the case of the DFT, there is a fast WHT, which can be computed by a technique similar to that used for the FFT.

5.2.4 Haar Transform

The *Haar transform* uses the Haar orthonormal functions (Haar 1910), and the 8- × -8 transform matrix looks as follows:

$$\mathcal{H}_8 = \begin{vmatrix} 1 & 1 & 1 & 1 & 1 & 1 & 1 & 1 \\ 1 & 1 & 1 & 1 & -1 & -1 & -1 & -1 \\ \sqrt{2} & \sqrt{2} & -\sqrt{2} & -\sqrt{2} & 0 & 0 & 0 & 0 \\ 0 & 0 & 0 & 0 & \sqrt{2} & \sqrt{2} & -\sqrt{2} & -\sqrt{2} \\ 2 & -2 & 0 & 0 & 0 & 0 & 0 & 0 \\ 0 & 0 & 2 & -2 & 0 & 0 & 0 & 0 \\ 0 & 0 & 0 & 0 & 2 & -2 & 0 & 0 \\ 0 & 0 & 0 & 0 & 0 & 0 & 2 & -2 \end{vmatrix} \quad (5.2.18)$$

There is a similarity between the Haar transform matrix and the Hadamard or Walsh–Hadamard transform matrix. In addition, the rows can be visualized as rectangular waves (with amplitudes 0, 1, −1, multiplied by powers of $\sqrt{2}$).

The first two rows of the Haar transform matrix are identical to the corresponding rows of the Walsh matrix (see Figure 5.4b). The remaining rows all contain some number of zeros, unlike the rows of the WHT matrix. Thus, whereas the WHT has a *global* property throughout—that is, each coefficient depends on *all* input samples—the Haar transform has this global property in only the first two coefficients.

The Haar and the Hadamard transforms were compared by Fino (1972), and it was found that, for some data sources, the Haar transform can perform as well as, and even faster than, the Hadamard transform.

In matrix form, the Haar transformation of the data sequence X is:

$$\text{HAAR} = \frac{1}{N} [\mathscr{H}_N][X] \tag{5.2.19}$$

and the inverse gives us:

$$X = [\mathscr{H}_N]^t[\text{HAAR}] \tag{5.2.20}$$

where t stands for transpose.

Example 5.4

Given: The sequence $X = 1, 2, 3, 4, 5, 6, 7, 8$
Find: The Haar transform and its inverse
The Haar transform is given by:

$$
\begin{bmatrix} \mathscr{H}(0) \\ \mathscr{H}(1) \\ \mathscr{H}(2) \\ \mathscr{H}(3) \\ \mathscr{H}(4) \\ \mathscr{H}(5) \\ \mathscr{H}(6) \\ \mathscr{H}(7) \end{bmatrix} = \frac{1}{8}
\begin{bmatrix}
1 & 1 & 1 & 1 & 1 & 1 & 1 & 1 \\
1 & 1 & 1 & 1 & -1 & -1 & -1 & -1 \\
\sqrt{2} & \sqrt{2} & -\sqrt{2} & -\sqrt{2} & 0 & 0 & 0 & 0 \\
0 & 0 & 0 & 0 & \sqrt{2} & \sqrt{2} & -\sqrt{2} & -\sqrt{2} \\
2 & -2 & 0 & 0 & 0 & 0 & 0 & 0 \\
0 & 0 & 2 & -2 & 0 & 0 & 0 & 0 \\
0 & 0 & 0 & 0 & 2 & -2 & 0 & 0 \\
0 & 0 & 0 & 0 & 0 & 0 & 2 & -2
\end{bmatrix}
\begin{bmatrix} 1 \\ 2 \\ 3 \\ 4 \\ 5 \\ 6 \\ 7 \\ 8 \end{bmatrix}
$$

$$\mathscr{H}(0) = \frac{9}{2}$$

$$\mathscr{H}(1) = -2$$

$$\mathscr{H}(2) = -\frac{\sqrt{2}}{2}$$

$$\mathscr{H}(3) = -\frac{\sqrt{2}}{2}$$

$$\mathscr{H}(4) = -\frac{1}{4}$$

$$\mathscr{H}(5) = -\frac{1}{4}$$

$$\mathscr{H}(6) = -\frac{1}{4}$$

$$\mathscr{H}(7) = -\frac{1}{4}$$

The inverse Haar transform is given by:

$$
\begin{bmatrix} X(0) \\ X(1) \\ X(2) \\ X(3) \\ X(4) \\ X(5) \\ X(6) \\ X(7) \end{bmatrix} =
\begin{bmatrix}
1 & 1 & \sqrt{2} & 0 & 2 & 0 & 0 & 0 \\
1 & 1 & \sqrt{2} & 0 & -2 & 0 & 0 & 0 \\
1 & 1 & -\sqrt{2} & 0 & 0 & 2 & 0 & 0 \\
1 & 1 & -\sqrt{2} & 0 & 0 & -2 & 0 & 0 \\
1 & -1 & 0 & \sqrt{2} & 0 & 0 & 2 & 0 \\
1 & -1 & 0 & \sqrt{2} & 0 & 0 & -2 & 0 \\
1 & -1 & 0 & -\sqrt{2} & 0 & 0 & 0 & 2 \\
1 & -1 & 0 & -\sqrt{2} & 0 & 0 & 0 & -2
\end{bmatrix}
\begin{bmatrix} \frac{9}{2} \\ -2 \\ -\frac{\sqrt{2}}{2} \\ -\frac{\sqrt{2}}{2} \\ -\frac{1}{4} \\ -\frac{1}{4} \\ \frac{1}{4} \\ \frac{1}{4} \end{bmatrix}
$$

$X(0) = 1$

$X(1) = 2$

$X(2) = 3$

$X(3) = 4$

$X(4) = 5$

$X(5) = 6$

$X(6) = 7$

$X(7) = 8$

5.3 QUANTIZATION FOR TRANSFORM CODING

Since the process of transformation involves transforming a *block* of N samples (or pixels) into a transform domain, schemes have been developed that attempt to optimize the quantization of the corresponding block of N transformed samples. This optimization typically takes the form of minimizing the total mean-square error between the original block samples and the reconstructed block samples, as shown in Figure 5.1. Quite naturally, these methods are called *block quantization.*

A benchmark paper on block quantization for transform coding was published by Huang and Schultheiss in 1963. In this paper they assumed that the total number of binary digits available for quantizing a block of N transformed Gaussian samples was fixed, and they developed a procedure for allocating these bits among the transformed samples. [They also found that the optimum mean-square-error transformation was the one that diagonalized the covariance matrix (the principal component)]. They developed this expression, which gives an approximate value for the number of bits to be assigned to the *i*th sample:

$$b_i = \bar{r} + \frac{1}{2} \log_2 \frac{\lambda_i}{[\det C_F]^{1/N}} \tag{5.3.1}$$

where: $\bar{r}$ is the average number of binary digits per sample available in the channel

λ_i is the *i*th eigenvalue of the covariance matrix, C_F

N is the number of transformed samples

It should be noted that the value of b_i as computed by (5.3.1) will not be typically an integer and may even be negative in some cases. For this reason, (5.3.1) should be used only as a starting point in developing the bit allocation for the transformed samples.

If we apply this procedure to Example 5.1, we proceed as follows. Let $\bar{r} = 3$ bits since the data sample shows no value > 6. The covariance matrix is:

$$C_f = \begin{bmatrix} 3 & -1 \\ -1 & 3 \end{bmatrix}$$

and the transformed covariance matrix is:

$$C_F = \begin{bmatrix} 2 & 0 \\ 0 & 1 \end{bmatrix}$$

so that $\lambda_1 = 2$, $\lambda_2 = 1$. Then

$$\det C_F = (\lambda_1)(\lambda_2) = 2$$

Using (5.3.1):

$$b_1 = 3 + \frac{1}{2}\log_2 \frac{2}{[2]^{1/2}} = 3 + \frac{1}{2}(0.5) = 3.25 \text{ bits}$$

$$b_2 = 3 + \frac{1}{2}\log_2 \frac{1}{[2]^{1/2}} = 3 + \frac{1}{2}(-0.5) = 2.75 \text{ bits}$$

Once again, we have to point out that this simple example is useful only to show the *procedure* one follows. If this were an actual system, then these results would indicate that we should use 3 bits for each sample. However, in a real system there not only would be larger matrices, but also one would expect a greater variation in the variances (λ's) and a corresponding variation in the b_i values.

It is important to remember that the result of equation (5.3.1) was obtained with the important assumption of a Gaussian distribution for the original samples. The obvious question then is: How well does this resulting scheme work for non-Gaussian distributions? Before this question can be answered, we must take into account the *changing* distribution of the original and transformed samples—an effect exaggerated by the fact that each block is typically a small fraction of the total data set or image to be compressed, and thus its distribution changes more rapidly than that of the entire data set or image. Fixed-block quantization schemes have been used in which a fixed transformation is followed by a quantization rule that assigns bits to samples on a predetermined basis, usually in decreasing numbers. These schemes can be improved in performance by making them *adaptive*.

5.4 ADAPTIVE TRANSFORM CODING

If we look at the operations involved in transform coding, we can identify three basic ones—sampling, transformation, and quantization—in that order. Each operation can be made adaptive, as described in the following sections (see Habibi 1977).

5.4.1 Adaptive Sampling

In adaptive sampling the sampling rate matches itself to the data set characteristics. Where there is high data activity (such as high detail in a picture), a higher sampling rate is used; where there is low data activity, a lower sampling rate is used. An example of this is a variable raster-scan rate in a video system. Of course, the scan rate would have to be transmitted to the receiver as additional information (usually called "side information") in order to maintain synchronization. Although this technique is theoretically very simple, it has seen little application in actual systems—perhaps because of the need to operate with a constantly changing synchronization pattern.

5.4.2 Adaptive Transforms

Of the four transformations described in Section 5.2, only one is suitable to be made adaptive, and that is the principal component (or Karhunen–Loève) transformation. The other three are fixed and independent of the data source statistics. But, the prinicpal component transformation might be considered already adaptive, so how can we make it more adaptive? While it is theoretically true that this transformation is adaptive, in actual practice the transformation is rarely used in its classical form. Instead of computing a new transformation matrix for each new data set, a single transformation matrix is developed from the eigenvectors of an "average" covariance matrix, which will be a fair match for most of the data sets expected. Obviously, some data sets will be poorly matched by this "average" transformation, so an alternate approach is to use a *set* of transformations that best fits certain classes of data sets.

Three such principal component transformations were used be Tasto and Wintz (1971) to compress 6- × -6 pixel images. The corresponding three classes of image blocks they used had the following characteristics:

Class 1.   Small correlation between picture elements (high detail and high spatial frequencies)

Class 2. Large correlation between picture elements and darker than average intensity levels

Class 3. Large correlation between picture elements and lighter than average intensity levels

5.4.3 Adaptive Quantization

Quantization is basically the mapping of a set of continuous amplitude samples into a set of discrete amplitude samples. In transform coding we use the term *bit allocation* to describe the assignment of the fixed total number of bits per block to the various transformed samples. In some bit allocation schemes we may wish to assign zero bits to a given sample—this is sometimes referred to in the literature as "sample selection." Two types of adaptive quantization procedures are primarily used in transform coding: threshold quantization and activity-index quantization.

In *threshold quantization*, a specific amplitude level is specified, and only those transformed samples that are above this threshold are quantized. Since the number and location of the above-threshold samples varies from block to block, this method is truly adaptive. But there is an important "overhead" requirement: namely, the location information (in the transform domain) for the selected samples. Such a scheme was used by Anderson and T. Huang in 1971 to compress images by a Fourier transformation. In their system, they used a run-length code to locate the above-threshold samples in the transform plane, and they made the number of quantization levels proportional to the standard deviation of the transformed pixels in the block. (Run-length coding and other position/time codes are covered in Chapter 8.)

Threshold quantizing should be differentiated from *zonal quantizing* wherein only those samples in a certain ordered range are quantized. In the Fourier transformation, this would correspond to low-pass, band-pass, or high-pass frequency component filtering. However, zonal quantizing does not adapt to different data set characteristics and is typically inferior in performance to threshold quantizing (see Andrews 1970).

One may use an *activity index* to classify the data blocks for quantization. The available bits can be assigned to blocks in different classes, according to the general rule that the higher activity-index classes are allocated more bits than the lower activity-index classes. Activity indexes that have been used include the sum of the squares of the transformed samples and also the sum of the absolute values of the transformed samples. An interesting example of this technique was applied to television. There are three activity indexes here corresponding to the three dimensions: horizontal, vertical, and temporal. Knauer (1976) used a 4- $\times$ -4 $\times$ -4 three-dimensional block with a Hadamard transform to compress black-and-white television with this approach. He monitored the appropriate vector to determine the degree of movement and allocated the available bits so as to minimize the distortion visible to the human observer. In order to achieve this, he applied more bits to the temporal (frame-to-frame) direction for rapid movement, and correspondingly more bits to the horizontal and vertical directions for slower movement.

In an interesting application of many of the ideas explained in this chapter, Zelinski and Noll (1977) developed the following adaptive transform coding scheme for speech signals:

1. A fixed cosine transformation

2. A bit allocation procedure based on an estimate of the variances of the transformed samples. These variances are used in the following formula for the number of bits in the ith sample [compare to equation (5.3.1)]:

$$b_i = \bar{r} + \frac{1}{2} \log_2 \frac{\sigma_i^2}{\left[\prod_{i=1}^{n} \sigma_i^2\right]^{1/N}} \qquad (5.4.1)$$

where: $\bar{r}$ is the average number of bits per sample

σ_i^2 is the variance of sample i (this variance is estimated from an average of the squared samples)

HIGHLIGHTS

- In transform coding the signal space is mapped into a transform space and the transformed samples are then compressed for transmission or storage by an efficient form of block quantization called bit allocation.
- The three operations involved in transform coding: sampling, transformation, and quantization may all be made adaptive.
- Four major linear transformations are: principal component (Karhunen—Loève), Fourier, Hadamard, and Haar.
- The principal component transformation is a discrete transformation that decorrelates data samples, resulting in a diagonal covariance matrix.
- The Fourier transformation may be either continuous or sampled; discrete Fourier transform (DFT) involves a discrete set of orthogonal functions; fast Fourier transform (FFT) is a rapid algorithm that can be used to compute DFT.
- The Hadamard transform uses a fixed transformation matrix in the form of a sampled two-level square wave; the present-day form is called the Walsh–Hadamard transform.
- The Haar transformation uses the Haar orthonormal functions.

SUGGESTIONS FOR FURTHER READING

The following items are suggested for further reading and study:

Ahmed, N., Natarajan, T., and Rao, K. R. "Discrete Cosine Transform." *IEEE Trans. on Computers*, vol. C-23, January 1974, pp. 90–93.
    The discrete cosine transform (DCT) is defined in this paper.

Ahmed, N., and Rao, K. R. *Orthogonal Transforms for Digital Signal Processing.* New York: Springer-Verlag, 1975.
    In this book, the authors cover the Fourier transformation, the fast Fourier transform (FFT), the Haar, the Walsh, and the Walsh-Hadamard transformation.

Anderson, G. B., and Huang, T. S. "Piecewise Fourier Transformation for Picture Bandwidth Compression." *IEEE Trans. on Comm. Tech.*, vol. COM-19, no. 2, April 1971, pp. 133–140.
    Adaptive block quantization is used in this paper for a Fourier transformation.

Andrews, H. C. *Computer Techniques in Image Processing.* New York: Academic Press, 1970.
    In this book, the Karhunen–Loève, Fourier, Hadamard, and Haar transformations are described, along with a number of related topics, such as quantization, sample selection, error effects, and so on.

Cooley, J. W., and Tukey, J. W. "An Algorithm for the Machine Computations of Complex Fourier Series." *Mathematics of Computation*, vol. 19, April 1965, pp. 279–301.
    In this paper, the fast Fourier transform (FFT) is introduced.

Fino, B. J. "Relations Between Haar and Walsh/Hadamard Transforms." *Proc. IEEE*, vol. 60, no. 5, May 1972, pp. 647–648.
    It is shown in some cases, that the Haar transform performs as well as the Hadamard transform. Also, for vector operations (of order 2^n), the Hadamard requires $n2^n$ operations whereas the Haar requires $2(2^n - 1)$ operations.

Habibi, A. "Survey of Adaptive Image Coding Techniques." *IEEE Trans. on Comm.*, vol. COM-25, no. 11, November 1977, pp. 1275–1284.
    In this survey, adaptive block quantization, as well as other adaptive transform coding methods, are covered.

Huang, J. J. Y., and Schultheiss, P. M. "Block Quantization of Correlated Gaussian Random Variables." *IEEE Trans. on Comm. Systems*, CS-11, no. 3, 1963, pp. 289–296.
    The principal component transformation is used for a set of Gaussian random variables. This is followed by block quantization using the same Gaussian assumption.

Knauer, S. C. "Real-Time Video Compression Algorithm for Hadamard Transform Processing." *IEEE Trans. on Electromagnetic Compatibility*, vol. EMC-18, no. 1, February 1976, pp. 28–36.
    An algorithm that implements an adaptive 4- ×-4- × -4 Hadamard transform for TV compression is described.

Kramer, H. P., and Mathews, M. V. "A Linear Coding for Transmitting a Set of Correlated Signals." *IRE Trans. on Info. Theory*, September 1956, pp. 41–46.
    The linear coding used in this paper is the principal component transformation based on the correlation coefficients of the original signals.

Pearl, J. "On Coding and Filtering Stationary Signals by Discrete Fourier Transforms." *IEEE Trans. on Info. Theory*, March 1973, pp. 229–232.

In this paper a theoretical development is given to show that the DFT of a stationary time series of data samples with uniformly bounded covariance matrix is asymptotically equivalent to the principal component (Karhunen–Loève) transformation.

Tasto, M., and Wintz, P. A. "Image Coding by Adaptive Block Quantization." *IEEE Trans. on Comm. Tech.*, vol. COM-19, no. 6, December 1971, pp. 957–971.

See Section 5.4.2.

Tescher, A. G. "Transform Image Coding." In *Image Transmission Techniques*, edited by W. K. Pratt. New York: Academic Press, 1979, pp. 113–155.

In this chapter Tescher gives a survey of the history and components of transform coding, both adaptive and non-adaptive.

Wintz, P. A. "Transform Picture Coding." *Proc. IEEE*, vol. 60, no. 7, July 1972, pp. 809–820.

This is a tutorial of transformation techniques as applied to images. An extensive list of references is given.

Zelinski, R., and Noll, P. "Adaptive Transform Coding of Speech Signals." *IEEE Trans. on Acoustics, Speech, and Signal Processing*, vol. ASSP-25, no. 4, August 1977, pp. 299–309.

This paper compares the performance of the Karhunen–Loève, Hadamard, discrete cosine, discrete Fourier, and discrete slant transforms for speech compression, and concludes that the discrete cosine is almost as effective as the Karhunen–Loève, and superior to the other three. An adaptive transform coding scheme is described, using a discrete cosine transform followed by an adaptive quantizer similar to the Huang-Schultheiss (1963) bit allocation scheme.

The following references are mentioned in this chapter primarily for their historical significance:

Haar, A. "Zur Theorie der Orthogonalen Funktionen-Systeme, (Inaugural Dissertation)." *Math. Ann:* 69, 1910, pp. 331–371.

Hadamard, J. "Resolution d'une Question Relative aux Determinants." *Bull. Sci. Math ser.* 2, vol. 17 Part I, 1893, pp. 240–246.

Hotelling, H. "Analysis of a Complex of Statistical Variables into Principal Components." *J. Educational Psych.*, vol. 24, 1933, pp. 417–441, 498–520.

Karhunen, H., "Über lineare Methoden in der Wahrscheinlichkeitrechnung." *Ann. Acad. Sci. Fenn.*, Ser. A. T. 37, Helsinki, 1947. (English translation: "On Linear Methods in Probability Theory," The Rand Corp. Doc. 131, August 1960.)

Loève, M. "Fonctions aléatoires de seconde ordre." In P. Levy, *Processus Stachastiques et Mouvement Brownien*. Paris: Hermann, 1948.

Rademacher, H. "Einige Sätze von allgemeinen Orthogonal functionen." *Math. Annalen*, vol. 87, 1922, pp. 122–138.

Walsh, J. L. "A Closed Set of Normal Orthogonal Functions." *Am. J. of Math.*, 1923, pp. 5–24.

CHAPTER 6

Predictive Coding

6.1 INTRODUCTION

In Chapter 5 we examined compression by means of transformations in which the signal was transformed or mapped into another space where it could be more efficiently quantized. In this chapter, we look at a form of compression in the *signal space*, typically the time domain, in which we predict the next sample and then encode the difference between the actual value of the next sample and its predicted value. This is called *predictive coding*. The motivation behind this technique is the fact that for most signal sets, the variance of the difference obtained in this way is less than the variance of the original signal, and thus more efficient quantization with fewer levels and hence greater compression is possible.

We discuss two well-known techniques: delta modulation and differential pulse code modulation (DPCM), both in the adaptive and nonadaptive modes. In addition, the general technique of block-to-block (frame-to-frame) predictive coding is introduced.

6.2 PREDICTION

If we could predict exactly what sample values would be available at the output of the data source as a function of time, then there would be no uncertainty about the data source and hence no information to be transmitted. In other words, we would have a zero-entropy source. In this situation there would be no need to transmit any data since we could *create* the data at the receiving end without any help from the transmitting end of the system. But how could we carry out such perfect prediction? We could predict (or create) the data perfectly if the data source could be perfectly represented by a mathematical model, and if the output data always matched the output of the model exactly. However, no real data source ever satisfies these two conditions, and the best we can strive for is a predictor that will predict the next sample with some degree of error that can be minimized.

Predictors are usually designed to use previous samples to predict the next sample in each case, rather than a model of the data source. The use of a model would be so complex and time-varying that in most cases it would be impossible to implement. In contrast, using the output samples does not involve the data source directly, so that prediction can be made a separate operation, not affecting the data source in any way.

Predictors using previous samples can be based on a linear or nonlinear function of these samples. Most of the work on prediction that has been used in predictive coding has been on *linear prediction.* Kolmogorov (1941) and Wiener (1942) did the pioneering work on linear prediction. Basically the problem is as follows: Given an error function based on the difference between the actual and the predicted values, and a set of time-sequential samples, find the constant weighting factor for each sample so that a prediction based on a linear sum of the weighted samples will minimize the error function. The error function that is normally used is the mean-squared error:

$$\text{mse} = E[(S_0 - \hat{S}_0)^2] \tag{6.2.1}$$

where: E is the expected value (or mean)

S_0 is the actual value of the next sample

$\hat{S}_0$ is the predicted value of the next sample

The design of a DPCM predictor outlined in Section 6.4.2 uses this error function.

It should be remembered that (6.2.1) is only one error function, and that others may be more appropriate for the actual application, such as in the case of speech (Chapter 13) or images (Chapters 15 and 16). It is also interesting to note that in the classic paper by Elias (1955) on predictive coding, the author does not use the mean-squared error. Elias observed that in a *coded* prediction system, the minimization of the mean-square error may not be an appropriate criterion since the coding may change the power, or in effect the mean-square value, of the error signal. Instead, Elias used the criterion of a minimum-entropy, average error-function distribution. This criterion ensures a minimization of the channel space required for transmission of the error signal, which is more in keeping with the idea of source coding as a two-step process than is the mean-square error criterion: First, a prediction is made of the next sample and the predicted and actual values are subtracted; second, this difference signal is encoded to match its entropy, which is typically less than the entropy of the original signal. In this way a compression takes place.

6.3 DELTA MODULATION

Delta modulation is a predictive coding technique in which the difference between a given sample and its predicted value is quantized into one of two levels, as shown in Figure 6.1. If the difference is positive, plus Δ is coded, and if the

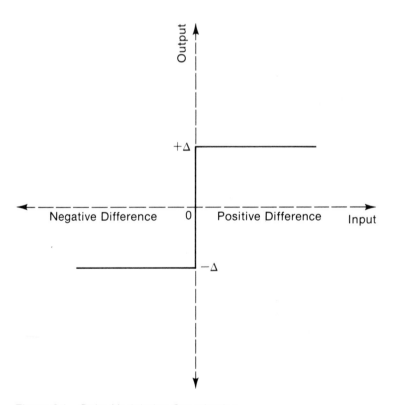

Figure 6.1 *Delta Modulation Quantization.*

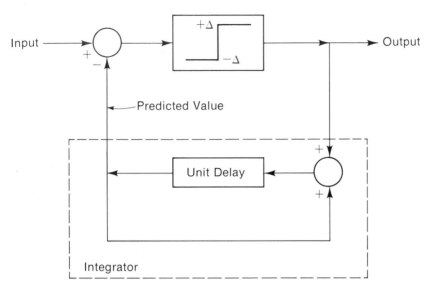

Figure 6.2 *Conventional Delta Modulator.*

difference is negative, minus Δ is coded. The important feature of delta modulation is that it allows only two possible levels to be coded and transmitted.
Because of this, it is sometimes called a "1-bit" system. There are two types of
delta modulation: conventional and adaptive.

6.3.1 Conventional Delta Modulation

The conventional delta modulator is shown in Figure 6.2. As can be seen from
this figure, the delta modulator is composed of three parts: a subtractor, a two-
level quantizer, and an integrator. The two-level quantizer is exactly the one
shown in Figure 6.1. The integrator is implemented by positive feedback around
a unit delay, as shown in the figure. In this way the delta modulator creates its
string of output plus or minus pulses based on the difference between the input
sample and the "predicted" value of that sample from the integrator. There is
no need for a buffer to store the values to be transmitted since a difference
signal $(+\Delta$ or $-\Delta)$ is always sent. Thus, the delta modulator provides a synchronous transmission signal, which is very desirable in some systems. The
string of pulses resulting from the delta modulation coding can be used to reconstruct a close approximation of the original waveform by using just the

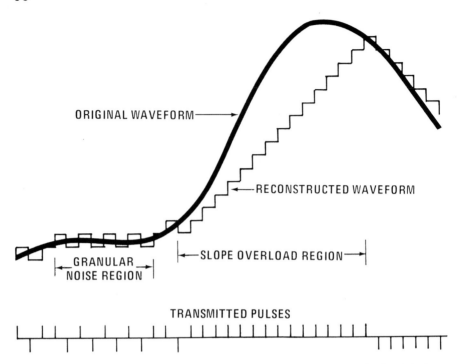

ORIGINAL WAVEFORM

RECONSTRUCTED WAVEFORM

SLOPE OVERLOAD REGION

GRANULAR
NOISE REGION

TRANSMITTED PULSES

Figure 6.3 *Examples of Slope Overload and Granular Noise in Delta Modulation.*

integrator of Figure 6.2. This is shown in Figure 6.3. As can be seen immediately in this figure, the reconstructed waveform may not "keep up" with the original waveform. This is one basic limitation of delta modulation, and it is called *slope overload*. Slope overload noise is caused by the inherent limitation of the staircase maximum slope, given by:

$$\text{Maximum slope} = (\text{step size}) \times (\text{sampling frequency}) \qquad (6.3.1)$$

Another limitation of delta modulation is evident around the zero-difference region of Figure 6.1. Where the difference is close to zero or at zero, random noise will perturb the original level and make the actual level either positive or negative, resulting in positive or negative pulses in some random pattern. This gives rise to a randomly alternating waveform that has to be smoothed to zero, the original level. In a typical case, this smoothing does not get rid of all of the variation about zero and we have what is known as *granular noise*. Slope overload and granular noise are illustrated in Figure 6.3.

Slope overload can be minimized by increasing the step size, but as the step size is increased, the granular noise increases. Thus, the signal-to-noise ratio for a given delta modulation system, when plotted as a function of step size, shows first an increasing characteristic (due to the minimization of slope overload) and then a decreasing characteristic (due to the increasing effect of granular noise).

6.3.2 Adaptive Delta Modulation

Examination of Figure 6.3 shows that the effect of slope overload can be minimized by simply increasing the step size. However, this increases the effect of granular noise, so some compromise must be reached in setting the step size. In most applications, such a compromise is not satisfactory and it is desirable to make the system adaptive.

A number of adaptive schemes for delta modulation have been proposed; most of them involve monitoring the slope of the incoming signal in order to make an appropriate adjustment to the step size. The slope can be monitored by keeping track of the string of pulses produced by the delta modulator. If polarity does not change, then we are in a potential slope overload condition, and the step size can be adjusted until the delta modulator output does change. Variations on this technique have been published by Abate (1967), Jayant (1970), and Song et al. (1971).

In the Song adaptive technique, the output of the delta modulator is considered either a $+1$ or a -1, and the step size is increased by 50% each time the output does not change and decreased 50% each time it does change, as follows. If E_{k+1} is the transmitted signal $(+1, -1)$, S_{k+1} is the present input sample, Δ_{k+1} is the step size, X_{k+1} is the predicted value, and $\Delta_{\min}$ is the minimum step size, then

$$E_{k+1} = \text{sgn}[S_{k+1} - X_k] \tag{6.3.2}$$

$$\Delta_{k+1} = \begin{cases} |\Delta_k| \left[E_{k+1} + \tfrac{1}{2} E_k \right] & \text{if } |\Delta_k| \geq \Delta_{\min} \\ \Delta_{\min} E_{k+1} & \text{if } |\Delta_k| < \Delta_{\min} \end{cases} \tag{6.3.3}$$

$$X_{k+1} = X_k + \Delta_{k+1} \tag{6.3.4}$$

(This adaptive function is shown in Figure 6.4.)

This adaptive approach simultaneously minimizes the effects of both slope overload and granular noise. In the slope overload condition, the step size is progressively *increased* by 50% in order to make the integrated signal "catch up" with the input signal. When an overshoot is reached (and the output changes sign), the step size is decreased by 50% in order to minimize granular noise. Examples of applications of the Song adaptive technique are given in the paper by Lei et al. (1977). The formulation just described is from this same paper.

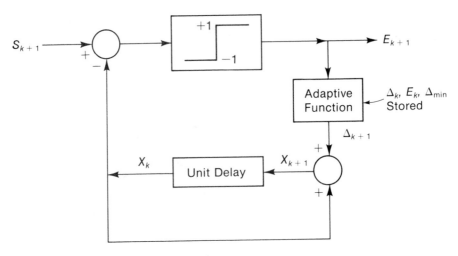

Figure 6.4 *An Adaptive Delta Modulator.*

6.4 DIFFERENTIAL PULSE CODE MODULATION (DPCM)

Pulse code modulation (PCM) was patented by Reeves in 1938. In PCM the original analog signal is time-sampled and each sample is quantized and transmitted as a digital signal. Of course, instead of quantizing each sample, one may predict the next sample and quantize the *difference* between the actual and predicted value. This, as we saw, is the basis of delta modulation, patented in 1946 by Deloraine et al., as well as of differential pulse code modulation (DPCM), patented in 1952 by Cutler. DPCM actually includes delta modulation as a special case—the "1-bit quantizer" case. Due to this relationship, many similarities exist between DPCM and delta modulation.

The basic concept of a DPCM system is shown in Figure 6.5. The difference between a given sample and its predicted value is quantized and transmitted. The predicted value, which is obtained from previous predicted values

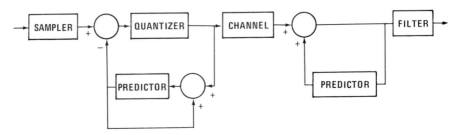

Figure 6.5 *Conceptual DPCM System.*

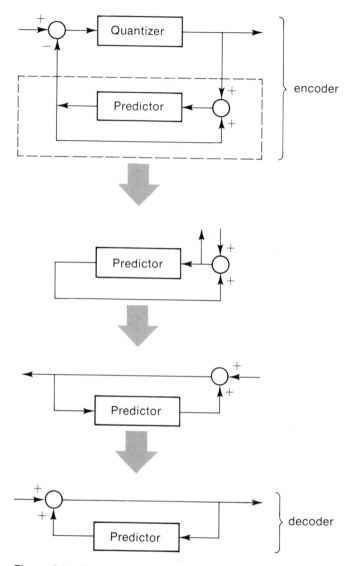

Figure 6.6 *Equivalence of the Integration Function in the DPCM Encoder and Decoder.*

and differences, is also available at the receiver, since the identical predictor is used there. The receiver adds this predicted value to the received quantized difference in order to produce an approximation to the original sample in each case.* The term *predictive quantizing* also has been used to describe DPCM.

---

* The equivalence of this "integration" function in the encoder and decoder can be seen graphically in Figure 6.6.

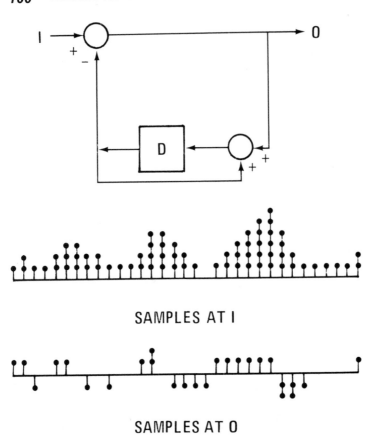

SAMPLES AT I

SAMPLES AT O

Figure 6.7 *Operation of a Simple Unit-Delay DPCM Encoder.*

The simplest form of the predictor shown in Fig. 6.5 is a unit delay of one sample period—the same as used in delta modulation. In this case, the next sample is always predicted to be equal to the previous sample.

6.4.1 DPCM Operation

The operation of the unit-delay predictor DPCM system is shown in Figure 6.7 where, for simplicity, the quantizer has been eliminated from the forward loop and the input signal is assumed to be already quantized. This figure shows the inherent compression ability of DPCM: namely, the output differences at point O occupy typically fewer quantization levels than the original input samples at point I. The state of the encoder for the first four samples is shown in Figure 6.8. Since the predictor in this simple example predicts the

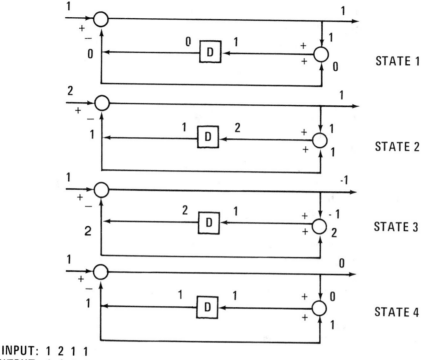

INPUT: 1 2 1 1
OUTPUT: 1 1 -1 0

Figure 6.8 *Example of DPCM Encoder States.*

next sample to be equal to the previous sample, the output is then the differences between successive samples. DPCM can utilize a more powerful predictor than the simple unit-delay loop (or integrator as it is called in delta modulation) shown in Figures 6.7 and 6.8. In many applications, a more accurate prediction can be obtained if more than just the previous sample is used. This is to be expected since many data sources produce sequential samples that are not independent. The number of previous samples to use for prediction and the predictor function itself depend upon the statistical properties of the data source. More will be said about this in the next section.

6.4.2 DPCM Design

As can be seen in Figure 6.5, there are two components to *design* in a DPCM system: the *predictor* and the *quantizer*. In the previous section a simple predictor and no quantizer was assumed just to illustrate the basic operation of a DPCM encoder. In this section, we examine design approaches for both the predictor and the quantizer.

Ideally, the predictor and the quantizer would be optimized together using a linear or nonlinear technique. In practice, however, this is not feasible, and what is actually done is a suboptimum design approach, as follows:

1. The predictor is designed as though it were outside the DPCM encoder using a linear predictor based on previous samples of the data source output. As can be seen in Figure 6.5, the actual predictor has as input previous *predicted* samples and quantized differences.
2. The quantizer is designed as a zero-memory quantizer, even though one of the inputs to the subtractor in Figure 6.5 is the output of the predictor, which does have memory.

In spite of all these simplifications, this suboptimal design approach produces systems that show reasonably good performance, in terms of signal-to-quantizing noise ratio. But for all these systems, the number of quantizing levels must be relatively large ($M > 8$) to achieve good performance. We will now look at the design of the predictor and the quantizer in some detail.

DESIGN OF THE DPCM PREDICTOR

If we assume a *linear* predictor using previous samples $S_1, S_2, \ldots, S_n$ to predict sample S_0, then the prediction* is [following O'Neal (1966)]:

$$\hat{S}_0 = a_1 S_1 + a_2 S_2 + \cdots + a_n S_n \tag{6.4.1}$$

Let

$$e_0 = S_0 - \hat{S}_0 \tag{6.4.2}$$

The best estimate of S_0 is that value of $\hat{S}_0$ for which the expected value of the squared error, e_0, is a minimum. To find that minimum, we compute the partial derivatives and set them equal to zero:

$$\frac{\partial E[(S_0 - \hat{S}_0)^2]}{\partial a_i} = \frac{\partial E[(S_0 - (a_1 S_1 + a_2 S_2 + \cdots + a_n S_n))^2]}{\partial a_i}$$

$$= -2E[(S_0 - (a_1 S_1 + a_2 S_2 + \cdots + a_n S_n))S_i]$$
$$(i = 1, 2, \ldots, n) \tag{6.4.3}$$

---

* *Note:* We are designing the predictor as though there were no quantizer and as though the predictor were operating on the *original* data.

$$E[(S_0 - (a_1 S_1 + a_2 S_2 + \cdots + a_n S_n))S_i] = 0$$
$$E[(S_0 - \hat{S}_0)S_i] = 0 \qquad (i = 1, 2, \ldots, n) \tag{6.4.4}$$

By definition, the covariance is given by:

$$R_{ij} = E[S_i S_j]$$

From (6.4.4),

$$E[S_0 S_i] = E[\hat{S}_0 S_i]$$
$$R_{0i} = E[a_1 S_1 S_i + a_2 S_2 S_i + \cdots + a_n S_n S_i]$$

or

$$R_{0i} = a_1 R_{1i} + a_2 R_{2i} + \cdots + a_n R_{ni} \tag{6.4.5}$$

where $i = 1, 2, \ldots, n$.

This is a set of a simultaneous equations from which we can find $a_1, a_2, a_3, \ldots, a_n$. When $\hat{S}_0$ comprises these optimized coefficients, a_i, then the mean-square error signal is:

$$\sigma_e^2 = E[(S_0 - \hat{S}_0)^2]$$
$$= E[(S_0 - \hat{S}_0)S_0] - E[(S_0 - \hat{S}_0)\hat{S}_0] \tag{6.4.6}$$

But $E[(S_0 - \hat{S}_0)\hat{S}_0] = 0$ from (6.4.3). Then

$$\sigma_e^2 = E[(S_0 - \hat{S}_0)S_0] = E[S_0^2] - E[\hat{S}_0 S_0]$$
$$\sigma_e^2 = R_{00} - (a_1 R_{01} + a_2 R_{02} + \cdots + a_n R_{0n}) \tag{6.4.7}$$

If we think of σ_e^2 as the variance of the error signal (or difference signal) and R_{00} as the variance of the original signal, then (6.4.7) clearly shows that the variance of the error signal is less than the variance of the original signal.

As can be seen from (6.4.5), the complexity of the predictor depends upon the number (n) of previous samples used in the linear prediction. This number depends on the covariance properties of the original signal. The simplest predictor uses only the previous sample and for this case:

$$a_1 = \frac{R_{01}}{\sigma^2} \tag{6.4.8}$$

DESIGN OF THE DPCM QUANTIZER

In Chapter 3, we saw that a *constant* discrete probability distribution has the maximum entropy for the signal limits of that distribution. However, in the case of a continuous distribution, the *Gaussian* probability density gives us the maximum entropy. The minimum entropy is achieved when there is only one possible level (with probability $= 1$) in the signal space, and this entropy is equal to zero. A typical distribution of the continuous difference signal is shown in Figure 6.9, along with the maximum and minimum entropy distributions. As can be seen in this figure, the difference signal distribution is highly peaked and more closely resembles the minimum entropy distribution than the maximum entropy distribution around the region of zero difference. This is not surprising since a "good" predictor would be expected to result in *many zero* differences between the predicted values and the actual values. Such differences allow for an error signal quantizer with fewer intervals than would normally be required for the original signal. Thus, the quantized error signal can be represented with fewer bits—and hence we have a compression.

As was stated in Section 6.4.2, the quantizer in the DPCM loop is designed as though there were no memory in the system. Also, the effect of the quantizer on the input to the predictor is neglected. These assumptions are necessary in order to make possible a suboptimum design of the quantizer, since a general optimization of the quantizer is not feasible due to the nonlinearity of the DPCM system. Arnstein (1975) optimized the quantizer in the loop, but only for the case of a two-level quantizer.

With these assumptions, one can proceed to design the quantizer following the approach of the zero-memory quantizer in Section 2.5. As in the design of any quantizer, it is important to be able to estimate the signal-to-quantizing noise ratio. We represent the quantizing noise by the symbol q_0 and show its propagation through the system in Figure 6.10.

The expression for quantizing noise in Section 2.5 was obtained for a uniform quantizer, assuming zero distortion in the overload regions. The result was:

$$\text{Mean-square distortion} = \frac{\Delta^2}{12} \qquad [\text{equation (2.5.7)}]$$

where $\Delta = 2V/M$, the input quantizing interval. The corresponding signal-to-noise ratio, assuming a uniform input signal probability distribution, was found to be:

$$\text{SNR} = 6n(\text{in dB}) \qquad [\text{equation (2.5.13)}]$$

where 2^n is the number of quantizing levels, M.

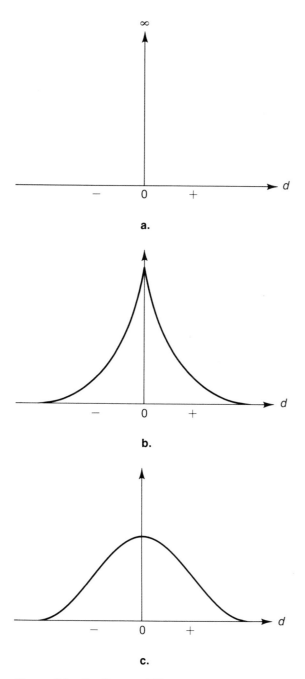

Figure 6.9 *Continuous Difference Signal Distribu-*
tions: a. Minimum Entropy, b. Typical, and c. Maxi-
mum Entropy.

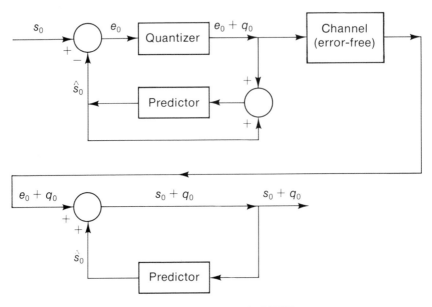

Figure 6.10   *Quantization Error Propagation in DPCM.*

This result shows the signal-to-noise ratio to be a linear function of the number of bits used to code the output levels of the quantizer. Even though this result is used extensively in the PCM literature and in PCM systems design, it is *not* appropriate for DPCM because the probability distribution of the input signal to the DPCM quantizer is not at all uniform. A typical shape for this distribution is shown in Figure 6.9b—a highly peaked distribution.

O'Neal (1966) developed an approximate expression for the quantizing noise in DPCM by using the nonuniform optimum quantizer approach described in Section 2.5. In this procedure, the spacing of the quantization levels is closer for the high probability intervals, and further apart for the low probability intervals. The criterion here is the minimization of the mean-square quantization noise. O'Neal used the expression developed by Panter and Dite (1951) for the minimum mean-square quantization noise (see Section 2.5), that is,

$$\sigma_q^2 = \frac{2}{3M^2} \left[\int_0^V [p(e)]^{1/3} de \right]^3 \tag{6.4.9}$$

where: M is the number of levels, with $M = 2^n$ for an n-bit system

   $p(e)$ is the probability density of the input to the quantizer

Equation 6.4.9 is actually equation (2.5.15), assuming an even, symmetric function for $p(e)$. Following O'Neal,* we use a Laplacian function to model $p(e)$, as follows:

$$p(e) = \frac{1}{\sqrt{2}\sigma_e} \exp\left(-\frac{\sqrt{2}}{\sigma_e}|e|\right) \tag{6.4.10}$$

where σ_e is the rms value of the quantizer input. Substituting (6.4.10) into (6.4.9):

$$\sigma_q^2 = \frac{2}{3M^2}\left[\int_0^V \frac{1}{(\sqrt{2}\sigma_e)^{1/3}} \exp\left(\frac{-\sqrt{2}}{3\sigma_e}|e|\right) de\right]^3 \tag{6.4.11}$$

When $V \gg \sigma_e$, as is typical, we can let $V \to \infty$, giving:

$$\sigma_q^2 = \frac{9\sigma_e^2}{2M^2} \tag{6.4.12}$$

This result in (6.4.12) shows the same inverse square function of M^2 as in the case of the uniform quantizer. For the uniform quantizer we had

$$\Delta = \frac{2V}{M}$$

so, we can rewrite equation (2.5.7) as

$$\text{Mean-square distortion} = \frac{V^2}{3M^2} \tag{6.4.13}$$

We can express the signal-to-quantizing-noise ratio for the nonuniform quantizer in DPCM as:

$$\text{SNR} = 10\log_{10}\frac{\sigma^2}{\sigma_q^2} \tag{6.4.14}$$

where σ^2 is the mean-square value of the original signal

$$\text{SNR} = 10\log_{10}\left(\frac{2M^2\sigma^2}{9\sigma_e^2}\right) \tag{6.4.15}$$

---

* O'Neal (1966) found that the Laplacian served as a good theoretical fit to the $p(e)$ curves obtained from actual measurements on real pictures.

Since $M = 2^n$,

$$\text{SNR} = 10\log_{10}\frac{2}{9} + 20n\log_{10}2 + 10\log_{10}\frac{\sigma^2}{\sigma_e^2} \tag{6.4.16}$$

$$\text{SNR} = -6.5 + 6n + 10\log_{10}\frac{\sigma^2}{\sigma_e^2} \tag{6.4.17}$$

To compare the signal-to-quantizing noise performance of DPCM to that of PCM, we have to reexamine the assumptions that were made in Section 2.5 for the PCM case, namely:

1. Zero contribution to quantization noise from the overload regions
2. Uniform probability distribution of the input signal to the quantizer

Assumption 2 is consistent with the uniform quantization law used, but assumption 1 does not reflect the more realistic situation wherein a finite noise contribution from the overload region is expected and a design attempt is made to minimize it. This is done under the constraint that the more one increases the overload point, V, to decrease the overload noise, the more the granular noise increases. The summary article on quantization by Gersho (1977) states that it is common practice to choose V as some multiple of σ, the input signal standard deviation. A common choice is $V = 4\sigma$, and this was the assumption used in Section 2.5 to develop the expression:

$$\text{SNR} = -7.27 + 6n \qquad \text{[equation (2.5.34)]}$$

If we compare (2.5.34) to (6.4.17), we see that the difference is in the constants and the term $10\log_{10}(\sigma^2/\sigma_e^2)$. O'Neal made a similar comparison for PCM and DPCM for television and found that by suitably arranging the synchronization pulse quantization and the video signal quantization, the constants in the SNR expressions could be made equal, leaving the term $10\log_{10}(\sigma^2/\sigma_e^2)$ as the only difference. We can do a similar adjustment here: If we assume that the overload point V equals 3.66σ instead of 4σ, then the SNR for the PCM case is:

$$\text{SNR} = -6.5 + 6n \tag{6.4.18}$$

giving the result that DPCM improves the signal-to-quantizing noise by

$$10\log_{10}\frac{\sigma^2}{\sigma_e^2}\,\text{dB}$$

This result is not surprising since we can do a "better job" in designing the quantizer for the highly symmetric, Laplacian-type distribution of the difference signal as compared to the input signal. And since the variance of the difference signal is less than that of the input signal, we would expect the improvement in SNR to be a function of the ratio σ^2/σ_e^2.

All of these formulations have been based on the mean-square error distortion measure. But as was stated in Section 6.2, this is not always the most appropriate measure, especially for pictures. Other measures have been used for pictures, and a good example is the one based on visual thresholds described in the paper by Sharma and Netravali (1977).

6.4.3 Adaptive DPCM

The usual assumption that is made in designing a DPCM system is that the input data is stationary.* With this assumption, we can design a predictor and a quantizer with fixed parameters, as was outlined in Section 6.4.2. But when the input data is far from stationary, these fixed-parameter designs will show inconsistent and generally poor performance—in terms of signal-to-quantizing-noise ratio. Adaptive designs have been used to advantage in these cases, and the design approach is really one of two choices: an adaptive predictor with a fixed quantizer, or a fixed predictor with an adaptive quantizer. Let's look at these options separately.

ADAPTIVE PREDICTION

The predictor design approach that was outlined in Section 6.4.2 utilized the covariance matrix of the incoming data to find the weighting factors to be applied to each previous sample value. If one were to recompute this covariance matrix and the corresponding weighting factors periodically, then the predictor could "keep up" with the changing statistics of the input data. A similar approach was used by Atal and Schroeder (1970) for an adaptive DPCM system for speech signals. In their scheme they updated the weighting factors every 5 msec, and even though they used only a two-level quantizer, they found that the results compared well with that of a 6-bit PCM system.

Although this method of making the predictor adaptive can be used for nonstationary data, it has become more common to use a fixed predictor with an adaptive quantizer, as will be covered in the next section.

ADAPTIVE QUANTIZATION

A number of techniques have been developed to make the quantizer in a DPCM loop adaptive, and we will look at a few representative ones here,

---

* See Section 2.3 for a definition of stationarity.

namely, error signal normalization, the switched quantizer, spatial masking, and the reflected quantizer.

Error Signal Normalization Since the quantizer in a DPCM loop is designed as a zero-memory quantizer assuming a Laplacian-type difference signal, knowledge of the standard deviation, σ_e, of this signal would allow one to change the quantizer intervals and levels accordingly. A practical variation on this method is to normalize the difference signals according to the standard deviation, and use a fixed quantizer.

Switched Quantizer Another approach involves changing the quantizer characteristics to match the difference signal, which is modeled as a Markov process, and using a few previous sample differences to determine the Markov state of the difference signal. Such a scheme was reported by Cohen for video (1972) and speech (1973). For video, two, and for speech, three, previous differences were used to control the quantizer.

Spatial Masking In the application of DPCM to images, it is common practice to use not only previous samples on the scan line in question, but also samples from the previous scan line—thereby taking advantage of the two-dimensional correlation between the samples. In the design of the quantizer, one can also use two-dimensional information in making it adaptive. The techniques is usually called *spatial masking*, and an example of it is given in the paper by Netravali and Prasada (1977), in which a masking function is developed from the weighted sum of the gradients around a given picture element. These masking functions are then used to segment the picture into blocks for "optimum quantization" of the difference signals on a block basis.

Reflected Quantizer It is important to remember that since the error signal in DPCM is a difference signal, it is either positive or negative. To preserve this polarity, one would normally use one binary digit to indicate it, and thus there would be one less bit available to represent the magnitude of the difference.

However, additional information about the polarity of the difference is carried by the predicted values. Musmann noted this fact in 1971, and in 1974 Bostelmann implemented a method of using this information, as follows.

An input sample of n bits has 2^n possible levels, from 0 to $2^n - 1$. If the predicted value has the same number of levels, then the difference signal $e = S - \hat{S}_0$, can be positive or negative and lie anywhere in the range of $-(2^n - 1)$ to $+(2^n - 1)$ or $(2 \cdot 2^n) - 1$ possible levels. (The 1 is subtracted to account for zero being common to the positive and negative range.) However, if we know the actual value of $\hat{S}_0$, then, where the difference is positive or negative, it has the ranges:

Positive difference range: $0 \leq e \leq (2^n - 1) - \hat{S}_0$

Negative difference range: $-\hat{S}_0 \leq e \leq -1$

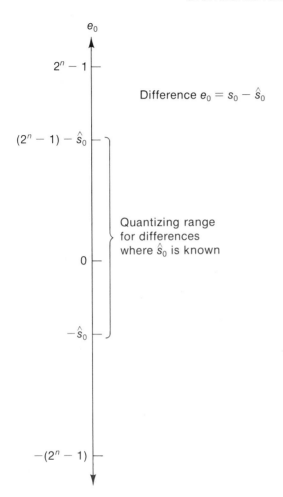

Figure 6.11 *Reduction of the Quantizing Range for the Quantized Difference Signal by Use of the Predicted Value, $\hat{S}_0$.*

Thus, the actual range of the difference, given $\hat{S}_0$, is from $-\hat{S}_0$ to $(2^n - 1) - \hat{S}_0$ or $2^n - 1$ levels. This is essentially half the possible number of levels if $\hat{S}_0$ is not known. Therefore, the sign bit is not necessary since an appropriate coding scheme can be used to differentiate between the positive and negative ranges. Such a scheme could utilize the complement for the negative range: If the positive differences are represented by their binary notation, and the negative differences are represented by their 2^n complement, then the level $2^n - 1 - S_0$ can be used as a test for polarity: less than the level is plus; greater than is minus (Bostelmann 1974). See Figure 6.11.

6.5 BLOCK-TO-BLOCK COMPRESSION

In the previous sections of this chapter, we have considered the prediction of the next *sample* in order to encode the difference between the predicted and actual values and thereby achieve a compression. This approach can be extended to include the prediction of *blocks* of samples, and the differences can be encoded in an appropriate way that allows unambiguous reconstruction of the "original" blocks at the receiving end of the system.

In most applications of block-to-block compression, the prediction is the simplest one possible: namely, that the next block is identical to the present block. This turns out to be a very useful prediction since in many applications, samples are not expected to change in subsequent blocks.

Two examples of this situation are: line-to-line compression of two-level facsimile and frame-to-frame compression of television. In two-level facsimile (such as in weather charts), there are large regions of white pixels that typically do not change on a line-to-line basis. In television, there are many scenes in which the *background* does not change from frame to frame over an appreciable number of frames. This is particularly true in television used for teleconferencing.

In such applications, only the differences that exceed a preset threshold are encoded so that the number of encoded differences is a small subset of the total number of original samples in the block. Because of this, the *location* of the samples that change has to be preserved. A number of schemes have been devised to accomplish this and they will be discussed in Chapter 8.

In the television application, some trade-offs can be made between the spatial and temporal resolution in designing the predictor and difference quantizer, and this will be discussed in Chapter 15.

HIGHLIGHTS

- Predictive coding involves compression in the time domain; in predictive coding the next sample is predicted and the difference between the actual and predicted value of the next sample is encoded.

- Delta modulation and differential pulse code modulation (DPCM) are two well-known predictive coding techniques.

- In delta modulation the sign of the difference between a given sample and its predicted value is coded into one of two equal and opposite-polarity levels; the two types of delta modulation are conventional and adaptive (the step size is adjusted to minimize slope overload and granular noise in the reconstructed signal).

- The two components that one attempts to optimize in a DPCM design are the predictor and the quantizer. Most DPCM predictors are linear and most DPCM quantizers are of the zero-memory type.

- The signal-to-quantizing noise ratio of DPCM compared to PCM, for the same code rate, is better by a factor that is approximately equal to the ratio of the original signal variance to the difference signal variance, σ^2/σ_e^2.

SUGGESTIONS FOR FURTHER READING

The following items are suggested for further reading and study:

Abate, J. E. "Linear Adaptive Delta Modulation." *Proc. IEEE*, *55*, no. 3, 1967 pp. 298–308.

Delta modulation is made adaptive by monitoring the derivative (the slope) of the incoming signal and changing the step size accordingly.

Arnstein, D. S. "Quantization Error in Predictive Coders." *IEEE Trans. on Comm.*, vol. COM-23, no. 4, April 1975, pp. 423–429.

The quantizer in a DPCM loop is optimized using an iterative procedure (and without the usual simplifying assumptions) to develop a two-level quantizer.

Atal, B. S., and Schroeder, M. R. See Chapter 13, Suggestions for Further Reading.

Bostelmann, G. "A Simple High Quality DPCM—Codec for Video Telephony Using 8 Mbit Per Second." *NTZ*, no. 3, 1974, pp. 115–117.

In this paper, the author presents a scheme for transmitting the output of the DPCM encoder *without* a sign bit.

Cohen, F. 1973. See Chapter 13, Suggestions for Further Reading.

Cohen, F. "A Switched Quantizer for Nonlinear Coding of Video Signals." *NTZ*, no. 12, 1972, pp. 554–559.

The transfer characteristic of the quantizer in the forward loop of a DPCM encoder is continually optimized by the method of Panter and Dite (1951) (see Chap. 2) depending on the previous state of the input, in order to match the quantizer to an assumed input Markov process.

Elias, P. "Predictive coding." Part I and Part II. *IRE Trans. Info. Theory*, IT-1, no. 1, 1955, pp. 16–33.

In this paper Elias proposed the concept of encoding the difference between a sample and its predicted value in order to minimize the entropy of the transmitted data.

Gersho, A. See Chapter 2, Suggestions for Further Reading.

Jayant, N. S. "Adaptive Delta Modulation with a One-bit Memory." *BSTJ*, 49, no. 3, March 1970, pp. 321–343.

This article concerns an adaptive delta modulator in which the step size is changed as a function of the previous two pulses coming from the encoder.

Lei, T. L. R., Scheinberg, N., and Schilling, D. L. "Adaptive Delta Modulation System for Video Encoding. " *IEEE Trans. on Comm.*, vol, COM-25, November 1977.

The Song adaptive delta modulation technique (see Song et al. 1971 in this section) is applied to video systems, and the effects of noise are examined.

Musmann, H. G. "Codierung von Videosignalen." *NTZ*, vol. 24, 1971, pp. 114–116. In this paper, the concept of the reflected quantizer in introduced.

Netravali, A., and Prasada, B. See Chapter 15, Suggestions for Further Reading.

O'Neal, J. B. "Predictive Quantizing Systems (Differential Pulse Code Modulation) for the Transmission of Television Signals." *Bell Systems Tech. J.*, 45, no. 5, 1966, pp. 689–721.
In this often-referenced paper, O'Neal analyzes DPCM, compares it to PCM, and presents actual experimental data for TV applications.

Panter, P. F., and Dite, W. See Chapter 2, Suggestions for Further Reading.

Sharma, D. K., and Netravali, A. N. "Design of Quantizers for DPCM Coding of Picture Signals." *IEEE Trans. on Comm.*, vol. COM-25, no. 11, November 1977, pp. 1267–1274.
In this paper, the number of levels of a quantizer is minimized, subject to the constraint of keeping the quantization error below a threshold of visibility.

Song, C., Garodnick, J., and Schilling, D. C. "A Variable—Step-size Robust Delta Modulator." *IEEE Trans. on. Comm. Tech*, vol. COM-19, no. 6, December 1971, pp. 1033–1044.
This paper analytically develops an adaptive delta modulation system for a Markov-Gaussian source by optimizing the transmitter and receiver separately. The resulting design increases the step size by 50% each time the output of the encoder does not change and decreases it by 50% each time it does change.

The following references are mentioned in this chapter primarily for their historical significance:

Cutler, C. C. Differential Quantization of Communication Signals. U.S. Patent No. 2 605 361, July 29, 1952.

Deloraine, E. M., Derjavitch, B., Van Mierlo, S. Delta Modulation. French Patent 932 140. August 1946.

Kolmogorov, A. N. "Interpolation and Extrapolation of Stationary Random Series." *Journal of the Soviet Academy of Sciences*, no. 5, 1941, pp. 3–14.

Wiener, N. *The Extrapolation, Interpolation, and Smoothing of Stationary Time Series with Engineering Applications.* Cambridge, Mass.: M.I.T. Press, 1942.

CHAPTER 7

Nonredundant Sample Coding

7.1 INTRODUCTION

Unlike the techniques in Chapter 6, there is a group of prediction techniques that does not transmit the difference between the new value and the predicted value, but only transmits the new value whenever this difference exceeds a threshold.

It has become customary to call new values that cause the difference to exceed the threshold *nonredundant*, and those that cause the difference to be equal to or less than the threshold *redundant*. A special code must be sent to indicate the presence of redundant samples, and it provides timing information that, together with the actual sample values, allows a complete reconstruction of the original sample sequence at the receiving end of the communication system. Many techniques can be used to send this timing information, and these are treated in Chapter 8.

Since the samples that are classified redundant are not transmitted, the output of this kind of predictor is asynchronous and must be buffered. This buffer requirement can represent a potential problem in the form of buffer overflow or underflow. The subject of buffer control is covered in Chapter 9.

In this chapter, we examine three classes of prediction techniques that transmit nonredundant samples and timing information: polynomial predictors, polynomial interpolators, and statistical predictors.

Polynomial predictors test the next sample to see if it lies (within an aperture) on an nth-order polynomial. The two most commonly used polynomials are the zero-order and the first-order polynomials. The zero-order polynomial has a special version called run-length coding, in which the timing information is sent in the form of the run lengths of the redundant samples.

Polynomial interpolators are similar to polynomial predictors, except that they allow the aperture to vary. The first-order polynomial interpolator is known as the *fan algorithm* and essentially fits straight-line segments to a data waveform.

Statistical predictors make use of a "learning period" of some number of previous samples to update a predictor function, which is applied to a smaller number of previous samples. Statistical predictors are adaptive in design as opposed to the polynomial predictors and interpolators, which are normally nonadaptive.

7.2 POLYNOMIAL PREDICTORS

One of the first data compression techniques that was considered for sampled data was the polynomial predictor (Medlin 1963). It has received much attention in the literature and has been applied to actual data in numerous experimental and simulation studies. The two most used forms of the polynomial predictor are the zero-order predictor and the first-order predictor.

In all polynomial predictors, the next sample is predicted to lie on an nth-order polynomial, as defined by $n + 1$ previous samples. Mathematically:

$$\hat{x}_t = x_{t-1} + \Delta x_{t-1} + \Delta^2 x_{t-1} + \cdots + \Delta^n x_{t-1} \tag{7.2.1}$$

where

$$\Delta x_{t-1} = x_{t-1} - x_{t-2}$$
$$\Delta x_{t-2} = x_{t-2} - x_{t-3}$$

and so on, and

$$\Delta^n x_{t-1} = \Delta^{n-1} x_{t-1} - \Delta^{n-1} x_{t-2}$$

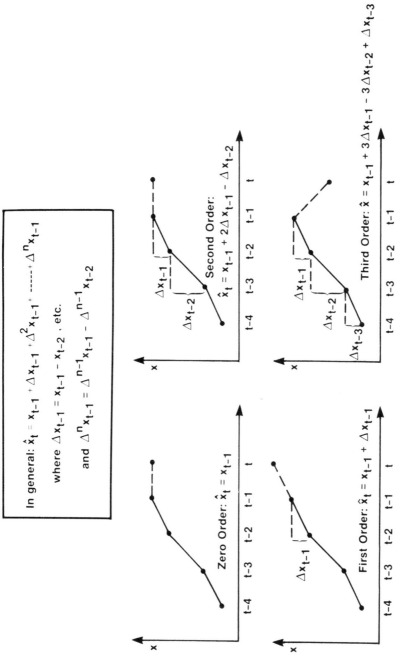

Figure 7.1 *Prediction by an nth-Order Polynomial.*

An illustration of (7.2.1) is given in Figure 7.1, where we see that it is possible to get a different prediction depending on the order of the polynomial. If the next sample lies on or in a well-defined vicinity of the nth-order polynomial, then it is considered redundant and is not transmitted. Otherwise, it is considered nonredundant and is transmitted.

In the following sections, we examine in more detail two forms of the polynomial predictor.

7.2.1 The Zero-Order Predictor

The *zero-order predictor* is given by the equation:

$$\hat{x}_t = x_{t-1} \tag{7.2.2}$$

In actual practice, a tolerance may be placed around this estimate, creating a window that is equal to, or a multiple of, the quantization interval. An algorithm for the zero-order predictor reads as follows:

ZERO-ORDER PREDICTOR ALGORITHM

1. Store and transmit first sample x_i and time of occurrence.
2. Put tolerance λ about x_i such that an aperture is obtained:

$$x_i - \lambda < \hat{x}_{i+1} < x_i + \lambda$$

3. Is next sample within aperture?
   If yes: Discard sample and test next sample.
   If no: Store and transmit sample and time of occurrence and repeat steps 2 and 3.

This algorithm is illustrated in Figure 7.2. The figure shows that of the 23 original samples in the pattern, 12 are classified as redundant. In the simplest form of time coding, a time word needs to be sent with each of the remaining 11 nonredundant samples. From a compression ratio standpoint, we have

$$\text{Sample compression ratio} = \frac{23}{11} = 2.09$$

However, the actual compression ratio would be considerably less than this number due to the overhead imposed by the time words. Various methods of time coding are examined in Chapter 8.

Periodic Sampling Pattern

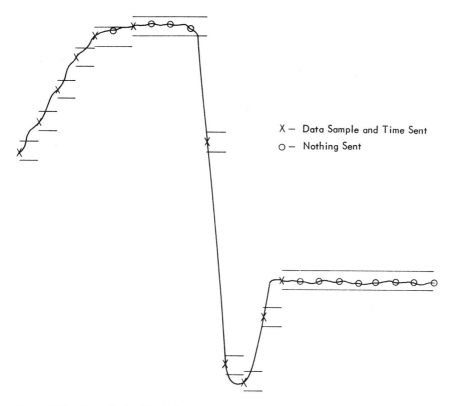

X — Data Sample and Time Sent

O — Nothing Sent

Figure 7.2 *Zero-Order Predictor.*

RUN-LENGTH CODING

Run-length coding is a special version of the zero-order predictor. Here, once the redundant samples have been eliminated, the requirement for sending the time information is met by sending the lengths of the redundant runs that occur between nonredundant samples.

For example, in Figure 7.2 if we used run-length coding, we would still send the same 11 nonredundant samples as before, but instead of sending 11 time words (one for each nonredundant sample), we would send 3 redundant run lengths. Very simply, if we used a fixed-length binary code to encode the time words and the run lengths, we would need a 5-bit word in both cases since there are 23 time slots. Computing the actual compression ratios then for each case, assuming 8-bit sample values:

$$\text{Simple time coding:}\quad \text{Actual Compression Ratio} = \frac{23 \times 8}{11 \times 8 + 11 \times 5}$$

$$= \frac{184}{143} = 1.29$$

$$\text{Run-length coding:}\quad \text{Actual Compression Ratio} = \frac{23 \times 8}{11 \times 8 + 3 \times 5}$$

$$= \frac{184}{103} = 1.79$$

This simple example suggests that the time coding method of sending a time word with every nonredundant sample is not always the best approach. More will be said about this in chapter 8.

Run-length coding has been used to compress images (see Section 14.3.2), and even though, as we will illustrate, it typically does not provide the highest compression ratio, its simplicity of implementation is an attractive design feature.

In order to develop an expression for the maximum compression ratio based on run lengths, we have to develop an expression for the entropy of the data source based on the run length as opposed to the sample (or pixel). Then

$$R_{\text{max}} = \frac{\log_2 M}{H_l} \tag{7.2.3}$$

where: M is the number of levels

H_l is the entropy on a run basis

This should be compared to the expression for maximum compression ratio defined in Chapter 3:

$$R_{\text{max}} = \frac{\log_2 M}{H} \qquad [\text{equation (3.4.1)}]$$

where H is the entropy on a sample basis.

We can derive an expression for H_l as follows. If we model a data source with M-level samples as a first-order Markov source, then the probability of a run exactly x samples long at the ith level is:

$$P(l_i = x) = P(i/i)^{x-1}\left[1 - P(i/i)\right] \tag{7.2.4}$$

Then the entropy of all the runs at level i is:

$$H_i(x) = -\sum_{x=1}^{\infty} P(l_i = x)\log_2 P(l_i = x))$$ (7.2.5)

or

$$H_i(x) = -\sum_{x=1}^{\infty} P(i/i)^{x-1}[1 - P(i/i)]\log_2 P(i/i)^{x-1}[1 - P(i/i)]$$ (7.2.6)

$$H_i(x) = -\sum_{x=1}^{\infty} P(i/i)^{x-1}[1 - P(i/i)]\{(x-1)\log_2 P(i/i) + \log_2[1 - P(i/i)]\}$$

(7.2.7)

$$H_i(x) = -[1 - P(i/i)]\log_2 P(i/i) \sum_{x=1}^{\infty}(x-1)P(i/i)^{x-1}$$

$$-[1 - P(i/i)]\log_2[1 - P(i/i)] \sum_{x=1}^{\infty} P(i/i)^{x-1}$$ (7.2.8)

But

$$\sum_{x=1}^{\infty} P(i/i)^{x-1} = \frac{1}{[1 - P(i/i)]}$$ (7.2.9)

and

$$\sum_{x=1}^{\infty}(x-1)P(i/i)^{x-1} = \frac{P(i/i)}{[1 - P(i/i)]^2}$$ (7.2.10)

Substituting:

$$H_i = \frac{-P(i/i)}{[1 - P(i/i)]}\log_2 P(i/i) - \log_2[1 - P(i/i)]$$ (7.2.11)

Now, to find the entropy of the runs at all M levels we have to average H_i over M:

$$H_l = \sum_{i=1}^{M} P(i)H_i$$ (7.2.12)

This computation of maximum compression ratio was made by Gray and Simpson (1972) for four different pictures taken on the moon as part of the Apollo program. Each picture was made up of 512×512 pixels, each quantized to 64 levels. The maximum compression ratio was computed both on a sample and on a run basis, and the interesting result was that the maximum compression ratio based on the run was about 60% that of the one based on the sample—independent of the picture.

Since the ratio of the maximum compression ratio on a run basis to that on a sample basis is really the ratio of the entropy on a sample basis to the entropy on a run basis [see equation (7.2.3) and equation (3.4.1)], we can look at it as the *efficiency* of the run-length coding as defined by equation (3.5.1). The above result of 60% should be compared to the typical efficiency of entropy coding (such as Huffman) of 95% and higher.

7.2.2 The First-Order Predictor

The *first-order predictor* is given by

$$\hat{x}_t = x_{t-1} + \Delta x_{t-1} \tag{7.2.13}$$

where $\Delta x_{t-1} = x_{t-1} - x_{t-2}$.

In the implementation of this first-order predictor, the actual algorithm may take on a number of different forms, depending on the definition of x_{t-1} and Δx_{t-1} in terms of tolerances. If we assume that $[x_{t-1} + \Delta x_{t-1}]$ has a tolerance λ placed about it equal to or greater than the quantization interval, then we can state the following algorithm.

FIRST-ORDER PREDICTOR ALGORITHM

1. Store and transmit first sample x_i and time of occurrence.
2. Store and transmit second sample x_{i+1}.
3. Compute $x_{i+1} - x_i$
4. Add $n(x_{i+1} - x_i)$ to last transmitted sample value, x_{i+1}, giving $\hat{x}_{i+1} = x_{i+1} + n(x_{i+1} - x_i)$, $n = 1$ initially.
5. Place tolerance around $\hat{x}$ so that an aperture is obtained:

$$x_{i+1} + n(x_{i+1} - x_i) - \lambda < \hat{x}_{i+2} < \hat{x}_{i+1} + n(x_{i+1} - x_i) + \lambda$$

6. Is next sample, $\hat{x}_{i+2}$, within aperture?
   If yes: Discard sample, replace n by $n + 1$, and repeat steps 4, 5, and 6, replacing i by $i + 1$ in step 6.
   If no: Repeat steps 1 through 6, considering x_{i+2} the first sample—that is, replacing i by $i + 2$, and letting $n = 1$.

This algorithm is illustrated in Figure 7.3. As can be seen in this example, 11 of the original 23 samples are classified redundant by the first-order predictor. Since the 12 remaining nonredundant samples occur in pairs by virtue of

Periodic Sampling Pattern

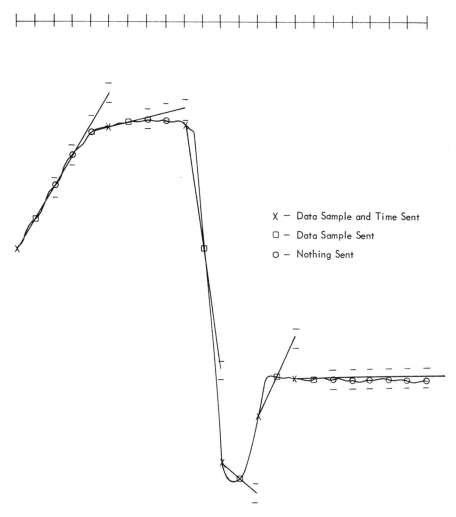

X — Data Sample and Time Sent

□ — Data Sample Sent

○ — Nothing Sent

Figure 7.3 *First-Order Predictor.*

the need to set a new slope each time, in the simplest approach to time coding only 6 time words need be sent. From a compression ratio standpoint:

$$\text{Sample compression ratio} = \frac{23}{12} = 1.92$$

As in the case of the zero-order predictor, the actual compression ratio will be reduced by the overhead imposed by the time words. More will be given on time coding in Chapter 8.

The first-order predictor's effectiveness depends on the probability of straight-line segments in the data. For a fixed number T of contiguous M-level samples, Lynch (1968) found an expression for the maximum number, N_L, of different straight-line segments (T samples long):

$$N_L = M + \sum_{S=1}^{S_m} 2\{M - S(T-1)\} \qquad (7.2.14)$$

where: S is the slope in levels per sample
         S_m is the maximum slope

The maximum slope, S_m is determined by

$$\left(\frac{M-1}{T-1}\right) - 1 < S_m = \text{integer} \le \frac{M-1}{T-1} \qquad (7.2.15)$$

The probability P_L of a straight-line sequence is then

$$P_L = \frac{N_L}{M^T} \qquad (7.2.16)$$

since there are M^T possible sequences as a maximum.

The curves in Figure 7.4 show that the number of straight-line sequences, T long, decreases as T increases and M (the number of levels) decreases. The probability of a straight-line sequence, however, decreases as T increases, but increases as M decreases.

7.2.3 Comparison of Polynomial Predictors

It is important to bear in mind that the sample compression ratio one obtains with a polynomial predictor depends to a large extent on how close the match is between the polynomial chosen (typically zero-order or first-order) and the actual amplitude vs. time behavior of the data. Extreme cases are obvious: For example, a zero-order predictor fits a staircase-type waveform, and a first-order predictor fits a sawtooth-type waveform. But actual data do not classify easily into such simple geometric waveforms, and in many cases only a *test* with representative data will indicate which order predictor should give the higher sample compression ratio. Recall that the method of time coding will affect the *actual* compression ratio, and it is this compression ratio that should be used for comparison purposes. The examples shown in Figures 7.2 and 7.3 are given

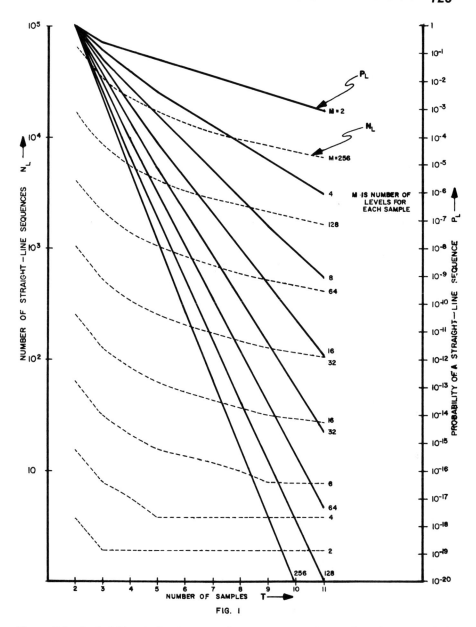

Figure 7.4 *Probability of a Straight-Line Sequence. From: Lynch, T. J. "The Probability of a Straight-Line Sequence from a Uniform Independent Sample Source." IEEE Trans. on Info. Theory, vol. IT-14, no. 5, Sept. 1968, p. 774. © 1968 IEEE.*

only to illustrate the operation of the zero- and first-order predictors, respectively. The sample compression ratios obtained from these examples should not be interpreted as a typical comparison of zero- and first-order predictors. On the contrary, to obtain a meaningful comparison, large representative samples of data should be tested and the results evaluated.

7.3 POLYNOMIAL INTERPOLATORS

In the literature, reference is made to the use of *interpolators* for compression (Ehrman 1967). Two are discussed: the zero-order and the first-order interpolator.

The zero-order interpolator is the same as the zero-order predictor except that the aperture is allowed to vary (within limits) in order to maximize the number of redundant samples. The first order interpolator, also called the "*fan algorithm*," has received much more attention and application. Basically, it is similar to the first-order predictor except that a new straight-line segment is always started at the end of the previous straight-line segment and the aperture is variable depending on the behavior of the sample sequence. Gardenhire (1964) and Davisson (1968) analyzed the fan algorithm.

The fan algorithm is illustrated in Figure 7.5. This figure shows two simple waveforms: (a) a straight-line waveform and (b) a simple curve waveform. The fan algorithm is applied to both as follows.

THE FAN ALGORITHM

1. Starting at sample 1, which is labeled nonredundant, draw a fan passing through tolerance limits placed around sample 2 and extending to the time slot of sample 3.

2. At sample 3 make the test: Is sample 3 within the fan?

3. If yes, label sample 2 redundant and start a new fan at sample 1 passing through the tolerance limits placed around sample 3. The new fan must have a smaller angle than the previous fan.

4. If no, label the previous sample (sample 2) nonredundant and start a new fan from this sample, passing through tolerance limits placed around sample 3.

5. Continue doing this until the end of the sample sequence. Label the last sample nonredundant.

6. Transmit each nonredundant sample and its time of occurrence.

7. At the receiving end of the system connect the nonredundant samples with straight lines.

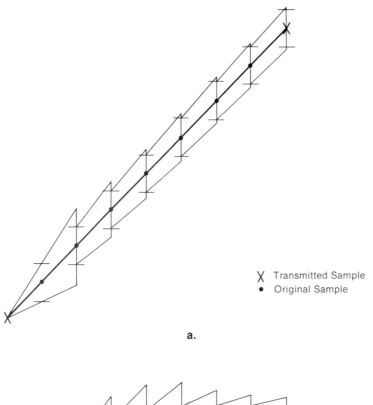

X Transmitted Sample
● Original Sample

a.

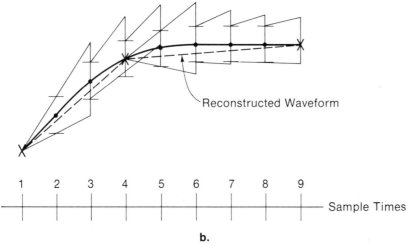

Reconstructed Waveform

Sample Times

1 2 3 4 5 6 7 8 9

b.

Figure 7.5 *The Fan Algorithm.*

When this algorithm is applied to the simple waveforms in Figure 7.5, only two nonredundant samples, the first and last, are found in part a, and three in part b. Note that sample 5 of part b falls outside the previously constructed fan, thus making sample 4 nonredundant.

7.4 STATISTICAL PREDICTORS

The effectiveness of the polynomial predictors and interpolators depends on the data source waveform. A poor match of the predictor technique to the data source may possibly result in an extremely inefficient system. The method of statistical prediction is aimed at solving this matching problem.

The procedure involves making a prediction of the next sample by using a linear or nonlinear function of some number of previous samples. If the absolute difference between the next sample and its predicted value is equal to or less than a preset threshold value, then this next sample is considered redundant. If this difference exceeds the threshold, then this next sample is considered nonredundant.

In statistical prediction, it is usually assumed that one can change the prediction function as time goes on. The prediction error can be monitored, and as the number of nonredundant samples increases, a decision can be made to change or update the predictor. Because of this feature, this kind of prediction is called *adaptive*.

The predictor is normally designed as a function of N previous samples. The parameters of the predictor function are determined from the characteristics of L previous samples, where

$$L \gg N \tag{7.4.1}$$

The L previous samples are sometimes referred to as "the learning period." For example, if a linear prediction function is used, then the next sample is predicted to be equal to the weighted sum of the N previous sample values. The weights are determined from the previous L samples, and if the criterion is minimum mean-square error, then the procedure of Section 6.4.2 would be followed wherein a set of N simultaneous covariance equations is solved for the N weights.

Statistical prediction for data compression was described by Balakrishnan in 1962 and applied in 1966 by Balakrishnan, Kutz, and Stampfl to video signals of weather satellite pictures. In this application, typical values of N and L were 3 and 20, respectively, and the actual compression ratios ranged between 2:1 and 3:1, depending on the picture.

HIGHLIGHTS

- In nonredundant sample coding a new sample value (called a nonredundant sample) is transmitted only when the difference between the new value and predicted value exceeds a threshold.
- Nonredundant sample coding requires buffering and time coding in every system.
- Three classes of nonredundant sample coding are: polynomial predictors, polynomial interpolators, and statistical predictors.
- In polynomial predictors, the next sample is predicted to lie on an nth-order polynomial; two forms are the zero-order predictor and first-order predictor.
- Run-length coding, a special form of the zero-order predictor, sends the time information by sending the lengths of redundant runs that occur between nonredundant samples.
- Polynomial interpolators are of two types: the zero-order interpolator (similar to the zero-order predictor) and the first-order interpolator, or fan algorithm (similar to the first-order predictor)
- Statistical predictors make predictions of the next sample by using a linear or nonlinear function of some number of previous samples and using a larger number of previous samples as a "learning period" to update the predictor function.

SUGGESTIONS FOR FURTHER READING

The following items are suggested for further reading and study:

Balakrishnan, A. V. "An Adaptive Nonlinear Data Predictor." *Proceedings of the National Telemetering Conf.* (*NTC*), vol. 2, no. 6–5. Washington, D. C., May 1962.

This paper describes the approach in designing a "statistical" predictor with a "learning" capability.

Balakrishnan, A. V., Kutz, R. L., Stampfl, R. A. "Adaptive Data Compression for Video Signals." NASA Technical Note, NASA TN D-3395, Washington, D. C., April 1966.

This report uses an adaptive "statistical" predictor to compress TV cloud cover pictures from the TIROS satellite and analyzes the results.

Davisson, L. D. "Data Compression Using Straight Line Interpolation." *IEEE Trans. on Info. Theory*, vol. IT-14, no. 3, May 1968, pp. 390–394.

Davisson analyzes the first-order interpolator (the fan algorithm), taking into account the effects of quantization.

Ehrman, L. "Analysis of Some Redundancy Removal Bandwidth Compression Techniques." *Proc. IEEE*, vol. 55, no. 3, March 1967, pp. 278–287.

In this article the zero-order predictor, the zero-order interpolator, and the fan algorithm are analyzed.

Gardenhire, L. W. "Redundancy Reduction, the Key to Adaptive Telemetry." *Proceedings of the National Telemetering Conf. (NTC)*, no. 1–5. Los Angeles, Calif., June 1964.
This paper compares the zero-order predictor, first-order predictor, and the fan algorithm.

Gray, K. G., and Simpson, R. S. "Upper Bound on Compression Ratio for Run Length Coding." *Proc. IEEE*, vol. 60, no. 1, January 1972, p. 148.
This short note computes the maximum compression ratios based on both run lengths and pixels, assuming a first-order Markov source model for four pictures, and finds that the run length R_{max} is typically 60% of the pixel R_{max}.

Lynch, T. J. "The Probability of a Straight-line Sequence from a Uniform Independent Sample Source." *IEEE Trans. on Info. Theory*, vol. IT-14, no. 5, September 1968, pp. 773–774.
In this article, for a uniformly distributed M-level, T-sample block of data, expressions for the number of different straight-line segments and their probabilities of occurrence are derived.

Medlin, J. E. "The Comparative Effectiveness of Several Telemetry Data Compression Techniques." *Proceedings of the International Telemetering Conf. (ITC)*, London, September 1963, pp. 328–340.
This paper describes the results when zero-order and first-order predictors are tested and compared using computer simulation.

CHAPTER 8

Time and Binary Source Coding

8.1 INTRODUCTION

In general, use of a redundancy-reduction technique requires that additional information be sent along with the *compressed* data so that the *original* data sequence or set can be reconstructed at the receiving end. This additional information is in the form of time or position information, and it must be coded in such a way as to minimize its "overhead" effect on the compression ratio, namely, the reduction of the compression ratio.

Not all source encoding or compression techniques require time coding. For example, the transformation techniques Karhunen–Loève, Fourier, and Hadamard require no special time information, and neither do the predictive coding techniques of differential pulse code modulation, and delta modulation. However, techniques such as polynomial and statistical predictors, which classify time samples into *redundant* and *nonredundant* categories, do require that special time information be sent along with the nonredundant samples. These techniques make use of a buffer in such a way that the periodicity of the original time sampling is lost. This periodicity is reinserted into the final reconstructed waveform by use of the time information. The requirement to send along additional time information with the nonredundant samples results in a compression ratio for the actual system that is always less than the idealized "sample compression ratio." In recent years, a number of coding schemes have been developed that may be used for time coding.

The basic information to be preserved by the time code is the *time of each nonredundant sample*. Different time codes supply this information in different ways. One important difference between time codes is the way in which the nonredundant sample value words are sometimes used in conjunction with the time code to supply the basic time information. Some time codes, called *total information time codes*, do not rely on this additional data, and consequently, can be compared directly to the entropy of the basic time information. But other codes, called *partial information time codes*, which supply only a part of the basic time information, cannot be compared to this entropy. For this reason, the time codes discussed in the following sections are compared to each other in performance, but the time information entropy is given for comparison only with the total information time codes.

There are basically three approaches to time coding a data source whose samples have been determined to be nonredundant (n) or redundant (r): (1) give the $n-r$ sequence; (2) give the time of each nonredundant sample; (3) give the length of each redundant and nonredundant run. Time code techniques have been developed for each approach, and in this chapter we examine various time codes and compare them on the basis of the average number of time code bits per original data sample. Two different source models, the independent sample model and the Markov sample model, are used for the time entropy formulation and code comparison. Special attention is given to the problem of discrimination between the time code and the nonredundant samples when they must be used together to supply the time information. Most of the material in this chapter is taken from a paper by the author on the same subject (Lynch 1974).

One type of data source—the binary data source—can be compressed directly by some of the codes described in this chapter. This type of source is found in two-level facsimile systems (Chapter 16) and in computer-based files (Chapter 17), among others. Basically, we try to code the binary source output so that the average *rate* is less than 1 bit per sample. As stated earlier, the *timing* information for a data source can be modelled as a binary source since the information it provides is used to label the output samples either redundant or nonredundant. Thus, time codes that operate independently of the nonredundant M-level samples can be considered candidates for the compression of binary sources. More is said about this in Section 8.5.

8.2 MATHEMATICAL MODELS FOR TIME INFORMATION

A source encoder that determines which samples are redundant according to some prescribed algorithm sends to a buffer the remaining samples, the nonredundant samples. We may think of these samples as one type of input to the buffer. Another type of input is the time information contained in the original sequence of nonredundant and redundant samples. This information may be coded in such a way that it is either stored in the buffer separately for subsequent transmission as a separate data block, or stored with the corresponding nonredundant samples for subsequent transmission in a combined sequence of time code words and nonredundant sample values. In the latter case, additional bits must sometimes be used to discriminate between the time code words and the nonredundant sample values.

For the time information we may use a mathematical source model that can be described in terms of its format and its statistical properties. The format of this model is a two-symbol sequence with the following characteristics:

1. Only two types of symbols are present: r symbols (corresponding to redundant samples) and n symbols (corresponding to nonredundant samples).

2. All symbols, whether r or n, occur at a fixed rate.

3. The output symbol pattern consists of alternating runs of r and n symbols, with a minimum run length of one symbol.

With the help of these characteristics it is possible to state the present problem of time coding in a mathematical sense—that is, to find a method of coding the time of the n symbols that results in a minimum average number of timing bits per symbol for the $n–r$ source.

The statistical properties are conveniently described in terms of the probabilities of the n and r symbols. Two statistical models for these probabilities are: the statistically independent symbol model, and the Markov model. Both are used in this chapter since both have been used widely in the literature, although the former is actually a special case of the latter, as will be shown.

8.2.1 Statistically Independent Symbol Model

In this model each symbol is assumed to be statistically independent, with P_n the probability of a nonredundant symbol, and $P_r = 1 - P_n$ the probability of a redundant symbol. The average run lengths are given by:

$$\bar{l}_n = \frac{1}{1 - P_n} \qquad (8.2.1)$$

and

$$\bar{l}_r = \frac{1}{1 - P_r} \qquad (8.2.2)$$

Similar models have been used by Elias (55) in studying run-length coding.

For estimates of P_n and P_r, we can introduce the *sample compression ratio* R, defined as

$$R = \lim_{S \to \infty} \frac{S}{S_n} \qquad (8.2.3)$$

where: S is the total number of samples in a sequence

S_n is the total number of nonredundant samples in the same sequence

In this case, a count of samples is the same as a count of symbols.

Then, P_n and P_r may be estimated by:

$$P_n \simeq \frac{1}{R}; P_r \simeq 1 - \frac{1}{R} \qquad (8.2.4)$$

Thus, for the average run lengths, we have:

$$\bar{l}_n = \frac{R}{R - 1} \qquad (8.2.5)$$

$$\bar{l}_r = R \qquad (8.2.6)$$

For this model, the entropy, on the basis of each symbol, is

$$H_s(\text{SI}) = -[P_n \log P_n + P_r \log P_r] \qquad (8.2.7)$$

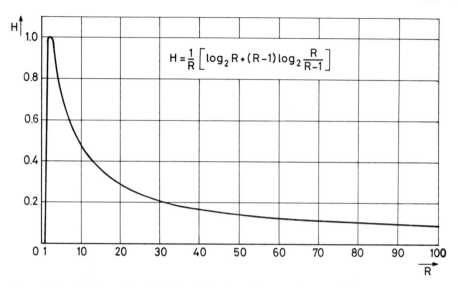

Figure 8.1 *Entropy of the Statistically Independent n–r Symbol Source. From: Lynch T. J. "Comparison of Time Codes for Source Encoding." IEEE Trans. on Communications, vol. COM-22, no. 2, Feb. 1974, p. 153. © 1974 IEEE.*

where all logarithms are to the base 2. Using (8.2.4)

$$H_s(\text{SI}) = \frac{1}{R}\left[\log R + (R-1)\log\frac{R}{R-1}\right] \tag{8.2.8}$$

This entropy function is plotted in Fig. 8.1.

8.2.2 Markov Model

If the assumption is made that each n or r symbol depends on the previous symbol, then the model of a first-order Markov process can be used. The process is described by six probabilities: $P(n)$, $P(r)$, $P(n/n)$, $P(r/r)$, $P(n/r)$, $P(r/n)$, where

$$P(n) + P(r) = 1 \tag{8.2.9}$$

$$P(n/r) + P(r/r) = 1 \tag{8.2.10}$$

$$P(r/n) + P(n/n) = 1 \tag{8.2.11}$$

$$P(r/n)P(n) = P(n/r)P(r) \tag{8.2.12}$$

This model has been used by Capon (1959).

The average run lengths are given by

$$\bar{l}_n = \frac{1}{1 - P(n/n)} \tag{8.2.13}$$

and

$$\bar{l}_r = \frac{1}{1 - P(r/r)} \tag{8.2.14}$$

For this model, the entropy on a symbol basis can be written as

$$H_s(M) = -[P(n)P(n/n)\log P(n/n) + P(n)P(r/n)\log P(r/n)$$
$$+ P(r)P(r/r)\log P(r/r) + P(r)P(n/r)\log P(n/r)] \tag{8.2.15}$$

Because of the symbol dependencies, the entropy of (8.2.15) will always be less than or equal to the entropy defined by (8.2.7).

For consistency with the statistically independent symbol model entropy, it is necessary to express the entropy in terms of the compression ratio. In the expression for the entropy in (8.2.15) there are six parameters; however, the entropy can be expressed in terms of only two of these parameters.

We choose as independent parameters, $P(n)$ and $P(r/r)$ since the compression ratio is approximated by $1/P(n)$, and the average redundant run length is given in terms of $P(r/r)$ (8.2.14).

We can write the following probabilities in terms of $P(n)$ and $P(r/r)$ using equations (8.2.9), (8.2.10), (8.2.11), and (8.2.12).

$$P(r) = 1 - P(n) \tag{8.2.16}$$

$$P(n/r) = 1 - P(r/r) \tag{8.2.17}$$

$$P(r/n) = \frac{[1 - P(r/r)][1 - P(n)]}{P(n)} \tag{8.2.18}$$

$$P(n/n) = 1 - \frac{[1 - P(r/r)][1 - P(n)]}{P(n)} \tag{8.2.19}$$

Then,

$$H_s(M) = -\left[P(n)\left\{1 - \frac{AB}{P(n)}\right\} \log\left\{1 - \frac{AB}{P(n)}\right\} + AB\log\frac{AB}{P(n)} \right.$$
$$\left. + AP(r/r)\log P(r/r) + AB\log B \right] \tag{8.2.20}$$

where: $A = 1 - P(n)$

$\qquad B = 1 - P(r/r)$

The entropy in (8.2.20) is plotted in Figure 8.2, versus $1/P(n)$ (the compression ratio) for different values of $P(r/r)$. All curves are not the same length because as $P(r/r)$ decreases, $P(n)$ must stay above an increasing lower bound in order to ensure that the other four probabilities that characterize the source all stay within the bound: $0 \le P \le 1$.

By applying $0 \le P(r/n) \le 1$ to (8.2.18), the lower bound on $P(n)$ is

$$P(n) \ge \frac{1 - P(r/r)}{2 - P(r/r)} \qquad\qquad (8.2.21)$$

The curves in Figure 8.2 have a special constraint on $P(n)$, which satisfies (8.2.21):

$$P(n) \ge 1 - P(r/r) \qquad\qquad (8.2.22)$$

for the following reason: If we substitute the equality of (8.2.22) into (8.2.17),

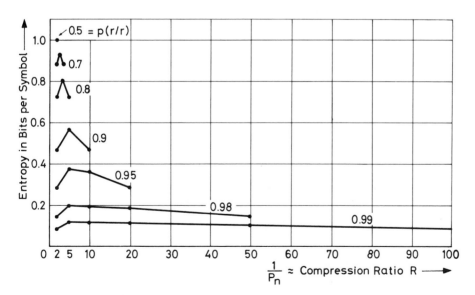

Figure 8.2 *Entropy of the Markov n–r Symbol Source. From: Lynch, T. J. "Comparison of Time Codes for Source Encoding." IEEE Trans. on Communications, vol. COM-22, no. 2, Feb. 1974, p. 154. © 1974 IEEE.*

(8.2.18), and (8.2.19), we can write the conditional probabilities as:

$$P(r/r) = 1 - P(n)$$

$$P(r/n) = 1 - P(n)$$

$$P(n/n) = P(n)$$

$$P(n/r) = P(n)$$

These equations show that the equality of (8.2.22) converts the Markov model into the statistically independent symbol model. We can see this from the Figures 8.1 and 8.2. The curve in Figure 8.1 is actually the locus of the points on the entropy curves in Figure 8.2, where

$$P(n) = 1 - P(r/r)$$

8.3 TIME ENCODING METHODS

In Section 8.1, three basic methods of sending time information were mentioned:

1. Send the n–r sequence.
2. Send the time of each nonredundant sample.
3. Send the length of each redundant and nonredundant run.

Time codes have been developed along these lines, and in the descriptions to follow, they will be broken down into similar categories:

1. Sequence time codes
2. Time of nonredundant sample (TNRS) codes
3. Run-length codes

Some of the time codes are designed to operate within a fixed time frame, others are not. However, all time codes could be utilized within a fixed time-frame basis. In the following description as well as in Section 8.4 we consider the sequence time codes, and the TNRS codes on a fixed time-frame basis, and the run-length codes on a frameless basis.

The frame synchronization will not be included in the design of the fixed time-frame codes since this is a function of the other system considerations, as in the case of time multiplexing.

As pointed out in Sections 8.1 and 8.2, some time codes contain all the time information and can be sent separately from the nonredundant samples, whereas other time codes contain only partial time information and must be sent in conjunction with the nonredundant sample values in order to supply the full time information. We now examine the various time codes.

8.3.1 Sequence Time Codes

BINARY SEQUENCE CODES

One may encode the pattern of the entire sequence of nonredundant and redundant samples as a single code word. The simplest way to do this is to represent a nonredundant sample by a 1 and a redundant sample by a 0. For a fixed time frame of N sample-time intervals, we have N samples per frame. If the first sample of the frame is always considered nonredundant, then there are $N - 1$ remaining samples to encode as either redundant or nonredundant. This results in a binary sequence time code of $N - 1$ bits.

We note that this time code does *not* depend on the statistical characteristics of the source. Since it requires 1 bit per n or r symbol, we may think of it as matched to the maximum entropy case of $P(r) = P(n) = 0.5$ and $H = 1$ bit per symbol.

Since the time word in this case has a fixed length, it can be easily distingished if it is sent separately at the beginning of the sequence of nonredundant sample values.

In this respect, this code has the advantage of having no requirement for additional code digits for discrimination between time code and nonredundant samples. The binary sequence code contains *all* the time information that is required to be sent from the n–r sequence. It is a total information time code.

LYNCH–DAVISSON CODE

Another method of encoding the pattern of nonredundant and redundant samples was developed by Lynch (1966) and Davisson (1966). Here the pattern of the sequence in the N-sample frame is represented by a number given by

$$T = \sum_{j=1}^{q} \binom{n_j - 1}{j} \tag{8.3.1}$$

where: q is the number of nonredundant samples, with $1 \leq q \leq N - 1$

n_j is the sample number of a nonredundant sample, with $1 \leq n_j \leq N - 1$

j is the index of the nonredundant sample, with $1 \leq j \leq q$

The encoding and decoding scheme of the Lynch–Davisson (LD) code can be represented in a coding matrix that can also be used to implement the scheme. Figure 8.3 shows this coding matrix, which is generated and extended by means of the Pascal triangle rule (as shown in the sample triangle). As an example, consider the 16-bit sequence:

0010000000100000

15	105	455	1365	3003	5005	6435	6435	5005	3003	1365	455	105	15	1	0
14	91	364	1001	2002	3003	3432	3003	2002	1001	364	91	14	1	0	0
13	78	286	715	1287	1716	1716	1287	715	286	78	13	1	0	0	0
12	66	220	445	792	924	792	495	220	66	12	1	0	0	0	0
11	55	165	330	462	462	330	165	55	11	1	0	0	0	0	0
10	45	120	210	252	210	120	45.	10	1	0	0	0	0	0	0
9	36	84	126	126	84	36	9	1	0	0	0	0	0	0	0
8	28	56	70	56	28	8	1	0	0	0	0	0	0	0	0
7	21	35	35	21	7	1	0	0	0	0	0	0	0	0	0
6	15	20	15	6	1	0	0	0	0	0	0	0	0	0	0
5	10	10	5	1	0	0	0	0	0	0	0	0	0	0	0
4	6	4	1	0	0	0	0	0	0	0	0	0	0	0	0
3	3	1	0	0	0	0	0	0	0	0	0	0	0	0	0
2	1	0	0	0	0	0	0	0	0	0	0	0	0	0	0
1	0	0	0	0	0	0	0	0	0	0	0	0	0	0	0
0	0	0	0	0	0	0	0	0	0	0	0	0	0	0	0

Figure 8.3   Coding Matrix for the Lynch–Davisson Code

The value of T can be computed from (8.3.1) as:

$$T = \binom{3-1}{1} + \binom{11-1}{2} = 47$$

And T can also be computed by adding the appropriate elements of the coding matrix. These matrix elements are found by letting n_j be the row number and j be the column number for each value of j, where the rows are numbered from bottom to top and the columns are numbered from left to right. In the present example

$$\text{element}_{3,1} = 2$$
$$\text{element}_{11,2} = 45$$

making $T = 47$. In order to decode T into the original sequence, we follow this procedure:

1. Start with the qth column and place T between two adjacent elements of the column such that

$$\text{element }_{k,q} \leq T < \text{element}_{k+1,q}$$

2. Subtract the lower element from T, obtaining the difference

$$D = T - \text{element}_{k,q}.$$

3. In the $(q - 1)$th column, place D such that

$$\text{element}_{l,q-1} \leq D < \text{element}_{l+1,q-1}$$

4. Subtract and continue until the first column is reached.
5. The sequence is defined by the locations of the 1s, and these locations are found from the row numbers of the *lower* elements in the preceding inequalities, where again the row number corresponds to n_j and the column number corresponds to j for $j = 1, 2, \ldots, q$.

In the present example, we see that

$$\begin{aligned}
&\text{Column 2:} \quad 47 - 45 = 2 \qquad n_j = 11, j = 2 \\
&\text{Column 1:} \quad 2 - 2 = 0 \qquad n_j = 3, j = 1
\end{aligned}$$

giving the original sequence: 0010000000100000.

The number T is unique for each sequence of q samples distributed over $N - 1$ positions. Since N is usually fixed, it is necessary to send the value of q along with T in order to uniquely identify the sequence. It can be shown that for a fixed N and q:

$$0 \leq T \leq \binom{N-1}{q} - 1 \tag{8.3.2}$$

The number of bits required for q and T is:

$$L_{\text{LD}} = k_q + k_T \tag{8.3.3}$$

where

$$2^{k_q - 1} < N \leq 2^{k_q}, \text{ or } k_q = \langle \log_2 N \rangle \tag{8.3.4}$$

and

$$2^{k_T-1} < \binom{N-1}{q} \le 2^{k_T}, \text{ or } k_T = \left\langle \log_2 \binom{N-1}{q} \right\rangle \qquad (8.3.5)$$

The LD codeword for the present example would look as follows:

$$k_q = \langle \log N \rangle = \langle \log 17 \rangle = 5$$

$$k_t = \left\langle \log_2 \binom{N-1}{q} \right\rangle = \left\langle \log_2 \binom{16}{2} \right\rangle = \langle \log 120 \rangle = 7$$

Then the LD codeword is:

$\underbrace{00010}_{q}$	$\underbrace{0101111}_{T}$

Davisson (1966) has shown that as the sequence length N approaches infinity, the number of code bits per symbol approaches the entropy of the statically independent symbol source. This will be shown in Section 8.5.1.

The Lynch–Davisson code is also a total information time code, and can be sent separately from the nonredundant samples.

8.3.2 Time of Nonredundant Sample (TNRS) Codes

STANDARD TNRS CODE

In this method, one sends the *time* of each *non-redundant* sample (TNRS) within a frame. The first sample of each N-sample frame is considered nonredundant, leaving a time interval corresponding to $N - 1$ samples to encode. A binary TNRS code would then be k bits long, where

$$2^{k-1} < (N - 1) \le 2^k, \text{ or } k = \langle \log_2(N - 1) \rangle \qquad (8.3.6)$$

The standard TNRS code is a total information time code, and can be sent separately or in conjunction with the nonredundant samples. In this latter case, each nonredundant sample value is accompanied by a TNRS time word, so no additional bits are required for time word discrimination.

MODIFIED TNRS CODE (CLUSTER CODE)

In this timing method, only the time of the *beginning* of a nonredundant run is given. Data reconstruction is accomplished by filling in redundant samples (as defined by the redundancy-reduction algorithm) from the last sample of a nonredundant run up to the first sample of the next nonredundant run, which is identified by the next time word. An example of this timing method is shown in Figure 8.4.

It is necessary to discriminate between time words and sample value words in the modified TNRS code. In spite of this additional redundancy, though, it

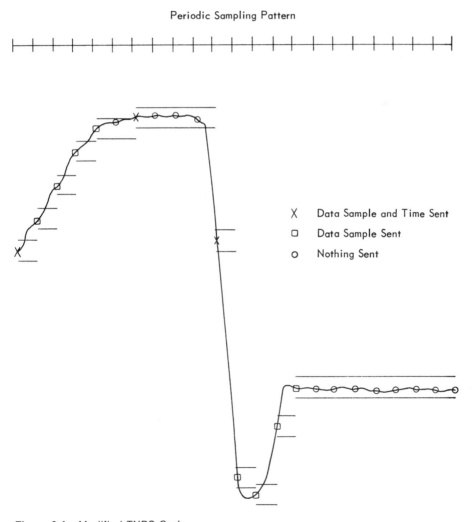

Figure 8.4 *Modified TNRS Code.*

is still possible to use fewer timing bits for the modified TNRS code than for the standard TNRS code. This is true in cases where most of the nonredundant samples occur in long runs. In the case where the nonredundant samples occur singly, the modified TNRS code requires more bits than the standard TNRS code due to the additional discrimination bits.

Lynch (1967) has analyzed and compared the standard TNRS code and modified TNRS code for a time-multiplexed telemetry system.

Since the modified TNRS code uses the count of the nonredundant samples, it is a partial information time code.

The *cluster code* is a special form of the modified TNRS code. Here, the start of a run of nonredundant samples is addressed with a time word, and the end of the run is signaled with a special flag word. This technique of time coding has been used for television frame-to-frame difference coding (Candy et al. 1971). The special flag word provides the required discrimination between the time words and the nonredundant sample value words.

8.3.3 Run-Length Codes

As explained in Section 8.2, the basic time information may be given by the r and n run lengths. Some time codes give both types of information, and others give only the redundant run lengths. In the literature, two-level sources have been compressed by encoding the alternating runs (Huang 1972). However, in the case of multilevel sources, it has been common practice to run-length encode only the redundant runs. The same procedure will be followed here.

FIXED-LENGTH CODE

The use of a *fixed-length* code for the redundant sample run lengths imposes an upper limit on the run length. In order to prevent a loss of data when a run exceeds this upper limit, we can proceed in two ways.

In the first way, a frame structure can be imposed on the sampled data stream with the frame length equal to or less than this upper limit. For a k-bit run-length code, and an N-sample frame:

$$2^{k-1} < (N-1) \leq 2^k, \text{ or } k = \langle \log_2(N-1) \rangle \tag{8.3.7}$$

This is equal to equation (8.3.6), or the code word length for the TNRS code is the same as that for the fixed-length, run-length code with the same frame size. However, since the run-length code will be interspersed with nonredundant sample value words, additional bits or words have to be added for the purpose of time word discrimination.

In the second way, a frame is not used to prevent run-length overflow, but instead the overflow is indicated by a special code word that may be repeated a number of times depending on the amount of overflow. Typically, for a k-bit code word, each overflow word adds a value of $2^k - 1$ to the run count, and a final k-bit code word gives the remainder of the run count (less than $2^k - 1$). Sheldahl (1968) and Preuss (1971) have discussed this technique of run-overflow coding. A similar method of using a variable number of fixed-length code words to encode a broad range of run lengths was described by Bradley (1969).

The fixed-length binary run-length code is a partial information time code.

HUFFMAN CODE

The Huffman code (Huffman 1952) provides a practical procedure for implementing the Shannon coding theorem (see Section 3.5). Specifically the procedure assigns a binary word of length m_i to each message from a source according to its probability P_i so that

$$\log \frac{1}{P_i} \le m_i < \log \frac{1}{P_i} + 1 \tag{8.3.8}$$

Such a code has the bound:

$$H \le \bar{l} < H + 1 \qquad [\text{equation (3.5.4)}]$$

where: $\bar{l}$ is the average number of output binary digits per input message

H is the entropy of the source in which the number of messages is finite

For the time code problem, we may think of the *redundant run lengths* as the messages from the source. We have, theoretically, an infinite number of run lengths. However, we cannot implement a Huffman code for the case of an infinite message set.

If we limit the maximum r-run length by the use of a data frame, then Huffman coding may be used directly on the r-run lengths. We again have the requirement of discrimination between the nonredundant samples and the Huffman code. Used in this way, Huffman coding still constitutes a partial information time code, since only the r-run lengths are coded.

It is possible to encode the n-run lengths as well; however, this method has been best utilized by the following code, the BNO code.

BINARY NONCONSECUTIVE ONE (BNO) CODE

Shannon (1948) suggested (but did not specify) a run-length encoding technique for a statistically independent source with two symbols in which the probability of occurrence of symbol A is much smaller than that of symbol B. The suggested code would consist of a special binary sequence for the infrequent symbol A, and a run-length code for the number of subsequent B symbols. The run-length code would not contain any code words that included the special sequence for symbol A, and as $P(A) \to 0$, the code would approach optimality provided the length of the special A sequence were properly adjusted.

Elias (1955) modified Shannon's coding scheme for the statistically independent two-symbol source. Essentially, for an $(m + 1)$ary code alphabet, he specified m-digits for the run-length code and one digit for the special infrequent-symbol code. For example, in order to use a binary code for the run lengths, the Elias code required a *ternary* code alphabet.

The idea of using a unique code or digit for the infrequent symbol in a two-symbol source is applicable to the present problem of discrimination between the nonredundant samples and the run-length code word, and this is clearly illustrated in the *binary nonconsecutive one* (BNO) code.

The binary nonconsecutive one (BNO) code was developed by Wai-hung Ng (1971), and in some ways it resembles the optimum two-symbol source code of Shannon described above. In this scheme, redundant-sample run lengths are encoded with variable-length binary code words that may have consecutive zeros, but not consecutive ones. (See Table 8.1.) A special consecutive one code

Table 8.1 *Binary Nonconsecutive One Code*

Run Length	BNO Code
1	0
2	1
3	00
4	01
5	10
6	000
7	001
8	010
9	100
10	101
11	0000
12	0001
13	0010
14	0100
15	0101
16	1000
17	1001
18	1010
19	00000
20	00001

Table 8.2 Classification of Time Codes for Source Encoding

Code Category	Name of Code	Time Information Coded	Type of Time Code	Separate Transmission
Time Sequence Codes	1. Binary Sequence Code	Complete *n–r* sequence pattern	Total Information	Yes
	2. Lynch–Davisson Code	Complete *n–r* sequence pattern	Total Information	Yes
Time of Nonredundant Sample (TNRS) Codes	3. Standard TNRS Code	Time of each nonredundant sample	Total Information	Yes
	4. Modified TNRS Code (Cluster Code)	Time of start of each *n*-run	Partial Information	No
Run-Length Codes	5. Fixed-Length Binary Code	Lengths of the *r*-runs	Partial Information	No
	6. Huffman Code	Lengths of the *r*-runs	Partial Information	No
	7. Binary Nonconsecutive One (BNO) Code	Lengths of the *r*-runs and the *n*-runs	Total Information	Yes

word is inserted between run-length code words and the nonredundant sample values for code discrimination. The special code word is always of the form:

$$\underbrace{111\ldots1110}_{2N_n}$$

where N_n is the number of nonredundant sample values that follow the run encoded by the previous BNO code. The format for the output sequence is then (according to Ng):

$$(\underbrace{111\ldots1110}_{2N_n})\,(A_1, A_2, \ldots, A_{N_n})\,(\text{BNO})\,(\underbrace{111\ldots1110}_{2N_n})\,(A_1, A_2, \ldots, A_{N_n})\,(\text{BNO})$$

where the A's are the sample values.

The BNO code is obviously a total information time code since it encodes both r-run lengths and n-run lengths. Because of this, it is possible to send the BNO and special code words separately from the nonredundant samples.

The salient features of all time codes are summarized in Table 8.2. In this table the total information and partial information codes are clearly identified.

8.4 COMPARISON OF TIME CODING METHODS

As discussed earlier, it is not possible to compare all the time codes discussed in this chapter to the entropy of the $n–r$ sequence (the time entropy) since all codes are not total information codes. Partial information codes depend on the nonredundant samples to carry some of the time information, and thus cannot be compared to the $n–r$ sequence entropy in a meaningful way. However, we may compare all time codes to each other on the basis of the number of *time* code *bits* per original data *sample* (TB/S). This measure of performance answers the practical question of how many bits must be added to the nonredundant samples in order to be able to reconstruct the original sampled data at the receiving end of the communication system.

It is still useful to consider the entropy of the $n-r$ sequence as a lower bound for the TB/S of the total information time codes. As shown in Section 8.2, the entropy depends on the mathematical source model that one assumes, and as before, we use the statistically independent source model and the Markov model for the appropriate entropies.

In the TB/S comparisons, it is also necessary to specify the source model, and again the same two models will be used. In order to formulate an expression for the TB/S, we need a definable sample interval so that:

$$\text{TB/S} = \frac{\text{Number of time code bits for sample interval}}{\text{Total number of original samples in interval}} \tag{8.4.1}$$

This sample interval will be the time frame in the case of the sequence codes and the TNRS codes. For the run-length codes, we will use a "typical segment" of the $n-r$ sequence, namely, an average-length n-run followed by an average-length r-run. We make comparisons separately under each source model.

8.4.1 Statistically Independent Symbol Model

For this model, we use equation (8.2.8), the entropy per symbol in terms of the sample compression ratio R:

$$H_s(\text{SI}) = \frac{1}{R}\left[\log R + (R-1)\log \frac{R}{R-1}\right] \qquad [\text{equation (8.2.8)}]$$

We also formulate expressions for the TB/S for the various time codes in terms of the compression ratio R. For the sake of comparison, the first data sample in a frame, or in a long frameless sequence, will be considered nonredundant. In addition, the TB/S can be expressed in terms of either "sample" or "symbol." We use the latter form in the rest of this chapter.

The average number of time code bits per symbol is formulated on the basis of an N-sample frame for the sequence time codes and the TNRS codes; and on the basis of an average n-run/r-run sequence segment for the run-length codes. For an N-sample frame, we can express:

$$\text{Timing bits per symbol} = \frac{(\text{No. of } n \text{ symbols}) \times \left(\begin{array}{c}\text{No. of timing bits} \\ \text{per } n \text{ symbol}\end{array}\right)}{\text{Total number of } r \text{ and } n \text{ symbols}}$$

or

$$\text{Timing bits per symbol} = \frac{\text{No. of timing bits per } n \text{ symbol}}{\text{Sample compression ratio}}$$

The notation $y = \langle \log x \rangle$ will be used to represent $2^{y-1} < x \leq 2^y$.

SEQUENCE TIME CODES

Binary Sequence Codes This code simply contains a replica of the n and r symbol sequence in binary form, and no discrimination bits are required. Therefore,

$$\text{Timing bits per symbol} = 1 \tag{8.4.2}$$

Lynch–Davisson Code In this code, it is necessary to send the sequence code T as well as the number q of nonredundant samples in the sequence. From (8.3.5) and (8.3.4) this requires $\left\langle \log \binom{N-1}{q} \right\rangle$ and $\langle \log N \rangle$ bits, respectively. From (8.2.3) we may express q in terms of the compression ratio R and $N - 1$,

$$q \approx \frac{N-1}{R}$$

No discrimination bits are required, and for $N - 1$ symbols,

$$\text{Timing bits per symbol} = \frac{\langle \log N \rangle + \left\langle \log \binom{N-1}{\frac{N-1}{R}} \right\rangle}{N-1} \tag{8.4.3}$$

TIME OF NONREDUNDANT SAMPLE (TNRS) CODES

Standard TNRS Code In this code, a time word is sent with each nonredundant sample. We assume that this time word is of constant length, and therefore no discrimination bits are necessary. We then have:

$$\text{Timing bits per symbol} = \frac{\langle \log(N-1) \rangle}{R} \tag{8.4.4}$$

Modified TNRS Code (Cluster Code) In this code, the time of the beginning of a nonredundant run is given, and discrimination bits are required between the last nonredundant sample value and the fixed-length time word. We assume that the discrimination word has the same length K as the sample value words but, of course, is not one of them. In order to obtain an estimate of the number of time words needed per frame, we recognize that a time word and a discrimination word will be needed for each nonredundant run. We can estimate the number of n runs in $N - 1$ samples by the ratio of the number of n samples to the n-run average length, or, using equation (8.2.5)

$$\text{Number of } n \text{ runs} \approx \frac{(N - 1)(R - 1)}{R^2} \tag{8.4.5}$$

Since the time word will have a length of $\langle \log(N - 1\rangle$, we can write for the frame:

$$\text{Timing bits per symbol} = \left(\frac{R - 1}{R^2}\right)[\langle\log(N - 1)\rangle + K] \tag{8.4.6}$$

RUN-LENGTH CODES

In the case of run-length codes, it is convenient to formulate the expression for the number of timing bits per symbol on the basis of a typical segment of the n- and r-symbol sequence. This segment is composed of an average-length n-run followed by an average-length r-run. In this way, the discrimination words can be accounted for in a consistent manner, since these special words are used in each n-run/r-run segment. We may write:

Timing bits per symbol

$$= \frac{\text{Average number of timing bits per } n\text{-run}/r\text{-run segment}}{\text{Average length of } n\text{-run}/r\text{-run segment}}$$

From Section 8.2, the average length of the n-run/r-run segment is:

$$\bar{l}_n + \bar{l}_r = \frac{R^2}{R - 1} \tag{8.4.7}$$

Fixed-Length Code In this code we impose an upper limit on the redundant run length, and set it equal to $N - 1$ for comparison purposes. A unique discrimination word is needed between the last nonredundant sample and the run-length code word, and again we assume that its length, K, is equal to the length of the nonredundant sample value word. Then

$$\text{Timing bit per symbol} = \left(\frac{R-1}{R^2}\right)[\langle \log(N-1)\rangle + K] \tag{8.4.8}$$

This is the same as (8.4.6)

Here we have an interesting result that shows the equivalence between using a fixed-length code word for the r-run-length coding, and using a fixed-length time word to code the beginning of each n-run.

Huffman Code   From equation (3.5.4), the average length of the Huffman code words will have a lower bound equal to the entropy of the r-runs. Because of the prefix code characteristic of the Huffman code we add a discrimination word of length K to mark the beginning only of the variable-length Huffman code word. Again, this unique word can be made equal in length to the nonredundant sample value words. Then we have as a lower bound:

$$\text{Timing bits per symbol} = \left(\frac{R-1}{R^2}\right)(H_{l_r}(\text{SI}) + K) \tag{8.4.9}$$

where it can be shown that [see equation (8.2.8)]

$$H_{l_r}(\text{SI}) = \log R + (R-1)\log\frac{R}{R-1} \tag{8.4.10}$$

BNO Code   Since the BNO code is a variable-length code, we must again use an average code-word length, designated as: $\overline{\text{BNO code}}$. This code has a special discrimination word of length K_{BNO} at the beginning of the nonredundant sample run, which gives the number, N_n, of these samples. As explained in Section 8.3 the number of bits in the discrimination word is: $2N_n + 1$. If we use the average of N_n, namely $\bar{l}_n$, we can write, with the help of equation (8.2.5):

$$K_{\text{BNO}} = 2\bar{l}_n + 1$$

or

$$K_{\text{BNO}} = \frac{3 - \dfrac{1}{R}}{1 - \dfrac{1}{R}} \tag{8.4.11}$$

We make the approximation:

$$\overline{\text{BNO code}} \approx \text{BNO code for } \bar{l}_r = \text{BNO code for } (l_r = R)$$

then,

$$\text{Timing bits per symbol} = \left(\frac{R-1}{R^2}\right)\left[(\text{BNO code for } l_r = R) + \frac{3 - \frac{1}{R}}{1 - \frac{1}{R}}\right]$$

$$(8.4.12)$$

8.4.2 Markov Symbol Model

As in the case of the independent symbol model, the sequence time codes and the TNRS codes will be handled on the basis of an N-sample frame, and the run-length codes on the basis of an average n-run/r-run sequence segment.
The following expressions will be used for TB/S:

SEQUENCE TIME CODES

Binary Sequence Code   See equation (8.4.2).

Lynch–Davisson Code   See equation (8.4.3).

TIME OF NONREDUNDANT SAMPLE (TNRS) CODES

Standard TNRS Code   See equation (8.4.4).

Modified TNRS Code (Cluster Code)   In order to estimate the number of time words and discrimination words needed per frame, we proceed as in the case of the statistically independent symbol model:

$$\text{Number of } n\text{-runs} = \frac{(N-1)(1 - P(n/n))}{R} \qquad (8.4.13)$$

Thus,

$$\text{Timing bits per symbol} = \frac{[1 - P(n/n)]}{R}\left[\langle\log(N-1)\rangle + K\right]$$

In order to write this expression in terms of $P(r/r)$ and R, we note that

$$1 - P(n/n) = P(r/n) = P(n/r)\frac{P(r)}{P(n)}$$

or

$$1 - P(n/n) = [1 - P(r/r)]\left[\frac{1}{P(n)} - 1\right] = [1 - P(r/r)][R - 1] \qquad (8.4.14)$$

Then,

$$\text{Timing bits per symbol} = \frac{[1 - P(r/r)][R - 1]}{R}\left[\langle \log(N - 1)\rangle + K\right]$$

$$(8.4.15)$$

Equation (8.4.13) can also be developed by finding the number of transitions from an n to an r symbol, which is given by

$$\left(\frac{N - 1}{R}\right)\left(\frac{P(n/r)\,P(r)}{P(n)}\right)$$

RUN-LENGTH CODES

As in the case of the statistically independent symbol model, we need an expression for the average length of an n-run/r-run segment. In this case,

$$\bar{l}_n + \bar{l}_r = \frac{1}{1 - P(n/n)} + \frac{1}{1 - P(r/r)}$$

$$\bar{l}_n + \bar{l}_r = \frac{1}{[1 - P(r/r)][1 - P(n)]}$$

or,

$$\bar{l}_n + \bar{l}_r = \frac{R}{[1 - P(r/r)][R - 1]} \qquad (8.4.16)$$

Fixed-Length Code

$$\text{Timing bits per symbol} = \frac{[1 - P(r/r)][R - 1]}{R}\left[\langle \log(N - 1)\rangle + K\right]$$

$$(8.4.17)$$

Huffman Code   As a lower bound:

$$\text{Timing bits per symbol} = \frac{[1 - P(r/r)][R - 1]}{R}\left[H_{l_r}(M) + K\right] \qquad (8.4.18)$$

where it can be shown that [see equation (7.2.11)]

$$H_{l_r}(M) = -\left[\frac{P(r/r)}{1 - P(r/r)} \log P(r/r) + \log(1 - P(r/r)) \right] \tag{8.4.19}$$

BNO Code   Here we use (8.2.13) for $\bar{l}_n$ and write:

$$K_{\text{BNO}} = \frac{2}{1 - P(n/n)} + 1 \tag{8.4.20}$$

Using equation (8.4.14):

$$K_{\text{BNO}} = \frac{2}{(1 - P(r/r))(R - 1)} + 1 \tag{8.4.21}$$

For the timing bits per symbol for the BNO code we also need the average-length BNO code. We make the approximation:

$$\overline{\text{BNO code}} \approx \text{BNO code for } \bar{l}_r = \text{BNO code for} \left(l_r = \frac{1}{1 - P(r/r)} \right) \tag{8.4.22}$$

Then we may write for the BNO code:

$$\text{Timing bits per symbol} = \frac{[1 - P(r/r)][R - 1]}{R}$$

$$\times \left\{ \left(\text{BNO code for } l_r = \frac{1}{1 - P(r/r)} \right) \right.$$

$$\left. + \frac{2}{[1 - P(r/r)][R - 1]} + 1 \right\} \tag{8.4.23}$$

The expressions for the entropy and the number of timing bits per symbol for both models are given in Tables 8.3 and 8.4. In order to plot the TB/S for each code we must assume some numerical values for $P(r/r)$, N, and K, as follows:

1. $P(r/r)$ can be either 0.9 or 0.99. This corresponds to $\bar{l}_r$ values of 10 and 100.
2. The frame size, $N = 101$ (for $P(r/r) = 0.9$) and $N = 1001$ (for $P(r/r) = 0.99$).
3. The nonredundant sample value word is of length 4 or 8 bits, so that $K = 4$ or 8 bits.

Table 8.3 *Timing Bits Per Symbol for the Statistically Independent Model*

Statistically Independent Symbol Model
$$H_s(\text{SI}) = \frac{1}{R}\left[\log R + (R-1)\log\frac{R}{R-1}\right]$$

1. Binary Sequence Code	$\text{TB/S} = 1$
2. Lynch–Davisson Code	$\text{TB/S} = \dfrac{\langle\log N\rangle + \left\langle\log\left(\dfrac{N-1}{R}\right)\right\rangle}{N-1}$
3. Standard TNRS Code	$\text{TB/S} = \dfrac{\langle\log(N-1)\rangle}{R}$
4. Modified TNRS Code (Cluster Code)	$\text{TB/S} = \left(\dfrac{R-1}{R^2}\right)[\langle\log(N-1)\rangle + K]$
5. Fixed-Length Run-Length Code (Binary)	$\text{TB/S} = \left(\dfrac{R-1}{R^2}\right)[\langle\log(N-1)\rangle + K]$
6. Huffman Code—Lower Bound	$\text{TB/S} = \left(\dfrac{R-1}{R^2}\right)[H_{l_r}(\text{SI}) + K]$
7. BNO Code	$\text{TB/S} = \left(\dfrac{R-1}{R^2}\right)$ $\times\left[(\text{BNO code length for } l_r = R) + \dfrac{3-\dfrac{1}{R}}{1-\dfrac{1}{R}}\right]$

The entropy and the TB/S for the total information codes are plotted in Figure 8.5. for the statistically independent symbol model, and in Figures 8.6 and 8.7 for the Markov model. The TB/S for the partial information codes are plotted in Figure 8.8 for the statistically independent model, and in Figures 8.9 and 8.10 for the Markov model.

As noted previously, the entropy can be considered a lower bound for the total information time codes only; in the case of the partial information time codes, it is plotted only for a relative comparison. Since the partial information time codes do not correspond to the full entropy as plotted, it is not surprising that some codes have a TB/S that falls below the time entropy, as in Figures 8.9 and 8.10.

Table 8.4 *Timing Bits Per Symbol for the Markov Model*

Markov Model
$$H_s(M) = -\left[P(n)\left\{1 - \frac{AB}{P(n)}\right\} \log\left\{1 - \frac{AB}{P(n)}\right\} + AB \log \frac{AB}{P(n)} \right.$$ $$\left. + AP(r/r) \log P(r/r) + AB \log B \right]$$
where: $A = 1 - P(n)$; $B = 1 - P(r/r)$

1. Binary Sequence Code	$\text{TB/S} = 1$
2. Lynch–Davisson Code	$$\text{TB/S} = \frac{\langle \log N \rangle + \left\langle \log\left(\dfrac{N-1}{R}\right) \right\rangle}{N-1}$$
3. Standard TNRS Code	$$\text{TB/S} = \frac{\langle \log(N-1) \rangle}{R}$$
4. Modified TNRS Code (Cluster Code)	$$\text{TB/S} = \frac{[1 - P(r/r)][R-1]}{R} [\langle \log(N-1) \rangle + K]$$
5. Fixed-Length Run-Length Code (Binary)	$$\text{TB/S} = \frac{[1 - P(r/r)][R-1]}{R} [\langle \log(N-1) \rangle + K]$$
6. Huffman Code—Lower Bound	$$\text{TB/S} = \frac{[1 - P(r/r)][R-1]}{R} [H_{l_r}(M) + K]$$
7. BNO Code	$$\text{TB/S} = \frac{[1 - P(r/r)][R-1]}{R}$$ $$\times \left[\left(\text{BNO code length for } l_r = \frac{1}{1 - P(r/r)} \right) \right.$$ $$\left. + \frac{2}{[1 - P(r/r)][R-1]} + 1 \right]$$

8.4.3. Conclusions

An examination of Figures 8.5–8.10 leads to the following observations:

1. The BNO code is the only total information code that is sensitive to the probability $P(r/r)$, or in other words, the average redundant run length. In the two cases, $P(r/r) = 0.9, 0.99$, the BNO code comes closest to the entropy.

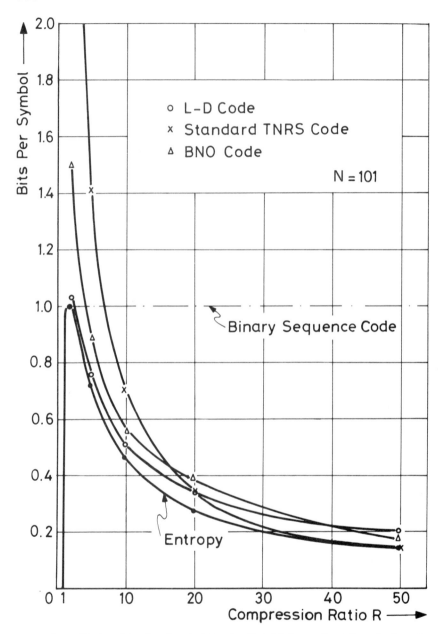

Figure 8.5 *Timing Bits Per Symbol for the Total Information Time Codes, As-suming Statistically Independent n–r Symbols. From Lynch, T. J. "Comparison of Time Codes for Source Encoding." IEEE Trans. on Communications, vol. COM-22, no. 2, Feb. 1974, p. 160. © 1974 IEEE.*

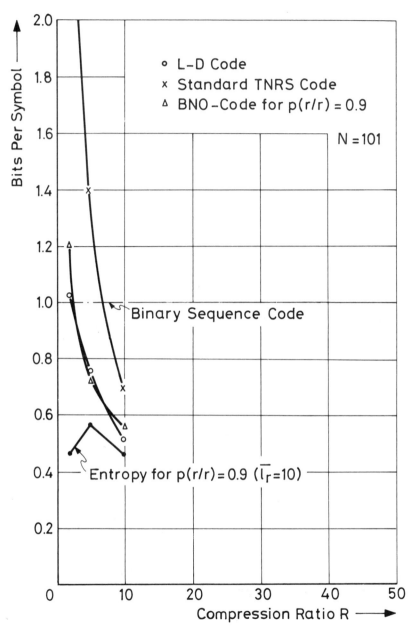

Figure 8.6 *Timing Bits Per Symbol for the Total Information Time Codes, Assuming Markov n–r Symbols With P(r/r) = 0.9. From: Lynch, T. J. "Comparison of Time Codes for Source Encoding." IEEE Trans. on Communications, vol. COM-22, no. 2, Feb. 1974, p. 160. © 1974 IEEE.*

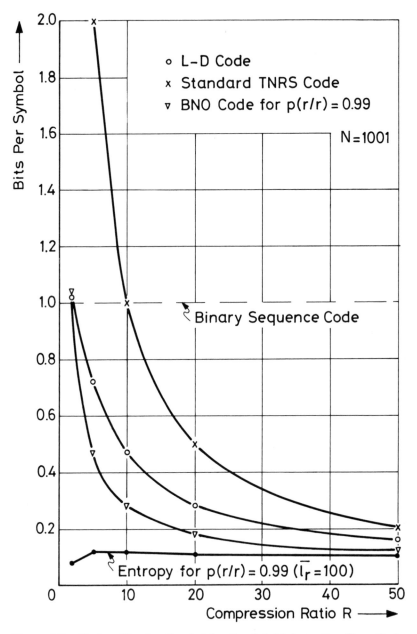

Figure 8.7 *Timing Bits Per Symbol for the Total Information Time Codes, Assuming Markov n–r Symbols With P(r/r) = 0.99. From: Lynch, T. J. "Comparison of Time Codes for Source Encoding." IEEE Trans. on Communications, vol. COM-22, no. 2, Feb. 1974, p. 161. © 1974 IEEE.*

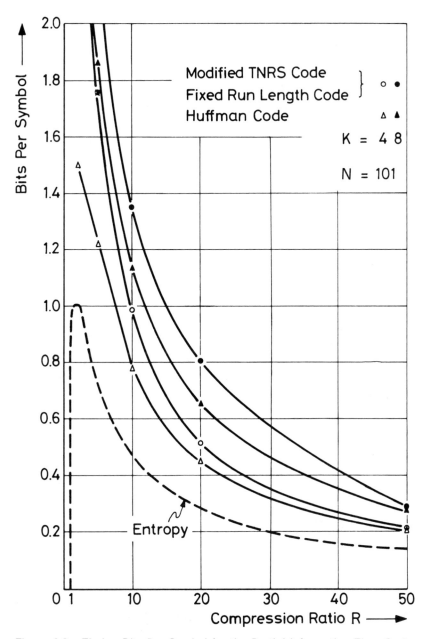

Figure 8.8 *Timing Bits Per Symbol for the Partial Information Time Codes, Assuming Statistically Independent n–r Symbols. From: Lynch, T. J. "Comparison of Time Codes for Source Encoding." IEEE Trans. on Communications, vol. COM-22, no. 2, Feb. 1974, p. 161. © 1974 IEEE.*

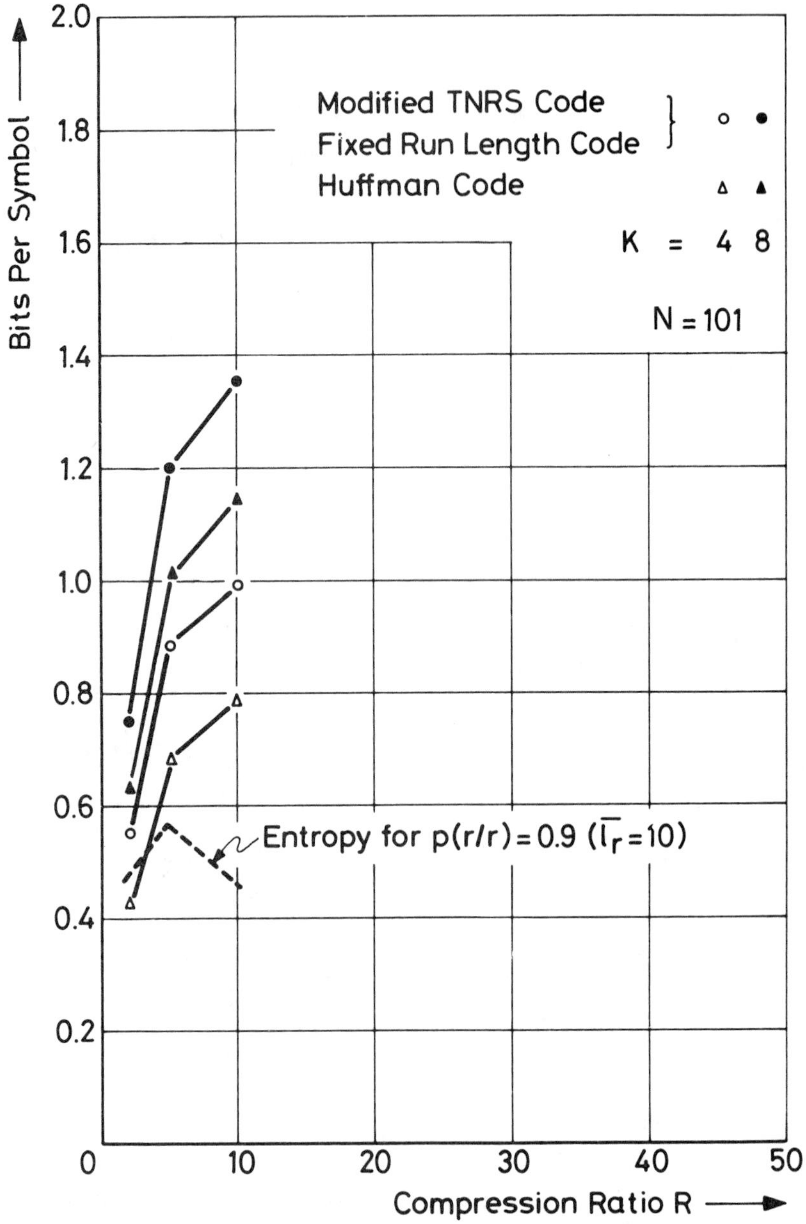

Figure 8.9 *Timing Bits Per Symbol for the Partial Information Time Codes, Assuming Markov n–r Symbols, With P(r/r) = 0.9. From: Lynch, T. J. "Comparison of Time Codes for Source Encoding." IEEE Trans. on Communications, vol. COM-22, no. 2, Feb. 1974, p. 161. © 1974 IEEE.*

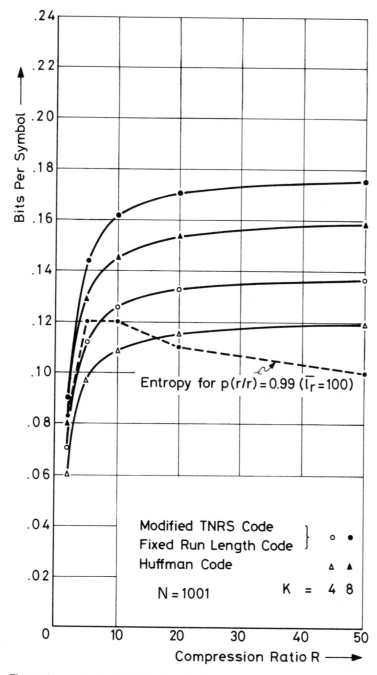

Figure 8.10 *Timing Bits Per Symbol for the Partial Information Time Codes, Assuming n–r Markov Symbols, With P(r/r) = 0.99. From: Lynch, T. J. "Comparison of Time Codes for Source Encoding." IEEE Trans. on Communications, vol. COM-22, no. 2, Feb. 1974, p. 161.* © *1974 IEEE.*

2. For the partial information codes, the Huffman code exhibits a consistently smaller TB/S than the modified TNRS or fixed run-length codes.

8.5 BINARY SOURCE CODING

A binary source, by way of review, is a source out of which can come only two levels, or symbols, with probabilities p and $1 - p$. The goal of binary source coding is to make the number of bits per source block (or binary string, as it is sometimes called) close to, or equal to, the entropy of that block.

As noted earlier, some of the time codes described in this chapter can be used for binary source coding. Other codes, some of them extensions of the codes in this chapter, are also suitable for binary source encoding (these will be noted later). Let us now look back at the categories of time coding that were discussed in this chapter and see which of the codes from this chapter would be candidates for binary source coding.

8.5.1 Sequence Codes

Under the category of sequence codes, two were described: the binary sequence code and the Lynch–Davisson (LD) code. The binary sequence code, if applied to a binary data source, would do nothing more than replicate the binary output of the source, giving a compression ratio of 1. The LD code, on the other hand, provides a compression ratio typically greater than 1, so let us look at it in some detail.

Some properties of the LD code are worth mentioning in regard to the code's being used as a binary source code. First, it operates on an entire sequence. Second, the design of the LD code is independent of the statistics of the sequence it is used to encode. Third, the rate of the LD code approaches the entropy of the binary output as the sequence approaches infinity. This last property was pointed out by Davisson in 1966, and since it later proved to have historical significance in the theory of source coding, we will reproduce Davisson's development of this property. For a review of the LD code see Section 8.3.1.

Given a binary source with the following output:

$$\text{Probability of} \begin{cases} 0 \text{ is} & p \\ 1 \text{ is} & 1 - p \end{cases} \tag{8.5.1}$$

We encode a sequence m bits long containing q 1s from the source by means of the LD code, where the rate is given by (see equation 8.3.3):

$$r(m) = \frac{1}{m}\left[\log_2 m + \log_2\binom{m-1}{q}\right]$$

(8.5.2)

To find an expression for the average rate as $m \to \infty$, we note that as $m \to \infty$, the ratio m/q converges to the average run length of 0s between 1s, where the average run length is given by (see equation 8.2.1):

$$\lim_{m \to \infty} \frac{m}{q} = \bar{l} = \frac{1}{1-p}$$

(8.5.3)

Since the ratio m/q will appear in the expansion of (8.5.2), then $r(m)$ is actually a function of p, and in order to find the average rate, we define:

$$\bar{r} = \lim_{m \to \infty} r(m)$$

(8.5.4)

$$\bar{r} = \left[\lim_{m \to \infty}\left(\frac{1}{m}\log_2 m + \frac{1}{m}\log_2\binom{m-1}{q}\right)\right]$$

(8.5.5)

But

$$\lim_{m \to \infty} \frac{1}{m}\log_2 m = 0$$

(8.5.6)

Then

$$\bar{r} = \lim_{m \to \infty}\left[\frac{1}{m}\log\binom{m-1}{q}\right]$$

(8.5.7)

As $m \to \infty$,

$$\binom{m-1}{q} \approx \binom{m}{q} = \frac{m!}{q!(m-q)!}$$

(8.5.8)

Stirling's formula gives an approximation to the factorial:

$$n! \approx e^{-n}n^n\sqrt{2\pi n}$$

(8.5.9)

Substituting in (8.5.8):

$$\binom{m-1}{q} \approx \frac{e^{-m}m^m\sqrt{2\pi m}}{(e^{-q}q^q\sqrt{2\pi q})(e^{-(m-q)}(m-q)^{(m-q)}\sqrt{2\pi(m-q)})}$$

(8.5.10)

or

$$\binom{m-1}{q} \approx \left(\sqrt{\frac{m}{(m-q)q2\pi}}\right)\left(\frac{m}{m-q}\right)^m\left(\frac{m-q}{q}\right)^q \tag{8.5.11}$$

Substituting in (8.5.7):

$$\bar{r} = \lim_{m \to \infty}\left[\frac{1}{m}\log_2\sqrt{\frac{m}{(m-q)q2\pi}} + \log_2\left(\frac{m}{m-q}\right)\right.$$
$$\left. + \frac{q}{m}\log_2\left(\frac{m-q}{q}\right)\right] \tag{8.5.12}$$

But,

$$\lim_{m \to \infty}\left[\frac{1}{m}\log_2\sqrt{\frac{1}{[1-(q/m)]q2\pi}}\right] = 0 \tag{8.5.13}$$

And from (8.5.3), in the limit as $m \to \infty$,

$$\frac{q}{m} = 1 - p, \quad \frac{m}{m-q} = \frac{1}{p}, \quad \frac{m-q}{q} = \frac{p}{p-1} \tag{8.5.14}$$

Substituting:

$$\bar{r} = -p\log p - (1-p)\log(1-p) \tag{8.5.15}$$

which is the same as equation (8.2.7), the entropy of a binary source.

The importance of this result is that it shows that an optimum source code can be designed without any knowledge of the statistical properties of the source. We recall that the Huffman code approaches the entropy of the source only if the probabilities of all source outputs are known in advance. The theory of optimum codes for sources with unknown statistics is known as *universal coding*. [See the paper by Davisson (1973).] An encoder is called universal if its performance, after being designed without knowledge of the source statistics, converges to the performance of an encoder designed *with* knowledge of the source statistics, as the block length approaches infinity. There are many forms of universal coding, with variations based primarily on the way the performances converge. One of the most referred-to forms is *minimax-universal*, in which the redundancy of the codes converge to zero as the block length approaches infinity. The LD code is thus a minimax-universal code. Other universal codes have been developed, and there is still a keen interest in finding more.

Through the years, sequence codes, both universal and nonuniversal, have been developed for binary sources. The following are a few examples in chronological order:

1972   Schalkwijk rediscovered the LD code method of ranking fixed-weight sequences, and suggested a method for variable-to-block coding.

1973   Cover developed a coding scheme for binary sources based on a ranking process and called this process *enumerative source coding*. The LD code thus became a special case of this type of coding.

1977   Lawrence developed a universal variable-to-block code based on Schalkwijk's 1972 paper.

1978   Ziv and Lempel developed a universal binary coding scheme in which a binary string is parsed into variable-length substrings and coded appropriately.

8.5.2 TNRS Codes

Two TNRS codes are described in Section 8.3.2: the standard TNRS code, and the modified TNRS code. Since the standard code requires the location of each n sample to be coded, we can eliminate this code for consideration for binary sources—it could in fact result in data expansion instead of data compression.

The modified TNRS code, however, could be used—but its performance would be very much a function of the distribution of 1s and 0s in the block. The ideal data set for this code would be one in which all 1s and all 0s occurred in clusters. Since this code encodes the beginning and end of one type of cluster (say a run of 1s), there would be a data compression if there were few clusters to a block. This could happen in two-level facsimile or in graphics, wherein each block corresponded to a scan line that contained a few segments of black lines separated by large intervals of white background. If the modified TNRS code were applied to printed material, however, a data expansion could occur. Perhaps for this reason, this type of coding has not seen much use in facsimile systems (see Chapter 16).

8.5.3 Run-Length Codes

Three forms of run-length coding can actually be used for binary source coding: fixed-length, variable-length (Huffman primarily), and BNO code. Even though in time coding it is customary to encode only the redundant runs, when run-length coding is used for a binary source, both the 1-runs and the 0-runs are coded. From this chapter, we have the following.

Fixed-length codes are used in a number of applications because they are easy to synchronize. A typical problem with fixed-length codes is code overflow on an extremely long run. In such cases, a special overflow code is used in conjunction with multiple code words to encode the long run.

Variable-length codes are typically Huffman-type codes which, of course, are prefix codes (self-synchronizing). Huffman codes must be matched to the probability distribution of the source, which may be changing.

The BNO code is a very efficient code and is not dependent on the statistics of the source. It actually encodes the runs of the two outputs of the binary source, as can be seen in Section 8.3.3.

There is a relatively new approach to binary string coding that is along the lines of arithmetic coding described by Langdon and Rissanen (1982). This approach separates the source model from the code so that the same code can be used for different models. The technique is actually a generalization of an earlier run-length coding technique of Golomb's (1966).

HIGHLIGHTS

- Some redundancy-reduction techniques require that sufficient information—in the form of time or position information—be sent with the compressed data so the original data sequence can be reconstructed.

- Nonredundant sample codes require that information about the time of each nonredundant sample be sent.

- Time codes can be classified as total information time codes (supply all time information) or partial information time codes (supply only a part of time information).

- Two statistical models for the time information are the statistically independent model and the Markov model.

- Three time encoding methods are used: sequence time codes, time of nonredundant sample (TNRS) codes, and run-length codes.

- Sequence time codes may be binary sequence codes (encode the pattern of the entire sequence as a single code word) or an enumerative code such as the Lynch–Davisson code.

- TNRS codes may be standard (the time of each nonredundant sample is sent within a frame) or modified (only the beginning of a nonredundant run is given).

- Run-length codes may be fixed-length codes, variable-length codes such as the Huffman code, or the binary nonconsecutive one (BNO) code.

- Time codes may be compared on the basis of TB/S, a measure of performance that describes how many bits must be added to nonredundant samples to reconstruct the original data at the receiving end. The time code comparisons in this chapter have shown the Huffman code to have the best TB/S performance of the partial information time codes and the BNO code to have the best TB/S performance of the total information time codes.

• The time codes described in this chapter may be applied to binary sources as well as other codes, such as arithmetic codes and parsing codes.

SUGGESTIONS FOR FURTHER READING

The following items are suggested for further reading and study:

Bradley, S. D. "Optimizing a Scheme for Run-Length Encoding." *Proc. IEEE*, vol. 57, no. 1, 1969, pp. 108–109.

This article describes an alternative to Huffman coding that involves coding black or white runs in a two-level image with combinations of fixed-length code words, depending on the length of the run.

Candy, J. C., Franke, M. A., Haskell, B. G., and Mounts, F. W. "Transmitting Television as Clusters of Frame-to-frame Differences." *Bell System Technical Journal*, vol. 50, no. 6, July–August 1971, pp. 1889–1917.

This paper describes the method of cluster coding for block-to-block difference coding.

Capon, J. "A Probabilistic Model for Run-Length Coding of Pictures." *IRE Trans. on Info. Theory* IT-5, December, 1959, pp. 157–163.

The author develops expressions for the entropy of single-level runs from a two-level Markov source.

Cover, T. M., "Enumerative Source Coding." *IEEE Trans. on Info. Theory*, vol. IT-19, no. 1, January 1973, pp. 73–77.

See Section 8.5.1.

Davisson, L. D. "Comments on 'Sequence Time Coding for Data Compression.'" *Proc. IEEE 54*, no. 12, 1966, p. 2010.

This article, together with the Lynch (1966) article, form the basis of the Lynch–Davisson code, an efficient code for encoding strictly monotonic number sequences.

Davisson, L. D. "Universal Noiseless Coding." *IEEE Trans. on Info. Theory*, vol. IT-19, no. 6, November 1973, pp. 783–795.

See Section 8.5.1.

Elias, P. See Chapter 6, Suggestions for Further Reading.

Golomb, S. W. "Run Length Encodings." *IEEE Trans. on Info. Theory*, vol. IT-12, no. 3, July 1966, pp. 399–401.

This short note describes a method of run-length coding of binary strings wherein the run lengths of one symbol follow a geometric distribution.

Huang, T. S., "Run Length Coding and Its extensions." In *Picture Bandwidth Compression*, edited by T. S. Huang, O. L. Tretiak. New York: Gordon and Breach, 1972. pp. 231–264.
   Run-length coding of a two-level source is described.

Huffman, D. A. See Chapter 3, Suggestions for Further Reading.

Langdon, G. G., and Rissanen, J. "A Simple General Binary Source Code." *IEEE Trans. on Info. Theory*, vol. IT-28, no. 5, September 1982, pp. 800–803
   This short note describes an arithmetic coding procedure for compressing binary strings. The code is separate from the source model so that the same code can handle different source models. A special case of this code is the Golomb code of 1966.

Lawrence, J. C. "A New Universal Coding Scheme for the Binary Memoryless Source." *IEEE Trans. on Info. Theory*, vol. IT-23, no. 4, July 1977, pp. 466–472. See Section 8.5.1.

Lynch, T. J. "Comparison of Time Codes for Source Encoding." *IEEE Trans. on Communications*, vol. COM-22, no. 2, February 1974, pp. 151–162.
   This paper compares seven different time codes for two different models of the time information. Most of the material in Chapter 8 is taken directly from this paper.

Lynch, T. J. "Data Compression with Error-control Coding for Space Telemetry." *NASA Technical Rep.*, NASA TR R-261, Washington, D.C., June 1967.
   In Chapter 4 of this report, the time-of-nonredundant sample (TNRS) method, the modified TNRS method, and the Lynch–Davisson method of time coding are compared.

Lynch, T. J. "Sequence Time Coding for Data Compression." *Proc. IEEE* 54, no. 10, 1966, pp. 1490–1491.
   This article, together with the Davisson (1966) article, form the basis of the Lynch–Davisson code, an efficient code for encoding strictly monotonic number sequences.

Ng, Wai-hung, "Binary Nonconsecutive One Code for Time-Tag Data Compression." *Proc. IEE*, vol. 118, no. 10, October 1971, pp. 1358–1360.
   The BNO code is introduced and described.

Preuss, D. "Redundanzreduzierende Codierung von Faksimilesignalen." *NTZ*, no. 11, 1971, pp. 564–568.
   Preuss proposes run-length coding for two-level facsimile with a special provision for overflow.

Schalkwijk, J. P. M. "An Algorithm for Source Coding." *IEEE Trans. on Info. Theory*, vol. IT-18, no. 3, May 1972, pp. 395–399.
   See Section 8.5.1.

Shannon, C. E. See Chapter 1, Suggestions for Further Reading.

Sheldahl, S. A. "Channel Identification Coding for Data Compressors." *EASCON '68 Record*, Washington, D.C., pp. 319–324.
   Run-length coding is analyzed using a special overflow code.

Ziv, J., and Lempel, A. "Compression of Individual Sequences via Variable-Rate Coding." *IEEE Trans. on Info. Theory*, vol. IT-24, no. 5, September 1978, pp. 530–536.
   See Section 8.5.1.

CHAPTER 9

Buffer Control

9.1 INTRODUCTION

A buffer is required at that point in a data system where the bit rate is to be changed from asynchronous to synchronous. In many data compression schemes a buffer is required for this same reason. For example, in the nonredundant sample techniques, only nonredundant samples and corresponding time words are to be transmitted, but the nonredundant samples occur randomly at the output of the data compressor and must be transmitted eventually over a synchronous channel—hence, the need for a buffer. This same requirement for a buffer would exist even if the channel were of the packetized type.

Not all data compression schemes need buffering. For example, delta modulation and DPCM* do not require buffering since they operate synchronously. In other words, as each original data sample comes in to the compressor, a compressed signal or word goes out. Some compression schemes require fixed-length buffers—for example, in the case of line-to-line or frame-to-frame differences. But these can easily be specified and are not the subject of this chapter.

In this chapter, we examine the double requirements of buffer design and buffer control for systems in which the output rate of

---

* It should be noted that when DPCM is used on a block or frame basis, a non-synchronous-to-synchronous buffer is required. See Section 15.3.2.

the data compressor is a random variable. The primary design consideration is the *size* of the buffer in terms of bits, and the primary control consideration is *data loss* due to *buffer overflow* or *buffer underflow*. In order to estimate the size of the buffer required in a given system, one needs a mathematical model of the compressor output so that the statistical properties of the buffer queue length can be estimated. This model is also of use in choosing an appropriate method for buffer overflow control and buffer underflow control.

9.2 MATHEMATICAL BUFFER MODEL

A buffer is required when the data rate has to be changed from asynchronous to synchronous. If we define the ratio of the buffer input rate to the buffer output rate as follows:

$$\rho = \frac{\text{Average number of inputs per unit time}}{\text{Number of outputs per unit time}} \tag{9.2.1}$$

we can develop an expression for the average queue length (or the average amount the buffer is filled) in terms of the parameter ρ.

It is common practice to use a Poisson process as a model for the input to the buffer since it represents the type of asynchronous output that is typical of data compression schemes such as polynomial predictors. For example, the Poisson process has been used to model the number of electrons emitted by a cathode in a vacuum tube, the number of telephone calls received at a central office, and the number of noise pulses that exceed a certain level. All of these processes are random and asynchronous and, as one can recall from Chapter 3, the purpose of most data compressors is to produce output samples that are more independent (more random) than the original samples. The Poisson distribution is as follows:

$$P(k) = \frac{m^k}{k!} e^{-m} \tag{9.2.2}$$

where: $P(k)$ is the probability of k events occurring per unit time

m is the average number of events per unit time

An interesting property of the Poisson distribution is that its variance is equal to its mean, m.

We assume a constant buffer output rate equal to the channel symbol rate, r_c. A modern exception to this involves packetized transmission, wherein the constant output rate is modeled only on a piecewise basis.

For simplicity, assuming a Poisson input process to the buffer with average rate m and a constant output rate r_c, then

$$\rho = \frac{m}{r_c} \tag{9.2.3}$$

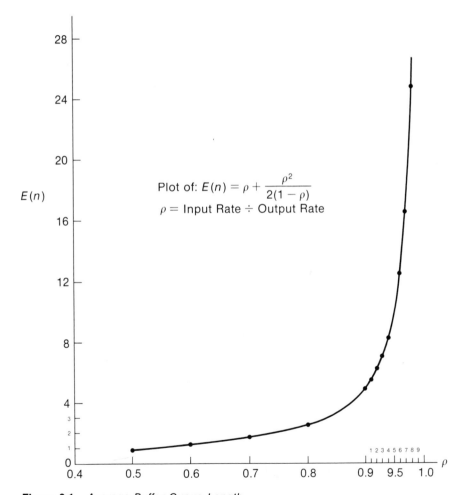

Plot of: $E(n) = \rho + \dfrac{\rho^2}{2(1 - \rho)}$

$\rho = $ Input Rate $\div$ Output Rate

Figure 9.1 *Average Buffer Queue Length.*

Using queuing theory, the following relationship is obtained (see Goode and Machol 1957, pp. 334–338) for the average buffer queue length:

$$E(n) = \rho + \frac{\rho^2}{2(1 - \rho)} \tag{9.2.4}$$

This function is plotted in Figure 9.1. As this figure shows, when ρ approaches 1, the average queue length increases rapidly. Herein lies a basic design trade-off: namely, the transmission rate vs. the compression ratio. If we can vary the transmission (or buffer output) rate (in many systems we cannot), we logically want to make it close to the average buffer input rate in order to preserve the compression ratio provided by the compressor. But as $r_c \to m$, $\rho \to 1$ and

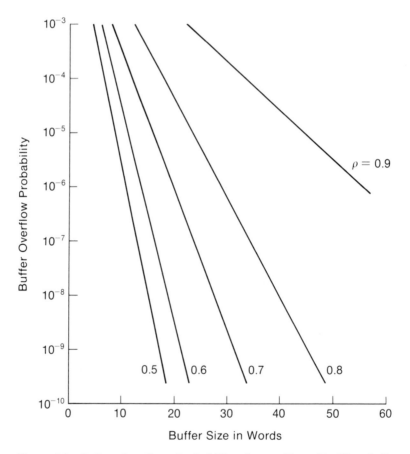

Figure 9.2 Buffer Overflow Probability. From: Chu, W. W. "Buffer Behavior for Poisson Arrivals and Multiple Synchronous Constant Outputs." IEEE Trans. on Computers, vol. C-19, no. 6, June 1970, p. 532. © 1970 IEEE.

$E(n) \rightarrow \infty$. Thus, to avoid buffer overflow, we have to *increase* the transmission rate; this, of course, has the effect of *reducing* the overall compression ratio.

9.3 BUFFER SIZE ESTIMATION

Since the curve of average queue length in Figure 9.1 is an *average* value, using it may occasionally lead to problems. If, for example, we were to build a buffer with a capacity equal to the average queue length, given the ratio of input to output rates ρ, then the result, on the average, would be a loss of input data as the buffer overflowed from time to time. In many design situations this loss of data is not allowable or at least must be minimized. What is needed, then, is a model that will predict the percentage loss of data due to buffer overflow. Such a prediction was made by Dor (1967) using a Poisson input and a constant rate output for the buffer. The single output case of Dor was extended to a multiple output case by Chu (1970). In Figure 9.2 the overflow probability is plotted against the buffer size for various values of ρ (based on Figure 1 in Chu's 1970 paper for the single output case). The curves in Figure 9.2 show that the reduction in overflow probability obtained by increasing the buffer size is less as the parameter ρ, sometimes called the *traffic intensity*, increases. For comparison purposes, for $\rho = 0.9$, a buffer with a capacity of about 33 words must be provided in order to keep the overflow probability less than or equal to 10^{-4}. In Figure 9.1, for $\rho = 0.9$, the average queue length is about 5, so it is apparent that a buffer size that is typically a large multiple of the average queue length must be used in order to maintain a reasonable overflow rate.

9.4 BUFFER OVERFLOW CONTROL

As we saw in the previous section, the buffer occupancy question is a statistical one. The possibility of buffer overflow is finite unless we overdesign the buffer and make it excessively large so that it will never overflow. This option is typically not a desirable one, however, since the cost of additional buffer capacity has to be included in the overall design. What is needed instead is a control system or procedure that will prevent the buffer from overflowing.

There are basically three methods of buffer overflow control: sampling control, filter control, and aperture control. These are shown schematically in Figure 9.3. In each method, buffer *fullness* is monitored continuously. When the buffer reaches a previously set level (percentage) of fullness, a signal is sent to the appropriate control mechanism.

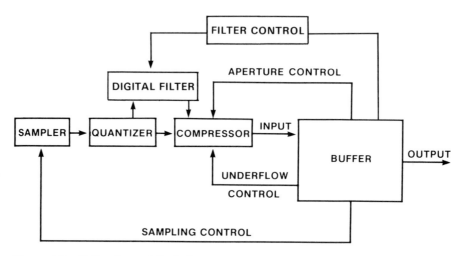

Figure 9.3 *Buffer Control Techniques.*

In *sampling control*, the signal is sent actually to delete samples before they are quantized. In a multiplexed data system this can take the form of low priority data channel deletion. In terms of the curves in Figure 9.2, this method involves moving from an initial operating point vertically downward (constant buffer length) to a line with a lower value of ρ. Of course, this is the *trend* relationship; in actual practice the change is temporary and it is assumed that, on the average, the operating point will stay on one curve and at a fixed buffer length.

In *filter control*, a digital filter is switched in between the output of the quantizer and the input of the compressor. The filter is typically the low-pass type and, as the cutoff frequency is reduced, fewer high-frequency components are passed on to the compressor. Accordingly, the compressor typically classifies more samples redundant, thus increasing the compression ratio and reducing the parameter ρ. As can be seen in Figure 9.2, for a constant buffer size, this results in a decrease in the buffer overflow probability.

In *aperture control*, the feedback signal causes the aperture (in the case of a polynomial or statistical predictor) to increase and thereby makes it possible for the data compressor to classify more samples as redundant. This, of course, increases the compression ratio and reduces ρ. Once again, we think of moving momentarily in Figure 9.2 from an initial operating point vertically downward to a lower value of ρ. As in the cases of sampling control and filter control, this movement has the effect of reducing the buffer overflow probability.

It should be mentioned that there is another way to prevent, or control, buffer overflow, and that is by *adaptively changing the size of the buffer*. This has a number of undesirable consequences, however, not the least of which is the fact that the probability of overflow is not decreased as fast as it is with the other three methods. This can be seen in Figure 9.2 where, with an adaptive buffer, one would move from some initial point on a line to a lower point on the same line (ρ does not change) corresponding to the larger buffer size. But the movement is typically *not* vertical, and therefore may not result in as large a decrease in buffer overflow probability as before.

In the literature these four methods are presented in the following order, which is also the order of preference:

Aperture control

Sampling control

Filter control

Adaptive buffer size

There is an interesting potential trade-off inherent in the first three of these methods and that is simply the fact that at the very time, or shortly thereafter, that the data source is increasing in activity so as to produce more nonredundant samples, we have to sharply reduce the resolution of the data by aperture widening, subsampling, or low-pass filtering: The trade-off becomes a choice between lower resolution data or no data at all.

The variable-length codes described in Chapter 3, such as the Huffman and Shannon-Fano, also require buffering. Even though the original sample rate is synchronous, when each sample is coded into a variable-length code word, this coded string must be buffered in order to maintain a synchronous output to the transmission channel. In this case, the Poisson model for the input to the buffer is not appropriate, and instead one can begin with a "worst case" approach in predicting buffer overflow. If the source symbol rate is 1/sec and there are k symbols per sample going into the block-to-variable-length coder, then the output code words will vary in length from the shortest, N_* symbols, to the longest, N^* symbols. (This latter notation is based on the 1968 paper by Jelinek.) The worst case would be the unlikely situation in which *all* the output words were N^* symbols long. In that case, to avoid buffer overflow, the channel symbol rate r_c should obey the inequality:

$$r_c \geq \frac{N^*}{k} \tag{9.4.1}$$

Also, the buffer will *underflow* occasionally as long as:

$$r_c > \frac{N_*}{k} \tag{9.4.2}$$

Buffer underflow is discussed in the next section.

9.5 BUFFER UNDERFLOW CONTROL

The opposite problem of buffer overflow is buffer underflow, a condition in which the buffer is empty, thus creating a data transmission gap. This can have a serious effect on synchronization and could lead to an eventual loss of data through synchronization loss.

Buffer underflow occurs because the data becomes highly redundant during a given period and only a few nonredundant samples are loaded into the buffer. Since the output rate of the buffer is fixed, the buffer will eventually empty.

An obvious approach to buffer underflow control is just the opposite to buffer overflow control; that is, *decrease* the aperture in the predictor so as to produce more nonredundant samples to fill the buffer. However, this approach has an inherent disadvantage in that the smaller aperture may be sensitive to *noise* in the data, which would tend to fill the buffer with digitized noise instead of actual data.

The method that seems to meet with general approval in the literature is that of priority control. In priority control, we assume that more than one data channel is being compressed and we assign priorities to the various channels in terms of their importance and activity. When a given channel becomes very inactive (highly redundant), we assign it a lower priority and load samples from other channels (channels that originally had a lower priority) into the buffer.

If there is only one channel, priority control obviously cannot be used and a simple "sample stuffing" or "bit stuffing" procedure can be used in the compressor to keep the buffer from emptying.

HIGHLIGHTS

- A buffer is required at that point in a data system where the bit rate is to be changed from asynchronous to synchronous.

- When a buffer is needed, buffer design (primarily its size in terms of bits) and buffer control (primarily data loss due to overflow or underflow) must be considered.

- A Poisson process is commonly used as a model for buffer input.

- Estimating buffer size requires a model that will predict the percentage loss of data due to buffer overflow.

- The three common methods of buffer overflow control are: sampling control (samples are deleted before they are quantized), filter control (fewer high-frequency components are passed to the compressor), and aperture control (aperture is increased, allowing more samples to be classified as redundant.)

- Buffer underflow is controlled by priority control, which allows lower priority channels to become active when higher priority channels become inactive. In the case of only one channel, "bit stuffing" is used.

SUGGESTIONS FOR FURTHER READING

The following items are suggested for further reading and study:

Chu, W. W. "Buffer Behavior for Poisson Arrivals and Multiple Synchronous Constant Outputs." *IEEE Trans. on Computers*, vol. C-19, no. 6, June 1970, pp. 530–534.

The single output buffer is treated and then extended to multiple output channels. The single output results agree with those of Dor (1967).

Dor, N. M. "Guide to the Length of Buffer Storage Required for Random (Poisson) Input and Constant Output Rates." *IEEE Trans. on Electronic Computers*, vol. EC-16, October 1967, pp. 683–684.

In this article, curves of fractional word loss due to buffer overflow vs. buffer size are given as a function of ρ, the ratio of input to output data rates.

Goode, H. H., and Machol, R. E. *System Engineering.* New York: McGraw-Hill, 1957, chapter 23.

In Chapter 23, the Poisson input model for a buffer is used to develop the expression for the average queue length [in our book, equation (9.2.4)].

Jelinek, F. "Buffer Overflow in Variable Length Coding of Fixed Rate Sources." *IEEE Trans. on Info. Theory*, vol. IT-14, no. 3, May 1968, pp. 490–501.

In this paper, a procedure is developed for designing a block-to-variable-length code with the overflow probability of the accompanying buffer a design constraint.

CHAPTER 10

Effects of Transmission Errors

10.1 INTRODUCTION

When a data source is compressed by a redundancy-reduction technique, the compressed data that is transmitted is more sensitive to transmission errors since an error in a transmitted sample affects more than one sample in the reconstructed data. The way in which transmission errors affect the reconstructed data depends, of course, on the compression scheme and the statistics of the transmission errors.

From a system design standpoint, the error control required to protect the compressed data has to be included in the overhead of the transmission system. This overhead, of course, has the effect of reducing the overall compression ratio, and herein lies an important consideration. Very simply, the noisier the channel, the more the need for error control, which has the effect of lowering the compression ratio. An interesting case to be avoided is the one in which error control is added to a system with a low compression ratio in such a way that the coding overhead reduces the compression ratio to near unity. The obvious alternative here is to leave the data uncompressed and uncoded.

In this chapter, we look at the general question of compression and error control and specifically examine the special requirements in three types of data compression: transform coding, predictive coding, and nonredundant sample coding. A brief review of error-control coding is given in Appendix A.

10.2 COMPRESSION RATIO AND DISTORTION

It is often necessary to be able to assess quantitatively the effects of compression and error-control coding on both the compression ratio and the overall distortion in the reconstructed data. Obviously, the goal is a high compression ratio with minimum distortion. In order to compare various combinations of compression and error-control coding some performance measures are needed, and these are described below. Most of the material in this section is based on the paper by Lynch (1967).

Two performance measures that are useful for trade-off analyses are the *average distortion* and *the actual compression ratio*. We can define these measures for three possible systems abbreviated as follows:

Uncompressed/uncoded	UU
Compressed/uncoded	CU
Compressed/coded	CC

These three systems represent increasing complexity as we go from UU to CU to CC. As we go from UU to CU, the distortion typically increases. From CU to CC the compression ratio decreases and, typically, the distortion decreases also. If we find that CC is no better than UU in terms of transmission rate and distortion, then there is no justification for adding the complexity of compression and error-control coding.

The actual compression ratio can be defined for the above three systems as follows. For the uncompressed, uncoded system, normalize it to 1:

$$R_{uu} = 1 \tag{10.2.1}$$

For the compressed, uncoded system, use the actual compression ratio:

$$R_{cu} = R_a \equiv \frac{\text{Total number of bits per block before compression}}{\text{Total number of bits per block after compression}} \tag{10.2.2}$$

For the compressed, coded system, multiply by the code rate, $k/n < 1$ (see Appendix A):

$$R_{cc} = R_a \left(\frac{k}{n}\right) \tag{10.2.3}$$

The average distortion, as discussed in Chapter 2, for a data source set M and a data user set Z involves parameters pertaining to the source $P(M)$, the channel $P(Z/M)$, and the eventual importance $D(M, Z)$, of each data error in the following way:

$$D = \sum_{M,Z} P(M)P(Z/M)D(M, Z) \qquad\qquad (10.2.4)$$

where: $P(M)$ is the first-order probability of the sampled and quantized source M

$P(Z/M)$ is the transitional probability matrix for the transmission of m_i to z_j

$D(M, Z)$ is a distortion measure matrix for transmission of m_i and final reception of z_j

The average distortion measure must take into account the distortion added to the signal from the point of input to the data compression operation to the output of the data reconstruction operation. This means that the distortion is not only a function of the channel noise, but also of the compression algorithm *and* the reconstruction algorithm. For example, in the case of transform coding the *transform coefficients* are transmitted and thereby are affected by the channel noise, but it is the distortion in the *data samples* produced by the inverse transformation that is of practical interest. Errors in the transmitted coefficients are reflected in the reconstructed samples as an *average* effect, as will be described in Section 10.3. In predictive coding, errors in the transmission of predictive coding differences will result in fixed-level offsets in the reconstructed data. In both of these situations, the distortion is a critical function of the compression scheme, especially if it is adaptive.

The most straightforward compression technique from a distortion measure viewpoint is nonredundant sample coding. Here we are transmitting nonredundant samples that will appear in the reconstructed data along with the reinserted redundant samples. We can use equation (10.2.4) since we know the source probability, the channel transitional probability matrix, and a distortion measure that relates transmitted and received signals. Since the ratio of the reconstructed samples to the nonredundant samples in a block is the sample compression ratio, we must multiply the average distortion by the average compression ratio to include the effect of error propagation in the reconstructed samples.

We use the nonredundant sample coding model to illustrate how distortion expressions for the three systems—UU, CU, and CC—can be developed in order to make consistent comparisons. The same general approach could be used in developing distortion expressions for transform coding and predictive coding, but these expressions would be different from the ones developed below, especially in the way errors in the transmitted data (coefficients in the case of transform coding, and differences in the case of predictive coding) affect the $P(Z/M)$ matrix in equation (10.2.4). More will be said about the peculiar error sensitivities of transform coding, predictive coding, and nonredundant sample coding in the following sections.

10.2.1 The Uncompressed-Uncoded System

The expression for D_{uu} is given by:

$$D_{uu} = \sum_{M,Z} P(M)_{uu} P(Z/M)_{uu} D(M, Z) \tag{10.2.5}$$

The first-order probability $P(M)_{uu}$ is that of the sampled and quantized (2^k levels) uncompressed source. The transitional probability $P(Z/M)_{uu}$ is the conditional probability of the *data user* obtaining sample level z_j, given that sample level m_i was sent. The reason the data user is specified here is because only the user can utilize a priori knowledge about, along with inherent redundancy in, the uncompressed data for the purpose of error control. This is an important consideration in trade-off comparisons between an uncompressed, uncoded system and a compressed, coded system. In order to quantitatively include this error-control ability on the part of the data user, we arrange the $P(Z/M)_{uu}$ matrix so that it takes account of this ability. One such arrangement is as follows. If the data user can detect large errors in the data, then the elements in $P(Z/M)_{uu}$ corresponding to these errors can be set equal to zero. The other elements of $P(Z/M)_{uu}$ now have to be suitably modified so as to ensure that $\sum_Z P(Z/M)_{uu} = 1$. Since $P(Z/M)_{uu}$ is a square matrix of order 2^k, this modification corresponds to setting all elements in the upper-right and lower-left regions equal to zero.

If we start with a $P(Z/M)$ matrix, whose elements are simply the word probabilities over a binary symmetric channel, then we can calculate all elements of this $P(Z/M)$ and obtain $P(Z/M)_{uu}$ by setting the corner regions equal to zero and then adding to the remaining elements in each column the total probability removed from that column. If we further assume that the data user performs error correction as well as error detection, then we add the total probability removed from each column to the *main diagonal element* in that column. The relative ability of a data user to perform error detection or correction can be represented by the *size* of the corners of $P(Z/M)_{uu}$ that are set to zero. For example, for a 3-bit, 8-level system, the $P(Z/M)$ matrix corresponding to transmission over a binary-symmetric channel has the form:

$$[P(Z/M)] =$$

Z \ M	000	001	010	011	100	101	110	111
000	q^3	q^2p	q^2p	qp^2	q^2p	qp^2	qp^2	p^3
001	q^2p	q^3	qp^2	q^2p	qp^2	q^2p	p^3	qp^2
010	q^2p	qp^2	q^3	q^2p	qp^2	p^3	q^2p	qp^2
011	qp^2	q^2p	q^2p	q^3	p^3	qp^2	qp^2	q^2p
100	q^2p	qp^2	qp^2	p^3	q^3	q^2p	q^2p	qp^2
101	qp^2	q^2p	p^3	qp^2	q^2p	q^3	qp^2	q^2p
110	qp^2	p^3	q^2p	qp^2	q^2p	qp^2	q^3	q^2p
111	p^3	qp^2	qp^2	q^2p	qp^2	q^2p	q^2p	q^3

$$(10.2.6)$$

where: p is the probability of a bit error

$$q = 1 - p$$

For a data user who can correct errors greater than four levels, we can construct the $P(Z/M)_{uu}$ matrix as follows:

$[P(Z/M)]_{uu} =$

Z \ M	000	001	010	011	100	101	110	111
000	$q^3 + p_1$	$q^2 p$	$q^2 p$	qp^2	$q^2 p$	0	0	0
001	$q^2 p$	$q^3 + p_2$	qp^2	$q^2 p$	qp^2	$q^2 p$	0	0
010	$q^2 p$	qp^2	$q^3 + p_3$	$q^2 p$	qp^2	p^3	$q^2 p$	0
011	qp^2	$q^2 p$	$q^2 p$	q^3	p^3	qp^2	qp^2	$q^2 p$
100	$q^2 p$	qp^2	qp^2	p^3	q^3	$q^2 p$	$q^2 p$	qp^2
101	0	$q^2 p$	p^3	qp^2	$q^2 p$	$q^3 + p_3$	qp^2	$q^2 p$
110	0	0	$q^2 p$	qp^2	$q^2 p$	qp^2	$q^3 + p_2$	$q^2 p$
111	0	0	0	$q^2 p$	qp^2	$q^2 p$	$q^2 p$	$q^3 + p_1$

$$(10.2.7)$$

where: $p_1 = 2qp^2 + p^3$
$p_2 = qp^2 + p^3$
$p_3 = qp^2$

10.2.2 The Compressed-Uncoded System

For D_{cu} we have the expression:

$$D_{cu} = R \sum_{M,Z} P(M)_{cu} P(Z/M)_{cu} D(M, Z) \tag{10.2.8}$$

where R is the sample compression ratio.

The expression for D_{cu} has the factor R because, on the average, an error in one sample of compressed data causes R samples to be in error in the reconstructed data.

The matrix $P(Z/M)_{cu}$ is the word probability of the entire system, but in this case, the data user has little or no redundancy left in the compressed data or the timing data to use in error control. For this reason, $P(Z/M)_{cu}$ can be written simply as the word probability imposed by the channel. For a 3-bit word system over a binary symmetric channel, $P(Z/M)_{cu}$ is in the same form as the $P(Z/M)$ shown in equation (10.2.6). However, the compression reduces the overall transmission rate, which allows an increase in the signal-to-noise ratio. This will be reflected in a lower bit-error probability, p, in the $P(Z/M)$ matrix and, of course, a correspondingly higher value of q.

10.2.3 The Compressed-Coded System

The third distortion, D_{cc}, is given by:

$$D_{cc} = R \sum_{M,Z} P(M)_{cu} P(Z/M)_{cc} D(M, Z) \tag{10.2.9}$$

Again, the factor R accounts for the fact that a sample that is in error in compressed, decoded data causes, on the average, R samples to be in error in the final reconstructed data. The compressed, uncoded data is the source for this channel encoding, and thus $P(M)_{cu}$ is used. Now the system transition probability matrix $P(Z/M)_{cc}$ has to take into account the error-control properties of the code.

The error-correction process provides a situation in which three things can happen to an n-bit transmitted word, assuming an (n, k) block code with k information bits (see Appendix A for a review of error-control coding):

1. No errors are introduced and the word is properly decoded.
2. The number of errors is equal to or less than t, and the t-error-correcting code decodes the k-bit words properly.
3. The number of errors is greater than t, and an original k-bit word is decoded into some other k-bit word.

We can compute the probability of the first two alternatives for a binary symmetric channel as:

$$P_c = \text{Probability of correct decoding} = q^n + \sum_{j=1}^{t} \binom{n}{j} q^{n-j} p^j \tag{10.2.10}$$

The probability of the third alternative is then given by:

$$\text{Probability of incorrect decoding} = 1 - q^n - \sum_{j=1}^{t} \binom{n}{j} q^{n-j} p^j \tag{10.2.11}$$

When a k-bit word is improperly decoded into some other k-bit word, a number of errors greater than the t-error-correcting capacity of the code changes bits in either the information or check sections of the code word, or in both of these sections. For each particular code one could examine the effect of all possible error patterns corresponding to more than t errors and compute the probability of a given word z_j being decoded, when word m_i $(i \neq j)$ was originally encoded. The number of cases one would have to examine would be equal to $2^k \sum_{i=t+1}^{n} \binom{n}{i}$. For a (13, 9) Hamming code* $(t = 1)$, for example, this number would be

$$2^9 \sum_{i=2}^{13} \binom{13}{i} = 2^9 \left(2^{13} - \sum_{j=0}^{1} \binom{13}{j}\right) = 2^9(2^{13} - 1 - 13) \approx 2^{22}$$

or approximately 4.6×10^6 cases.

For the purposes of trade-off analysis, wherein codes of different lengths and different error-correcting capabilities may be compared, it is reasonable to make an approximation and assign equal transition probabilities to the *incorrectly* decoded word pairs. This probability is given by:

$$\left.\begin{array}{l}\text{Probability of each} \\ \text{incorrectly} \\ \text{decoded word pair}\end{array}\right\} = \frac{1 - q^n - \sum_{j=1}^{t} \binom{n}{j} q^{n-j} p^j}{2^k - 1} = \frac{1 - P_c}{2^k - 1} \qquad (10.2.12)$$

Then the $P(Z/M)_{cc}$ matrix is constructed by using the following values for elements:

Each main diagonal element $= P_c$ $\qquad (10.2.13)$

Every other element $= \dfrac{1 - P_c}{2^k - 1}$ $\qquad (10.2.14)$

10.2.4 Use of the Performance Measures

The distortion measure matrix, $D(M, Z)$, used in all three D expressions assigns a relative cost to word errors. In general, each element of the $D(M, Z)$ matrix may be any function of the dissimilarity between m_i and z_j. One distortion measure is the absolute difference between m_i and z_j or

$$d(m, z) = |z_j - m_i| \qquad (10.2.15)$$

Another measure that is widely used in evaluating systems is the squared difference or

$$d(m, z) = (z_j - m_i)^2 \qquad (10.2.16)$$

---

* See Appendix A.

Having computed the compression ratios and average distortions for each system, UU, CU, and CC, one can compare them and answer the following questions, given the system specifications:

1. Will the CU system meet the maximum distortion limitation of the entire data system?
2. If not, will the CC system meet the compression ratio requirement of the system?

10.3 ERROR CONTROL FOR TRANSFORM CODING

Four linear transformations were presented in Chapter 5: principal component, Fourier, Hadamard, and Haar. All of these transformations except the Haar transformation create transform coefficients, each of which is a linear combination of *all* the data samples. And inversely, the reconstructed samples are each a linear combination of *all* the coefficients. In the Haar transformation, only the first two coefficients are linear functions of all the samples, the other coefficients being functions of fewer than all the samples. The situation for the inverse Haar transformation is similar—no reconstructed samples are functions of *all* the coefficients. See Example 5.4.

What does this mean in the situation where there are transmission errors? In a typical system incorporating transform coding data compression, the transform coefficients are sent over the transmission channel and, thus, they are subject to error effects. If we assume that the transmission is in PCM, then random nosie will effectively change some 1s to 0s and vice versa. Depending on the time of occurrence of these noise pulses, various coefficients will be increased or decreased in magnitude. If, over a given block of data, some coefficients are increased and some are decreased, we have the so-called averaging effect of transmission noise on transformations. When the original samples are reconstructed, each one now has the weighted sum of the changes (due to errors) in the various coefficients added to its "true" value. Since some coefficients are increased and some are decreased, we can expect a partial balancing or averaging of the overall error effect on the reconstructed samples. Obviously, this averaging effect depends on the noise characteristics, but experimental results have shown that for the same bit-error probability, the noise effects are reduced by the intervening transformation (Andrews 1970).

Another way of looking at the effect of these channel errors is through the model of a filter applied to the transmitted coefficients. For example, this filter would be a function of *frequency* if the transformation were Fourier.

Typically, the signal energy is not uniformly distributed throughout the various transform coefficients. Most linear transformations tend to "pack" more energy into the lower-ordered coefficients, with the principal component transformation doing this to the greatest degree. Because of this tendency to have more energy in the lower-ordered coefficients, errors in these coefficients are more serious than errors in the higher-ordered coefficients. Accordingly, it has been suggested that more error-control coding be applied to the lower-ordered coefficients (Andrews 1970).

This discussion of the relative low sensitivity to channel errors, or the "robustness," of transformation techniques really applies to the *nonadaptive* case. In an adaptive transformation system, the words added to the transmitted block that indicate the *mode* of compression in terms of the sample selection, quantization rule, and so on are extremely critical. An error in one of these words can cause a large block of data to be lost, and for this reason, special error-protection coding is usually applied to these mode words.

The Huffman code is a fixed-to-variable-length word transformation, and it is much more vulnerable to noise effects than the linear transformations. Because it is a *prefix code*, that is, no short word is the same as the beginning of a longer word, all bits must be preserved in order to maintain word synchronization. A single bit error could wipe out an entire block of data, where we define a block of data as being between synchronization words.

10.4 ERROR CONTROL FOR PREDICTIVE CODING

In predictive coding we are sending the difference between a predicted sample, pixel, line, or frame and the actual value of that sample, pixel, line, or frame. At the receiving end, these differences are accumulated, and when a difference is in error because of transmission noise effects, the entire string of samples following the erroneous difference is offset in amplitude by the amount of the difference error. As subsequent errors occur, subsequent samples are offset by the algebraic sum of all the preceding difference errors. In predictive coding there is usually a periodic reinitialization of the sample values. For example, in a scanned image, this takes place at the beginning of a scan line. The error effect can be spread over more than the intervening samples (between the error and the reinitialization point), depending on the *prediction* function. This is illustrated in the following sections.

Now we look at the error effects in three types of predictive coding covered in Chapter 6: delta modulation, DPCM, and block-to-block compression.

10.4.1 Noise Effects in Delta Modulation

Delta modulation, as described in Section 6.3 transmits binary pulses that are then integrated and low-pass filtered to form the output signal. As channel noise increases, some pulses are changed from one polarity to the other. We have to look at the effect of these "flipped" pulses in the nonadaptive and adaptive versions of delta modulation.

In nonadaptive delta modulation, the error due to a single pulse polarity inversion is simply

$$\text{Error} = \pm 2\Delta \tag{10.4.1}$$

where Δ is the step size. This results in a fixed offset whose sign depends on the original polarity of the flipped pulse. If the erroneous pulse was initially positive, then the offset error is negative and vice versa. This is illustrated in Figure 10.1. As more errors occur in the pulse train, the cumulative reconstructed error for a total of N pulse errors is:

$$\text{Cumulative error} = \sum_{i=1}^{N} 2q_i\Delta \tag{10.4.2}$$

where $q_i = \begin{cases} +1, \text{ original pulse negative} \\ -1, \text{ original pulse positive} \end{cases}$

If the errors are random, and if over a given time period as many positive pulses are "flipped" as negative ones, then the cumulative error in (10.4.2) will

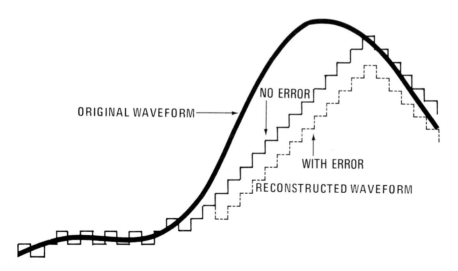

Figure 10.1 *Error Propagation in Delta Modulation.*

be zero. This, of course, is not likely to happen, but it illustrates the robustness of delta modulation to channel noise, namely, a certain averaging of the error effects over time. Obviously, if errors occur during a time period when the signal is monotonically increasing or decreasing, then the effect of the errors will be cumulative. Wolf (1966) used a Markov model to analyze the effect of errors on delta modulation, and his result shows the signal-to-noise ratio (SNR) at the output of the receiver to be a function of the reciprocal of the square of the bit-error probability. In terms of an asymptotic behavior, this functional relationship exhibits a "graceful degradation" of SNR with channel degradation.

In *adaptive delta Modulation*, the effect of errors is different from that of the nonadaptive case. Since the adaptive scheme is typically monitoring the *trend* in the data, the effect of an error is highly dependent on its time location in the data stream. For example, in the adaptive delta modulation algorithm by Song (1971) described in Section 6.3.2, the following rules apply:

Output polarity does not change: increase step size by 50%

Output polarity changes: decrease step size by 50%

It is obvious that a "flip" in a single pulse affects *two* polarity changes, the change from the previous pulse to the flipped pulse and the change from the flipped pulse to the next pulse. We can illustrate these effects if we consider three pulses and allow only the second one to be "flipped" in order to compare the effects, assuming the same initial step size, Δ, in each case. The results are shown in Table 10.1.

As Table 10.1 shows, for four different original pulse patterns, there are two *different* cumulative offsets. This is in contrast to the case of nonadaptive

Table 10.1

Delta Modulation Pulse Pattern at Receiver				Step—Size—Pattern at Decoder			Total Offset $\sum$(Step)	
Original	1	1	1	$+\Delta$	$+1.5\Delta$	$+2.25\Delta$	4.75Δ	4Δ
With error	1	-1	1	$+\Delta$	-0.5Δ	$+0.25\Delta$	0.75Δ	
Original	1	-1	1	$+\Delta$	-0.5Δ	$+0.25\Delta$	0.75Δ	4Δ
With error	1	1	1	$+\Delta$	$+1.5\Delta$	$+2.25\Delta$	4.75Δ	
Original	1	1	-1	$+\Delta$	$+1.5\Delta$	-0.75Δ	1.75Δ	2Δ
With error	1	-1	-1	$+\Delta$	-0.5Δ	-0.75Δ	-0.25Δ	
Original	1	-1	-1	$+\Delta$	-0.5Δ	-0.75Δ	-0.25Δ	2Δ
With error	1	1	-1	$+\Delta$	$+1.5\Delta$	-0.75Δ	1.75Δ	

delta modulation, where the offset due to a single pulse error is fixed. Also in the adaptive case, there is less chance of *error averaging*, since the location of the error is critical to the offset thereof.

10.4.2 Noise Effects in DPCM

When we look at the noise effects in DPCM, we see some similarities to delta modulation but also important differences. As was pointed out in Chapter 6, delta modulation is really a 1-bit version of DPCM.

As in the case of nonadaptive delta modulation, a transmission error in DPCM causes an offset that affects all subsequent samples until the next error or the next reinitialization occurs. Unlike nonadaptive delta modulation, however, the DPCM offset is not always the same and depends on which bit position is affected by the error. For this reason, we can't say there is an "error averaging" effect in DPCM as we can in nonadaptive delta modulation. In fact, DPCM has an error response closer to adaptive delta modulation than nonadaptive delta modulation.

Since the two main parts of a DPCM encoder are the quantizer and the predictor, we will look at each part in terms of the effect of errors. We saw in Section 6.4.2 that the quantizing noise in DPCM is less than that of PCM (assuming the same number of levels) by the amount

$$10 \log_{10} \frac{\sigma^2}{\sigma_e^2} \quad \text{in dB}$$

Another way of looking at this improvement with DPCM is to say that for a given amount of quantizing noise, DPCM allows transmission of the same information at a lower bit rate than PCM. On the other hand, transmission errors are more serious in DPCM than in PCM.

O'Neal (1966) developed an expression for the decoded noise in DPCM as follows. In the decoder shown in Figure 6.10 we can follow the progress of a noise pulse, η, as follows: The decoded output would have the noise sequence:

$$\eta \quad a_1\eta \quad a_1^2\eta \quad a_1^3\eta \quad a_1^4\eta \quad \cdots$$

The noise energy would look as follows:

$$\text{Noise energy} = \eta^2 + (a_1\eta)^2 + (a_1^2\eta)^2 + (a_1^3\eta)^2 + \cdots \tag{10.4.3}$$

$$\text{Noise energy} = \eta^2(1 + a_1^2 + a_1^4 + a_1^6 + \cdots) \tag{10.4.4}$$

$$\text{Noise energy} = \eta^2 \left(\frac{1}{1 - a_1^2} \right) \tag{10.4.5}$$

For the simple case of a predictor that uses only the previous sample, we have, from Section 6.4.2:

$$a_1 = \frac{R_{01}}{\sigma^2} \qquad \text{[equation (6.4.8)]}$$

Then

$$\frac{1}{(1 - a_1^2)} = \frac{1}{1 - \dfrac{(R_{01})^2}{\sigma^4}} \qquad (10.4.6)$$

But

$$\sigma_e^2 = R_{00} - a_1 R_{01} \qquad \text{[equation (6.4.7)]}$$

Since $R_{00} = \sigma^2$, we may divide equation (6.4.7) by σ^2 to obtain:

$$\frac{\sigma_e^2}{\sigma^2} = 1 - \frac{(R_{01})^2}{\sigma^4} \qquad (10.4.7)$$

Substituting (10.4.7) into (10.4.6),

$$\frac{1}{(1 - a_1^2)} = \frac{\sigma^2}{\sigma_e^2} \qquad (10.4.8)$$

Now (10.4.5) shows that the DPCM operation *increases* the channel noise energy by a factor of σ^2/σ_e^2, or in dB, $10\log_{10}(\sigma^2/\sigma_e^2)$. We thus have the interesting result that the decrease in quantizing noise is exactly equal to the increase in channel noise in a DPCM system.

The predictor operates on the previous predicted samples and, in the case of a linear predictor, computes a weighted sum of these samples to be used as the predicted value. When an error is made in transmission, the error has a cumulative effect on the reconstructed signal since the same predictor function is used in the decoder (see Figure 6.10.) However, there are situations, especially in image coding, in which the effect of channel errors can be lessened to some degree by virtue of the fact that some of the predicted samples included in the linear prediction function are from a previous line or block that may *not* have been affected by the channel error that is affecting the samples on the present line. Lippmann (1976) investigated this effect and Figure 10.2 illustrates his results.

In image coding, a DPCM error *propagates*, resulting in the characteristic streak in a reconstructed line-scanned image. A method of shortening this streak, or error propagation has been developed, which is nothing more than

Geometry

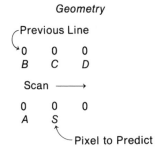

Previous Line

$$0 \quad 0 \quad 0$$
$$B \quad C \quad D$$

Scan $\longrightarrow$

$$0 \quad 0 \quad 0$$
$$A \quad S$$

Pixel to Predict

Predictors and Appearance of Errors

$\hat{S} = (31/32)A$	STREAKS
$\hat{S} = (1/2)A + (15/32)C$	BLOTCHES
$\hat{S} = (3/4)A - (17/32)B + (3/4)C$	TRIANGLES

Figure 10.2 *Error Effects in One- and Two-dimensional in DPCM. After: Lippmann, R. "Influence of Channel Errors on DPCM Coding." Acta Electronica, vol. 19, no. 4, 1976, pp. 289–294.*

attenuation in the predictor loop, as shown in Figure 10.3. This attenuation is usually shown as an amplifier with a gain close to, but less than, 1; it is usually referred to as the *leak*. It is possible to show that in the absence of transmission errors, the original signal will be reconstructed with the leak in place, and the effect of a transmission error, where it occurs, will *decay* with time because of the leak, as shown in Figure 10.4.

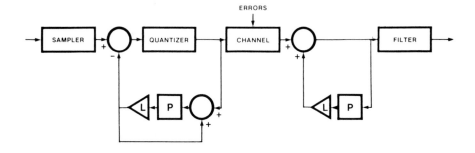

L = Leak Attenuator
P = Predictor

Figure 10.3 *DPCM System With Error Propagation Control.*

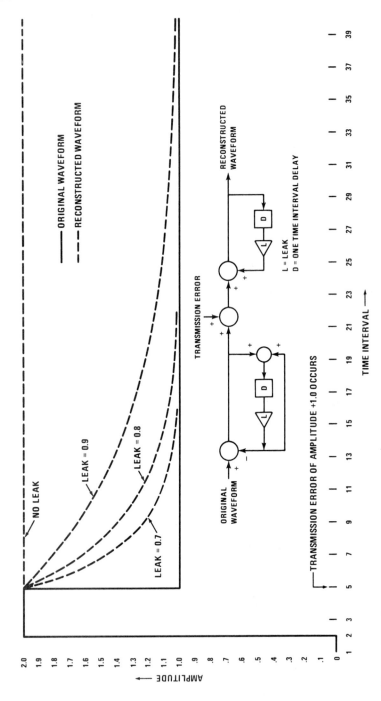

Figure 10.4 *Reduction of DPCM Error Propagation by Leak Attenuator.*

10.4.3 Noise Effects in Block-to-Block Coding

In Chapter 6, block-to-block coding was the general name given to line-to-line and frame-to-frame coding. In general, the prediction in these types of predictive coding is the simplest—namely, that the next line or frame is identical to the previous one. In effect, then, what are transmitted are the differences between successive blocks. If we think of the prediction as being done on a pixel basis from block to block, we could say that the error propagation is in the *direction* of prediction. In the case of one-dimensional DPCM, the prediction is normally done from pixel to pixel within a block. Error propagation in this case creates a horizontal streak in a line-scanned image. In the case of line-to-line image coding, the streak is vertical, and in frame-to-frame image coding, the effect is a pixel with a permanent amplitude offset.

In both line-to-line and frame-to-frame coding, the differences often occur in *clusters*, so the technique of cluster coding (see Chapter 8) is used to reduce the time/position coding overhead. Cluster coding, in its simplest form, involves coding the time or position of the *beginning* of each cluster. Then, only the nonzero (or above-a-threshold) differences have to be transmitted, along with their cluster start position. Obviously, an error in the cluster start position code will shift the entire cluster and result in a large error propagation. Thus, in block-to-block coding, the *type* of error, from the standpoint of the overall effect on the reconstructed signal, is very important.

10.5 ERROR CONTROL FOR NONREDUNDANT SAMPLE CODING

The discussion of nonredundant sample coding in Chapters 7 and 8 described basically three kinds of information that is sent in this type of compression technique: the nonredudant sample values, the timing information, and finally, discrimination information between the first two. An error in any one of these categories will result in some error propagation in the reconstructed data. How much error propagation will occur depends on two things: the type of nonredundant sample coding used and the location of the error(s) in the above categories. In order to do a complete analysis of all possible situations, one would have to examine the combinations of choices in these categories:

TYPE OF NONREDUNDANT SAMPLE CODING

Polynomial predictors

Interpolators

Statistical predictors

TYPE OF TIME CODING

Time sequence codes

Time of nonredundant sample codes

Run-length codes

ERROR LOCATION

Nonredundant sample values

Timing information

Discrimination information

Having done this, one would attempt to choose error-control techniques for each combination. Since the number of combinations is large, a more practical, alternate approach is usually followed: to study the more general case in order to develop a better understanding of the relative effects of errors in the various nonredundant sample coding techniques. This approach is taken in the next section, followed by an example using a specific time code.

10.5.1 General Case

All Nonredundant sample techniques partition the original data set into two classes: nonredundant and redundant. In so doing, the compression scheme develops the need to send along timing information, and this, in turn, creates the need to send along discrimination information so that time words will not be interpreted as nonredundant samples, and vice versa. In general, we can represent the typical sequence of compressed data words to be transmitted as shown in Figure 10.5. This figure simply shows that we are sending *n* consecutive nonredundant samples and a time code, with discrimination words before and after the time code.

We can now make the following general statements about the effect of errors on the format shown in Figure 10.5:

1. An error in the consecutive nonredundant sample values will affect only the sample in error except when this sample happens to be the *last* or *next-to-last* sample in the string. In the case of Figure 10.5, this would be NRS(*n*) in

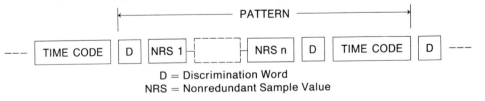

D = Discrimination Word
NRS = Nonredundant Sample Value

Figure 10.5 *Nonredundant Sample Coding General Format*

the case of a zero-order predictor, and NRS($n - 1$) and NRS(n) in the case of a first-order predictor. When these samples are in error, then all the redundant samples following this cluster of nonredundant samples will be in error. Such error propagation is equivalent, on the average, to a multiplication of the distortion due to a single sample error by the compression ratio.

2. An error in a time code will cause a time shift in the reconstructed data. This shift will be in effect until the next time reference is sent. For this reason, errors in time codes are usually more serious than errors in the nonredundant samples. Three categories of time codes are covered in Chapter 8:

a. *Sequence time codes.* There are two codes in this category: the binary-sequence code and the Lynch–Davisson code.

The binary-sequence code, although the most inefficient time code of all, has some robustness in the case of channel errors. Since this code is merely a binary representation of the labels assigned by the compressor to the original samples, either nonredundant or redundant, an error changes only one sample from nonredundant to redundant, and vice versa. But the location of the "flipped" sample is important. If the error changes an *n* (for nonredundant) to an *r* (for redundant), then the situation is the same as that discussed in statement 1: Error propagation occurs only when the flipped sample is the last, or next-to-last sample in the nonredundant cluster. If the error changes an *r* to *n*, then all the *r* samples following this change in the *r*-run are in error.

The Lynch–Davisson code is a two-part code. The first part gives the number of nonredundant samples in the block, and the second part gives their location by means of a unique pattern code. For this code, an error in either part is very serious since the entire block is affected.

b. *Time of nonredundant samples (TNRS) codes.* There are two TNRS codes: the standard and the modified. The latter is sometimes called the cluster code.

In the standard TNRS code, the time of each nonredundant sample is given. An error in one of these time words will change some values of reconstructed samples in the interval from the previous nonredundant sample to the next nonredundant sample, assuming that the time error has not violated the strictly increasing monotonic pattern of the time words. Obviously, if the error produces a time word out of order, then it is easily detected as an error.

In the modified TNRS code or cluster code, only the time of the beginning of a cluster of nonredundant samples is sent. When an error occurs in this time word, the entire cluster is shifted, causing all the shifted nonredundant samples to be in error as well as those redundant samples changed by the shift. If the cluster is *b* samples long, and the shift *s* samples, then the number of samples affected is:

$$\text{Number of samples affected} = b + s \tag{10.5.1}$$

c. *Run-length codes.* Run-length codes are used to encode the length of the *redundant* run lengths, so that an error in the run-length word will result, upon reconstruction, in an erroneously long or short run of redundant samples. The three types of run-length codes discussed in Chapter 8 are: fixed-length binary, Huffman, and BNO. An error in the fixed-length binary will cause the shortening or lengthening of the redundant runs as stated above. An error in the Huffman code will have the same effect but, in addition, word synchronization could be lost due to the fact that the Huffman code has to be decoded as a variable-length prefix code. The BNO code is an interesting case, since it was designed just for the purpose of encoding the redundant runs in a nonredundant sample compression scheme. It will be examined in the next section as an illustrative example.

3. An error in a discrimination word will affect all reconstructed data up to the next discrimination word. In Figure 10.5, two discrimination words are shown in the basic pattern. It is possible to use only one discrimination word in some schemes (as in the case of the BNO code). But the overall effect of errors in the discrimination word is still the same: nonredundant samples are interpreted as time codes and vice versa.

10.5.2 An Example

The binary nonconsecutive one Code is an interesting example of a coding system specially designed for the nonredundant sample class of compression techniques. It was described in detail in Section 8.3.3, and a typical sequence looks as follows:

$$\overbrace{(111\ldots 1110)}^{\text{pattern}} \underbrace{(A_1, A_2, \ldots, A_{N_n})\,(\text{BNO})}_{2N_n} \quad \overbrace{(111\ldots 1110)}^{\text{pattern}} \underbrace{(A_1, A_2, \ldots, A_{N_n})\,(\text{BNO})}_{2N_n}$$

In each of these two patterns, we have in this order:

Discrimination word:	$(111\ldots 1110)$
Nonredundant sample values:	$(A_1, A_2, \ldots, A_{N_n})$
Time Code:	(BNO)

Comparing this pattern to Figure 10.5 shows that the *second* discrimination word in Figure 10.5 has been eliminated from here. This second word is not necessary because, in the BNO scheme, the discrimination word includes the *number* of nonredundant samples to follow it, so that by simply counting these samples we can find the beginning of the time code, the actual BNO code. Let us now briefly check the BNO scheme against the three considerations in Section 10.5.1:

1. *Error in a nonredundant sample.* What was stated in Section 10.5.1 holds for the BNO scheme as well.

2. *Error in the time code.* The time code is the BNO code, and since it has no consecutive ones, an error that creates two or more consecutive ones will make it look like the discrimination word, which *always* has consecutive ones. Since the discrimination word always has an *even* number of consecutive ones, an erroneous BNO code with an *odd* number of consecutive ones could be detected as an error. When an error changes one BNO code into another legitimate BNO code, as shown in Table 8.1, then we have the shortening or lengthening of the redundant runs, as discussed earlier.

3. *Error in the discrimination word.* Since the discrimination word must have an even number of consecutive ones, a single error will be detectable except in some special case. For example, if the *second* one in the discrimination code were changed to a zero *after* a BNO code ending in a zero, then the BNO code would be changed to another BNO code, and the discrimination word would have us count one less nonredundant sample following it. This would affect the *next* BNO code as well.

This example shows how the location of errors in the basic pattern is so critical to the overall error effect.

HIGHLIGHTS

• Data compressed by redundancy-reduction techniques is very sensitive to transmission errors, since one error will affect more than one sample in the reconstructed data.

• When the effects of compression and error-control coding on the compression ratio and overall distortion must be assessed, two useful performance measures are average distortion and the actual compression ratio, and they can be defined and compared for three systems: uncompressed/uncoded, compressed/uncoded, and compressed/coded.

• In transform coding, the transform coefficients are subject to error effects but an averaging effect tends to reduce the overall error effect on reconstructed samples.

- In predictive coding, errors in differences between predicted and actual sample values can offset an entire string of samples at the receiving end; the error effects are typically worse in DPCM than in delta modulation.

- In nonredundant sample coding, an error in any type of information that is sent—non-redundant samples, time words, discrimination words—will result in error propagation in the reconstructed data.

- In general, error effects are worse in adaptive redundancy-reduction techniques than in nonadaptive techniques.

SUGGESTIONS FOR FURTHER READING

The following items are suggested for further reading and study:

Andrews, H. C. See Chapter 5, Suggestions for Further Reading.

Lippmann, R. "Influence of Channel Errors on DPCM Picture Coding." *Acta Electronica*, vol. 19, no. 4, 1976, pp. 289–294.

The effect of channel errors is analyzed as a function of different predictor functions in the forward DPCM loop. In particular, two-dimensional prediction is analyzed for picture coding.

Lynch, T. J. "Performance Measures for Compressed and Coded Space Telemetry Systems." *IEEE Trans. on Aerospace and Electronic Systems*, vol. AES-3, no. 5, September 1967, pp. 784–795.

Two performance measures based on rate distortion theory are developed to compare systems with different combinations of source and channel coding. These measures include the effects of the compression ratio and channel errors on the overall distortion.

O'Neal, J. B. See Chapter 6, Suggestions for Further Reading.

Song et al. See Chapter 6, Suggestions for Further Reading.

Wolf, J. K. "Effects of Channel Errors on Delta Modulation." *IEEE Trans. on Comm. Tech.*, vol. COM-14, no. 1, February 1966, pp. 2–7.

In this paper, the author used a first-order Markov model for the data source and developed an expression for the signal-to-noise ratio at the output of a delta modulation system as a function of the channel bit-error rate. This result predicts a "graceful degradation" for delta modulation with a degrading channel as opposed to a "threshold effect."

CHAPTER 11

System Design

11.1 INTRODUCTION

The incorporation of data compression into a larger data system has to be planned carefully, with a number of trade-offs considered if the compression operation is to obtain the maximum benefit. The simplistic approach of adding compression as a "black box" at some appropriate point in series with other data operations, with little or no consideration of its impact on the rest of the system, could have disastrous effects.

An obvious response to this warning is to consider each case separately and to exhaustively try all combinations of algorithms and designs. In this chapter, however, we try to provide a more structured approach to the system design of data compression, drawing heavily on the material in Part II as well as that in Part I. In Part III, actual examples of data compression systems will be given in terms of types of applications.

In this chapter, we revisit the question of entropy reduction as compared to redundancy reduction in the light of system requirements. An algorithm selection procedure is given using the actual compression ratio, and finally, the use of cascaded redundancy reduction is discussed.

11.2 ENTROPY REDUCTION AND REDUNDANCY REDUCTION

In Part I the differences between entropy reduction and redundancy reduction were described. Basically, entropy reduction is irreversible, whereas redundancy reduction is reversible. Typically, one can obtain a higher compression ratio with entropy reduction, but at the cost of lost information. In Part II we have described both types of techniques since there is interest in applying them to a wide variety of systems—as will be seen in Part III.

An important fact to keep in mind is that redundancy-reduction techniques *do* introduce some minimal distortion even though we characterize them as reversible. The detailed descriptions of the different techniques of nonredundant sample coding (Chapter 7) show this to be the case.

In any system design, we usually start with a set of requirements, specifications, constraints, and so on. Let us do the same here for data compression. A system that needs data compression needs a reduction in the volume of data transmitted per unit time or stored per unit volume. This need for compression can be based on one of two considerations: system operability or system cost.

System operability means that there is no way the system can function without data compression. An example of this is a communication system in which it is necessary to transmit the output of a data source over a channel of insufficient bandwidth. Obviously, the only choices are to compress the output of the data source or to buffer it and transmit at a much slower rate. The latter option may not be feasible in many cases, so we may have to perform data compression.

System cost seems self-explanatory, but sometimes it is not obvious how much of a saving one realizes with data compression since it may be necessary to factor in additional cost requirements for time coding, buffering, and error-control coding.

Having established a legitimate need for data compression, one needs to identify the important parameters that are part of the system requirements. In a very general sense, there are three such parameters:

Compression ratio

Average distortion

Complexity

COMPRESSION RATIO

Compression ratio is the first requirement that comes to mind. As noted, there is often a need, for one or another compelling reason, to compress data. Thus, one might imagine that the higher the compression ratio the better—but it has been shown that if *some* compression is good, *more* is not necessarily better. As we keep increasing the compression ratio by more powerful algorithms or concatenated algorithms, a point is reached (the entropy) beyond which we cannot go without introducing distortion—or to put it another way, without losing information. This fact has been discussed in detail in Chapters 2 and 3, but the important relationship to keep in mind is the following: In an *n*-bit system, the maximum distortionless compression ratio that one can ever achieve is equal to *n* divided by the entropy or

$$R_{\max} = \frac{\log_2 M}{H} \qquad [\text{equation } (3.4.1)]$$

where *M* is the number of quantization levels

Having computed this upper bound on the compression ratio (for zero distortion), we can compare it to the actual compression ratio required. Obviously, if the required value is less than the maximum, we can plan to use redundancy reduction exclusively and the choice of algorithm hinges primarily on the complexity factor. If the required compression ratio is greater than the maximum value, then some combination of entropy reduction and redundancy reduction will have to be found.

The above comparisons are preliminary, of course, because it is the actual compression ratio that has to be compared to the required compression ratio, and the actual value is always less than the computed maximum value. The actual compression ratio is discussed in Section 11.3.

The required compression ratio may have to be modified depending on the maximum compression ratio predicted and the feasibility of using combinations of entropy reduction and redundancy reduction. If the basis of the compression ratio requirement is *system cost*, then this adjustment can be made by suitable trade-off analyses. However, if the basis is *system operability*, then the required compression ratio remains the dominant design driver and cannot be changed.

AVERAGE DISTORTION

Average distortion is typically the second consideration in setting requirements for data compression. To many data users, it is not clear why the average distortion cannot be zero in all cases. Of course, if only redundancy reduction is used, this is theoretically possible. But obviously, entropy reduction introduces distortion and so do channel errors (as described in Chapter 10). In addition, the fact that some redundancy-reduction techniques introduce some minimal distortion is important when the application requires little or no distortion. In these cases, the *type* of distortion becomes the important consideration, and the simple specification of the average distortion magnitude will not fully describe the distortion requirement.

In most cases of redundancy reduction, the distortion due to channel errors is a dominant factor in the design of the entire system since it leads to the need for error-control coding, which, of course, affects the actual compression ratio and overall complexity.

COMPLEXITY

Complexity is a system requirement that one wants to minimize, obviously. But the total complexity is made up of the complexity at the encoding end as well as at the decoding end, and herein lies an important selection factor for data compression algorithms. Some algorithms have simple encoders and more complex decoders and vice versa.

The need for time coding, buffering, and error control for some redundancy-reduction schemes adds to the total system complexity, so that some systems may be prohibitively complex after data compression is added.

11.3 CHARACTERISTICS OF DATA COMPRESSION TECHNIQUES

Before one can select a data compression technique that will meet the system requirements of the specific application, one should be able to compare the various compression techniques in terms of their characteristics.

Let us look at three types of data compression algorithms: transform coding, predictive coding, and nonredundant sample coding. Each type of compression has its own peculiar characteristics that have to be considered in a system design selection. Obviously, the goal in system design is to choose a compression scheme or a cascade of compression schemes that will meet the two system requirements of *compression ratio* and *distortion* with a minimum of complexity. We review these three types of data compression from the standpoint of their unique characteristics. In particular, we look at the following characteristics from a system design standpoint:

1. Timing requirements
2. Buffer requirements
3. Inherent distortion
4. Error effects and error control
5. Actual compression ratio

11.3.1 Transform Coding

As was described in Chapter 5, there are two basic operations in the data compression system called transform coding. They are: transformation and quantization (including sample selection). The compression occurs because the transformation makes possible a more efficient quantization within the transform domain before transmission. Now we look at the five characteristics in relation to transform coding.

1. TIMING REQUIREMENTS

The timing requirements are minimal and relatively simple in transform coding. Data samples are transformed in blocks of predetermined size that are buffered before and after the transformation. Quantization is done on a block basis. The timing requirement, therefore, is more of a block synchronization requirement. The compressed blocks typically will not be the same length, so it is necessary to provide an indication for the "start of block." In nonadaptive schemes, the selected coefficients are contiguous and are transmitted in order, so there is no need to identify them; in adaptive schemes, however, the location of the coefficients (for example, those that fall above a set threshold) has to be transmitted. Also, adaptive schemes that use different quantization procedures require that information about the quantization parameters be sent as they are changed.

2. BUFFER REQUIREMENTS

Since data is transformed in blocks, a fixed buffer size can be specified for both the pre- and posttransformation buffering, as the latter will contain even fewer words because of sample selection.

The other requirement for buffering comes about when a block-to-variable length code, such as a Huffman code, is used after quantization. In this case, we can start with a "worst case" design, as outlined in Section 9.4, and make the output buffer large enough to handle a block of words of maximal length in the variable-length code. The size of the buffer can be reduced from this maximum size since we know that the average output word length is less than $\log_2 M$, where M is the number of quantization levels.

3. INHERENT DISTORTION

By inherent distortion, we mean the distortion that is introduced by the data compression scheme itself in the absence of any transmission errors. In the case of transform coding the distortion is introduced in two ways: (1) by the sample selection process, in which some samples (or coefficients) are discarded, and (2) by the special quantization of the remaining coefficients. Typically, the larger contributor to the total distortion is the first, the sample selection. In the case of the principal component transformation, the distortion can actually be predicted, as follows (from Section 5.2.1):

$$\text{Mean-square error} = \sum_{\text{discarded}} \sigma_k^2 \tag{11.3.1}$$

which says that the mean-square error is the sum of the variances of the discarded coefficients. In the case of the principal component transformation, this error can be kept low.

The quantizing noise is low due to the fact that optimum quantizing techniques can be used, as explained in Chapter 2.

4. ERROR EFFECTS AND ERROR CONTROL

The transmission error effects in transform coding, as discussed in Section 10.3, show a certain "robustness" of this compression scheme to transmission errors. For example, the worst effect in the case of image compression would be low-frequency noise in the reconstructed image. This is true of the nonadaptive case; the adaptive case is much more sensitive to transmission errors.

Of course, the total distortion is the aggregate of the inherent distortion and the distortion due to errors that are undetected by the error-control code. Particular attention has to be paid to the use of variable-length codes (like Huffman), which lose word synchronization if bits are in error.

5. ACTUAL COMPRESSION RATIO

In terms of sample selection, the compression ratio depends on the number of coefficients in the transform domain that are selected for transmission. But the "optimum" coding and quantization also contribute to the compression ratio. If error-control coding is used, then this represents another factor in the overall compression ratio. Representing everything in terms of a block of data to be transformed, we have, for the nonadaptive case:

$$R_a = \left[\frac{(S_u)(k_u)}{(C_s)\bar{k}_c + \text{sync}} \right] \left(\frac{k}{n} \right) \tag{11.3.2}$$

where: S_u is the original number of samples in the block

k_u is the number of bits per original sample

C_s is the number of selected coefficients in the transformed block

$\bar{k}_c$ is the average number of bits per selected coefficient

sync is the number of bits in the block sync word

k/n is the error-control code rate, where $k/n < 1$

The range of actual compression ratios obtainable through transform coding is from 2:1 to some upper value, typically under 10:1, and the upper value depends very strongly on the data statistics and inherent distortion requirements of the given system.

11.3.2 Predictive Coding

Predictive coding includes delta modulation, differential pulse code modulation (DPCM), and block-to-block compression. In each of these techniques, the approach is the same: Predict the next data sample or sequence and send an indication of the difference between the predicted and the actual values. In delta modulation, we send only the fact that the difference is positive or negative; in DPCM we send the actual difference (assuming the DPCM quantizer does not overflow); and in block-to-block compression we send the actual differences. A common feature of predictive coding is *synchronous operation*. With the exception of block-to-block compression, no buffering is required, and a difference word or block is sent for every original sample or block.

We now look at the five characteristics, keeping in mind the important differences among delta modulation, DPCM, and block-to-block compression.

1. TIMING REQUIREMENTS

Basically, there are *no* timing requirements for difference techniques. Only in the case of block-to-block compression, where frame replenishment (see Chapter 15) is used, is there a need to identify the *location* of the changed samples, or clusters of samples. Cluster coding, as described in Section 8.3.2 would be used in this situation. Delta modulation and DPCM are synchronous in operation, so once an initialization sync word has been transmitted, there should be no need for further synchronization, except as required by the communication channel.

2. BUFFER REQUIREMENTS

As already stated, buffering is required only in block-to-block compression, and here the requirement is easy to specify since it is fixed by the size of the block in question. Typically, we must store *two* blocks at one time in order to take the differences.

The only other possible requirement for buffering would come about from use of a variable-length code such as a Huffman code. But here we have an upper bound on the buffer size, determined by the longest variable-length code word.

3. INHERENT DISTORTION

We look at each type of difference technique from the standpoint of inherent distortion.

A. *Delta modulation.* As described in Section 6.3.1, conventional delta modulation has inherent distortion of two types: slope overload and granular noise. Adaptive delta modulation attempts to minimize these effects by changing the step size adaptively.

B. *DPCM.* Even though conventional DPCM does not exhibit granular noise as does delta modulation, it does have the same potential problem of slope overload. This is particularly noticeable in an image wherein there are high contrast edges. The DPCM quantizer cannot handle the large differences at these edges, and hence overflows, resulting in an edge blur in a single image or an "edge busyness" in a television image. Two techniques designed to alleviate this problem are: (1) the use of a nonuniform quantizer and (2) the use of more than one quantizer, sometimes called the "switched-quantizer" approach. The nonuniform quantizer can code large amplitude changes, but with less fidelity, since the quantizer intervals are spaced farther and farther apart as we move out, in a positive or negative direction, from zero. The switched-quantizer approach allows for accurate tracking of large differences (by larger quantizers), but there is an overhead requirement to send the *mode* of the quantizer switch.

An interesting alternative to these two solutions to slope overload involves the use of a full-range uniform quantizer, followed by a Huffman code. In this technique, the full-range quantizer handles the larger differences and the Huffman code provides the compression.

As was explained in Section 6.4.3 the quantizer noise in DPCM is less than that of PCM by the ratio: σ^2/σ_e^2.

C. *Block-to-block compression.* The same comments that were made for DPCM also apply to block-to-block compression. However, in many cases, especially in television, where we are taking frame-to-frame differences, compression is achieved by virtue of the fact that usually only a small subset of the picture elements (pixels) change at all from frame to frame. The pixels that change are usually quantized at full range and coded in clusters by means of cluster coding. So, block-to-block compression should have little or no inherent distortion, with most of its *overall* distortion being due to the effects of transmission errors.

4. ERROR EFFECTS AND ERROR CONTROL

In Section 10.4 a description of error effects in predictive coding was given; that will be summarized here. In all cases, the overall effect is one of error propagation.

A. *Delta modulation.* For conventional delta modulation, two effects are to be expected: first, the error effect caused by a single error is no more than twice the step size; and second, the overall effect in the presence of multiple random transmission errors is one of *error averaging*. For adaptive delta modulation, the situation is more serious, since the offset due to an error is not fixed, but rather depends on the *location* of the error, as explained in Section 10.4.1.

B. *DPCM*. From the treatment of noise effects in DPCM in Section 10.4.2, we have the following results. The DPCM encoding tends to increase the channel noise by the same factor it decreases the quantizing noise, σ^2/σ_e^2. The error propagation that normally takes place in DPCM can be shortened in duration by means of an attenuation factor in the predictor loop called the "leak." In an adaptive DPCM system that used switched quantizers, an error in the quantizer mode word would be very serious.

C. *Block-to-block compression*. This type of compression usually uses some form of cluster coding to locate the beginning of a cluster of samples that have changed from block to block. An error in such a location code will shift an entire cluster to an erroneous position in the block.

5. ACTUAL COMPRESSION RATIO

A. *Delta modulation*. Since 1 bit is being sent for every original k_w-bit word in delta modulation, the compression ratio is:

$$R_a = k_w \left(\frac{k}{n}\right) \tag{11.3.3}$$

where k/n is the error-control code rate.

B. *DPCM*. The compression achieved in DPCM comes about in the quantizer, but it is not a 1-bit quantizer as in the case of delta modulation, but instead a k_D-bit quantizer. Thus, the actual compression ratio is:

$$R_a = \left(\frac{k_w}{k_D}\right)\left(\frac{k}{n}\right) \tag{11.3.4}$$

It is worthwhile to point out that the rate k_w/k_D is usually somewhere between 2 and 3, so that the actual compression ratio of DPCM is somewhat greater than 2:1, but not much greater.

C. *Block-to-block compression*. Since we are typically sending clusters of changed samples and a cluster code for each cluster, the actual compression ratio would be:

$$R_a = \frac{(S_u)(k_u)}{S_c k_c + \text{cluster code}}\left(\frac{k}{n}\right) \tag{11.3.5}$$

where: S_u is the original number of samples in the block

k_u is the number of bits per original sample

S_c is the number of cluster samples in the difference block

k_c is the number of bits per cluster sample

$\dfrac{k}{n}$ is the error-control code rate

11.3.3 Nonredundant Sample Coding

As was discussed in Chapter 7, nonredundant sample techniques classify all data samples into two categories: redundant and nonredundant. The way in which this is done depends on the algorithm being used. Some form of time coding and buffering is required by all algorithms of this type since redundant samples are removed and must be replaced at the receiving end of the system. The time coding techniques described in Chapter 8 are directly applicable to the nonredundant sample techniques. Likewise, the buffer models described in Chapter 9 are appropriate for this type of compression.

We now look at the five system characteristics for nonredundant sample compression.

1. TIMING REQUIREMENTS

There *is* a system requirement for time information to be sent along with the nonredundant samples, and this time information represents a significant overhead in the calculation of the actual compression ratio. In Chapter 8, seven different time codes are analyzed and compared using two different statistical models for the time information. For the type of time code that must be sent in its proper place in the compressed data sequence (a partial information code), the most efficient one was found to be the Huffman code, which is not too surprising. However, for the type of time code that can be sent separately since it contains all the time information (a total information code), the most efficient one was found to be the binary nonconsecutive one (BNO) code. This is a special type of run-length code.

2. BUFFER REQUIREMENTS

In Chapter 9, a Poisson function was used to model the buffer input and output behavior for a nonredundant sample system. This resulted in an expression for the average queue length in the buffer:

$$E(n) = \rho + \frac{\rho^2}{2(1 - \rho)} \qquad \text{[equation (9.2.4)]}$$

where: $\rho = m/r_c$, with m the average input rate and r_c the constant output rate

However, in order to meet a specification of probability of buffer overflow, we must make the buffer larger than this average value, and the curves in Figure 9.2 allow us to do this for a given value of ρ.

3. INHERENT DISTORTION

The inherent distortion in nonredundant sample techniques comes from the use of an aperture in the test for redundancy. In a zero-order predictor, for example, an aperture equal to some multiple of the quantization interval is placed around a given sample. If the next sample falls within this aperture, it is considered redundant. Obviously, the larger the aperture, the larger the number of redundant samples and the higher the compression ratio. But this also increases the inherent distortion, so the aperture is the critical parameter in the trade-off of compression ratio vs. distortion.

4. ERROR EFFECTS AND ERROR CONTROL

In Section 10.5 we saw that errors can affect three different kinds of information to be transmitted: the nonredundant sample values, the timing information, and the discrimination information. In general, errors in the timing and discrimination information are more serious than errors in the nonredundant samples. The most efficient total information time code, the BNO code, has some robustness to errors, but all other practical time codes are extremely vulnerable to transmission errors. For these reasons, error-control coding is usually a system requirement with nonredundant sample techniques.

5. ACTUAL COMPRESSION RATIO

The definition of actual compression ratio is as follows:

$$
R_a = \frac{\text{Uncompressed bits in time interval } \Delta T}{\text{Compressed bits in time interval } \Delta T}
$$

$$
= \frac{(S_u)(k_d)}{(S_n)(k_d) + (TB/S)(S_u)} \tag{11.3.6}
$$

where: S_u is the number of uncompressed samples in ΔT

S_n is the number of nonredundant samples in ΔT

k_d is the number of data bits per sample value

TB/S is the number of timing bits (including discrimination bits) required in ΔT per original sample.

Then we may write:

$$R_a = \cfrac{1}{\cfrac{1}{R} + \cfrac{(TB/S)}{k_d}}$$

(11.3.7)

where R is the ratio of S_u to S_n—often referred to in the literature as the "sample compression ratio." Likewise, we may include the effect of error-control coding in terms of the ratio k/n, where n is the number of coded bits in a block that contained k bits before encoding. Then (11.3.7) becomes:

$$R_a = \left[\cfrac{1}{\cfrac{1}{R} + \cfrac{(TB/S)}{k_d}} \right] \left(\frac{k}{n} \right)$$

(11.3.8)

11.4 COMPRESSION ALGORITHM SELECTION

In order to make a rational choice of a compression algorithm, it is necessary to ensure that the compression operation is enhancing the overall system and not degrading it. A poor choice of algorithm could result in a large increase in complexity and cost with little increase in performance over the original system. It is desirable, therefore, to have a logical procedure for algorithm selection.

The following is a procedure that utilizes most of the material presented so far; assume that the required compression ratio and maximum distortion are given:

1. Compute the entropy and maximum compression ratio [See equations (3.3.4), (3.3.5), and (3.4.1).]

2. Compare the maximum compression ratio with the required compression ratio. If the required compression ratio exceeds the maximum compression ratio, then a combination of entropy reduction and redundancy reduction will have to be used. In this case, go to step 6.

3. If the required compression ratio does not exceed the maximum compression ratio, then select two or more candidate redundancy-reduction algorithms that should meet the compression ratio requirement.

4. Compare these candidate algorithms on the basis of overall distortion (including inherent distortion and transmission-error distortion) and complexity.

5. Choose the algorithm that has an actual compression ratio that meets the required compression ratio, and that meets the distortion requirement with the minimum complexity. This completes the selection.

6. In the event that a combination of entropy reduction and redundancy reduction is required, choose an entropy-reduction scheme that will introduce less than the maximum allowable distortion and will provide a compression ratio approximately equal to the quotient of the required value divided by the maximum value.

7. Select two or more redundancy-reduction algorithms that will provide the theoretical maximum compression ratio.

8. Go to steps 4 and 5.

This procedure assumes that there *is* more than one potential redundancy-reduction algorithm available that will meet the compression ratio requirement and distortion requirement. In some cases, it may be possible to use transform coding or predictive coding as redundancy reduction schemes, depending upon the allowable distortion.

Another situation, which has a special selection criterion, also exists, and that is a *high data rate source*. This involves uncompressed data rates in the order of 10^2–10^3 Mbps. At these rates, the number of operations on each sample required by the algorithm in question becomes a critical factor, since it would be possible for some algorithms to "fall behind" the incoming data due to the speed limitations of the hardware technology.

11.5 CASCADED ENCODERS

We have already seen some instances where it is desirable to use a cascaded arrangement of data compression techniques. One example uses a DPCM encoder with a full-range quantizer in the forward loop, followed by a Huffman encoder. A typical reason for such an arrangement is to avoid edge distortion in images.

In other cases, two or more compression algorithms are cascaded to achieve a certain overall compression ratio requirement, such as in the case of entropy reduction followed by redundancy reduction. An example of this is a fixed number of scan lines to be skipped in an image, followed by some form of redundancy reduction on the remaining lines. For reconstruction, the reconstructed lines will be repeated (see example in Section 14.3.2). There is often an advantage in images to compress first in the horizontal direction and then in the vertical direction, thus utilizing horizontal and vertical redundancies, respectively.

The amount of cascading that can be done is limited by the entropy-derived maximum compression ratio and system complexity.

HIGHLIGHTS

- Incorporating data compression into a larger system involves a number of design trade-offs if the maximum benefit is to be obtained.
- The need for compression may be based on system operability or system cost.
- Three important parameters should be part of the system requirements: compression ratio, average distortion, and complexity.
- Each data compression technique can be evaluated on the basis of timing requirements, buffer requirements, inherent distortion, error effects and error control, and actual compression ratio.
- A cascaded arrangement of two or more data compression techniques is sometimes desirable and feasible.

PART III

Applications

CHAPTER 12

Introduction to Data Compression Applications

12.1 INTRODUCTION

In Part I, a theoretical background of data compression was given as a basis for understanding the various techniques covered in Part II. In Part III we look at the various applications of data compression in recognizable fields such as television and speech transmission. These examples of practical applications illustrate the many uses to which the techniques described in Part II can be put. The special design considerations of certain applications are also illustrated.

12.2 BRIEF HISTORY OF DATA COMPRESSION TECHNIQUES

When did data compression start? Many writers consider the invention of the VOCODER by Dudley in 1939 the first practical example of compression. The VOCODER (from VOice CODER) partitioned the voice spectral energy into a finite number of frequency bands and transmitted the energy level in each band, thus providing a high (> 100) compression ratio. If we think of the Morse code as a variable-length code, then we could say that Morse, in the nineteenth century, was actually the first to compress data since he followed a scheme for selecting code lengths that resulted in efficient transmission (short codes for the more probable letters and longer codes for the less probable letters—as in the Shannon–Fano code, which was developed in 1948).

Delta modulation was invented in 1946, and the related technique of differential pulse code modulation (DPCM) was invented in 1952. Both delta modulation and DPCM were applied to speech and video for bandwidth compression. The Huffman code was developed in 1952 and has been used as an optimum variable-length code for many applications.

Transform techniques, such as Fourier, Hadamard, and so on, were applied to a number of applications, particularly images and speech, in the 1960s. During that same time, nonredundant sample techniques, such as run-length coding, were applied to a number of applications, including telemetry data transmission. Binary coding techniques were developed in the 1960s [Golomb's run-length code (1966), the LD code (1966)]; in the 1970s [Schalkwijk's variable-to-block code (1972), Cover's enumerative code (1973), Ziv and Lempel's parsing code (1978)]; and in the 1980s [Langdon and Rissanen's arithmetic code (1982)].

Quantization has been a topic of great interest in data compression, up to, and including, the present. Originally, all quantization techniques were zero memory type; that is, they quantized one sample at a time. The nonuniform quantization schemes of Panter and Dite and Lloyd and Max in the 1950s were all zero memory. As noted above, other forms of quantization were also developed in the 1950s (predictive coding) and in the 1960s (transform coding). Now in the 1980s, vector quantization, or the optimum quantizing of a whole block of samples to 1 bit per sample, has been developed and applied to speech compression. In particular, vector quantization has been successfully applied to the newest version of the VOCODER, the linear predictive coder (LPC), which, unlike the original VOCODER, operates in the time domain.

12.3 WHAT TO COMPRESS AND WHY

Since Part III is concerned with data compression applications, it is useful to reconsider two basic questions in data compression:

1. What is it we want to compress?
2. Why?

In Section 1.1, we saw that the object of compression is usually three interrelated parameters:

> Data volume
> Time
> Bandwidth

which are related as follows:

$$\text{Volume} = f(\text{time} \times \text{bandwidth}) \qquad [\text{equation } (1.1.1)]$$

Obviously, in a given application, we do not compress all three simultaneously. In any given system, only one of the three parameters is usually the critical item to compress.

This leads to the second question: Why? There are typically two reasons why we compress data:

1. To meet an operational constraint
2. To realize a cost saving

For example, one part of a given system may have a limited bandwidth channel whose capacity is exceeded by the output data rate of the source. Here, we compress the source to reduce the output rate so it is compatible with the channel. Similar situations can be found in which we are forced to compress the time of transmission or the data volume.

Compression for cost saving sounds, as noted earlier, like an obvious thing to do, but one must be careful from a total system and total cost standpoint. In some systems, the introduction of compression may require additional complexity (such as in buffering and error-control coding) that may in fact negate the cost saving provided by the compression alone. The different degree of complexity that each type of compression technique creates is described in Chapter 11 (Part II).

12.4 THE APPROACH AND CONTENTS OF PART III

In Chapters 13–17, examples are given of data compression applications to practical systems. The *what* and the *why* of the compression question are addressed and the special or unique requirements in each application field are described. Finally, some actual compression systems are described and illustrated. Wherever appropriate, these descriptions will reference the techniques described in Part II.

Any description of data compression applications has to be open-ended, since new applications are being discovered all the time. Nevertheless, the applications covered here are basic, and new applications might reasonably be expected to be only special modifications of one or more of the fundamental techniques described in Part II. In short, the techniques will not change—only the way in which they are implemented in hardware or software in the actual systems.

The data compression applications presented in this part cover the following fields, in this order:

Speech

Telemetry

Television

Pictures

Data Bases

This order is not arbitrary—it corresponds roughly to the historical development of data compression techniques and their applications described in Section 12.2.

12.4.1 Speech Compression

There is now, and has been for many years, an interest in compressing speech in order to transmit it over narrower bandwidth channels. Speech compression techniques have been grouped into two categories. The first category, called waveform coding, compresses the speech signal in such a way that it can be reconstructed at the receiving end, in the manner of a redundancy-reduction technique. The second category, called voice coding, extracts sufficient parameters from the speech signal at the transmitting end that a facsimile of the speaker's voice may be synthesized at the receiving end with some minimal distortion, as in the case of entropy reduction. Typically, a higher compression ratio [compared to pulse code modulation (PCM)] is obtained with voice coding techniques than with waveform coding techniques—which is consistent with the comparison of entropy reduction to redundancy reduction.

12.4.2 Telemetry Compression

The telemetry data from missiles, rockets, and satellites is often characterized by periods of high redundancy, and is thus amenable to compression. In more recent years, satellites have been transmitting images from space, and compression has been applied to reduce the bandwidth required for this transmission.

Another type of telemetry data that is compressed is seismic data. There are two reasons for this: First, it is desirable to reduce the large volume of seismic data that has to be stored for analysis, and second, it is sometimes necessary to reduce the data rate from the remote seismometer to the central processing facility.

A more recent application of compression to telemetry has been in the field of medicine, specifically, electrocardiogram (ECG) measurements. As in the case of seismic data, there is a need to reduce the volume as well as the data rate of the signals. The data rate reduction is of interest since there are situations where it is useful to transmit the ECG data over telephone lines.

12.4.3 Television Compression

The motivation behind television compression is the desire to reduce the required transmission bandwidth, especially in the case of PCM. Television compression techniques can be grouped into two broad categories: intraframe and interframe. The intraframe techniques include some of the techniques of Part II as well as some television-unique techniques such as: dithering, slant transform, and slow-scan. Interframe techniques are usually of the predictive coding type, but on a frame basis as opposed to a sample basis. Two interframe coding techniques are called frame replenishment and motion compensation. The latter technique is aimed at solving one of the inherent problems in interframe compression, namely, blurred images caused by a compression scheme that can't keep up with rapid movement. There has been at least one example of combined intraframe and interframe compression, and this scheme used a three-dimensional Hadamard transform.

One of the most recent applications of compression to television has been in TV teleconferencing, where the system takes advantage of some of the characteristics of the conference television images, such as no rapid movement.

Compression has been applied to television from remotely-piloted-vehicles, and newer applications for TV compression are in the fields of Videotex and high-definition TV.

12.4.4 Picture Compression

In addition to television pictures, some *still* pictures also have to be compressed before transmission, and these fall into two categories: two-level and multilevel. The two-level images comprise facsimile and newspapers. It is interesting to note that facsimile compression has become so commonplace that international standards for facsimile compression have now been proposed. The multilevel images include: multilevel facsimile, multispectral imagery, and x-rays.

Many of the techniques from Part II are used for picture compression, especially two-dimensional versions of these techniques since there is two-dimensional redundancy in the pictures.

12.4.5 Data Base Compression

Data base compression is used not only to reduce the volume of the data base, but also to reduce the access time in querying the data base. Since data bases are often accessed remotely, this access time is very important in the operation of the entire data base/remote terminal network.

Compression has been applied to the two basic parts of a data base system: the data files and the file index.

CHAPTER 13

Speech Compression

13.1 INTRODUCTION

Speech compression has been of interest for many years. The VOCODER (VOice CODER) was invented by Dudley in 1939 to reduce the bandwidth required to send speech over a telephone line. Ever since, extensions and variations on the original VOCODER concept have been developed. This concept involves simply analyzing the speech spectrum into frequency bands and transmitting the energy measure in each band instead of the original speech signal. The transmitted information is used to create a synthetic version of the speech at the receiver.

The VOCODER concept is not the only approach to speech compression. Many of the techniques described in Part II are used for speech compression, with appropriate designs to suit the speech signal.

In this chapter, various techniques of speech compression will be discussed, including VOCODERs. Examples of the techniques involved will be given, including some recent implementations in hardware.

Some of the techniques described in this chapter (such as linear predictive coding, or LPC) have applications in other areas besides communication channels, such as computer voice response systems and speaker recognition systems. A discussion of these latter two areas is outside the scope of this book, but for an introduction to these areas see Rabiner and Schafer (1978, chapter 9) as well as the survey article by Flanagan et al. (1970).

13.2 SPEECH AS A DATA SOURCE

In every data communication system there is a data source, a data channel, and a data receiver. If we wish to model a communication system involving speech, we need to model each of these three parts. Typically, the data source is the human voice, the channel is a telephone system, and the receiver is the human ear and brain. Since we can model all parts of this system, it would seem likely that we could efficiently compress the data, and so we can.

The human voice is produced by the vocal tract, wherein two different types of sounds are generated when a person speaks. The first type of sound is called a *voiced* sound, and it is produced by quasi-periodic pulses generated by the vocal cords. The second type of sound is called an *unvoiced* sound, and it is produced by air passing through constrictions in the vocal tract. Both types of sounds are further modulated by the action of the speaker's mouth, lips, and nasal passage.

This description of the voice generation model has been used to design speech compression systems. The goal in these systems is always to preserve the characteristics in the speech signal that provide intelligibility (what is said) and recognizability (who is saying it).

From a digital data source standpoint, the voice can be characterized as an information source and the information rate of the voice in bits per second can be estimated. In his book (1972), Flanagan estimated the entropy of the human voice source and developed this estimation, as follows. If we regard each mutually exclusive sound that can be made by the human voice (normally referred to as a *phoneme*) as a distinct message from the source, and know the frequency of occurrence of each phoneme, then we can compute the entropy. For 42 distinct phonemes, the entropy, assuming a statistically independent source, is computed to be 4.9 bits. In conversational speech, about ten phonemes are uttered per second, making the information rate from the source 49 bits per sec (bps). How does this compare to the transmission rate that is normally used to transmit speech over a telephone line?

Shannon (1948) developed the fundamental expression for the capacity of the Gaussian white noise channel as follows:

$$C = B \log_2[1 + (\text{SNR})] \qquad \text{(bits per sec)} \tag{13.2.1}$$

where: B is the channel bandwidth in hertz

SNR is the signal-to-noise ratio

For a telephone voice channel with a bandwidth of 3000 hertz (200–3200 Hz) and a SNR of 30 dB, $C \approx 30,000$ bits per sec. In a PCM voice transmission system, where the sampling rate is 8000 samples per second and each sample is quantized with 7 bits (with a SNR higher than 30 dB), we have a resulting bit rate of 56,000 bits per sec. Telephone channels, then, appear to have excess capacity in terms of handling a 49 bps voice signal. The computation of this voice rate (49 bps), however, takes into consideration only the *intelligibility* of the voice, not the *quality* (that is, its recognizability). It is the voice quality that allows the listener to recognize the identity of the speaker and to pick up subtle characteristics that indicate something about the speaker's mood, intention, and so on.

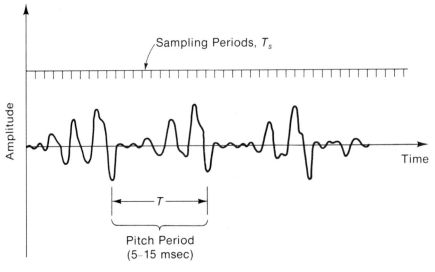

Time Domain

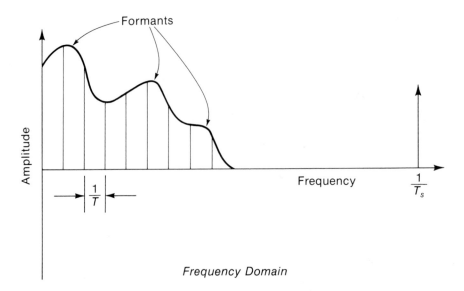

Frequency Domain

Figure 13.1 *Idealized Speech Waveform and Spectrum.*

Consideration of voice quality requires additional information, but not so much that it "fills up" the available capacity of the telephone channel. So we indeed have the possibility of reducing the transmission rate of speech.

Figure 13.1 is an idealized time domain and frequency domain representation of a voiced speech waveform. (Unvoiced speech has a smaller amplitude noiselike waveform.) There is a periodicity in the time domain waveform on the order of 5–10 msec, which is called the *pitch period*. This appears in the frequency domain as a line spectrum, the envelope of which is a function of the actual time domain waveform of the voiced signal. The spectral envelope has an upper frequency limit, usually between 3 and 4 kHz, and it exhibits maxima that are called "formants" or "resonances." When the speech signal is sampled, the Nyquist rate is twice the highest frequency component, and so in fact it is normally 8000 samples per sec.

In the sections that follow, voice compression techniques are described under two broad groups: waveform coding and voice coding. Waveform coding utilizes many of the techniques described in Part II, especially transform coding (Chapter 5) and predictive coding (Chapter 6). But voice coding techniques are more unique to speech compression since they utilize a priori information about the human voice, and in particular, the mechanism that produces it. Because of these inherent characteristics, voice coders do not reconstruct the actual voice at the receiving end, as is the case with waveform coders, but rather a synthetic facsimile of it. Waveform coders usually operate at bit rates above 4.8 kbps, whereas voice coders usually operate at bit rates below 4.8 kbps.

In the next section we look at waveform coders and note, in particular, how they are adapted to speech signals.

13.3 WAVEFORM CODING

As can be seen in Figure 13.1, the speech waveform can be *sampled* and, therefore, subsequently coded by many of the techniques described in Part II. For speech coding, these techniques can be divided into time domain and frequency domain techniques.

13.3.1 Time Domain Waveform Coding

In the following sections the techniques of pulse code modulation (PCM), differential pulse code modulation (DPCM), delta modulation (DM), adaptive predictive coding (APC), and variable speech control (VSC), are applied to speech compression.

PULSE CODE MODULATION (PCM)

Pulse code modulation is not normally thought of as a speech compression system, but when it is used with nonuniform quantization (companding, the logarithmic *A*-law or *μ*-law type; see Section 2.5), it becomes a *reference* against which the performance of other speech compression schemes are measured. (A typical PCM speech system has 8000 samples per sec and 7 bits per sample or 56,000 bits per sec.)

The speech signal itself has a probability distribution that closely resembles the gamma distribution (Paez and Glisson 1972) as follows:

$$P(x) = \left[\frac{\sqrt{3}}{8\pi\sigma|x|} \right]^{1/2} e^{-\frac{\sqrt{3}|x|}{2\sigma}} \qquad (13.3.1)$$

From this model of the distribution, a zero-memory quantizer can be designed, and in fact this was done by Paez and Glisson (1972).

Three other types of quantization used for speech signals are: vector quantization, adaptive quantization, and tree coding. *Vector quantization* is another name for block quantization (see Section 2.5), and such quantizers have been designed for real and simulated speech signals down to 1 or 2 bits per sample. For an overview of vector quantization, see Gersho and Cuperman (1983). Also see Linde et al. (1980), Buzo et al. (1980), and Abut et al. (1982).

Adaptive quantizing for speech signals means changing the quantizer characteristics as a function of time to track the power levels of the speech signal. The power levels vary slowly enough to allow such tracking. If the control of the quantizer characteristic is made a function of only the previous sample quantizer output, then the adaptation can be followed by the receiver without any additional information from the transmitter (Flanagan et al. 1979).

Tree coding is actually a form of sequential quantization (see Section 2.5) in which we "look ahead" to find the "best" sequence of quantized samples to fit the input data. Anderson and Bodie (1975) showed that tree coding could provide an SNR gain of 7 dB over DPCM with 2 or 3 bits per sample. Matsuyama and Gray (1982) developed a tree code for speech that operates at 1 bit per sample.

DIFFERENTIAL PULSE CODE MODULATION (DPCM)

Differential pulse code modulation was described in Section 6.4. Basically, the difference between a sample value and its predicted value is transmitted and since the difference distribution is expected to have a smaller variance than the original sample amplitude distribution, compression is achieved. In a DPCM system, two components must be designed: the predictor and the quantizer.

The predictor can be fixed or adaptive. The fixed DPCM predictor is usually a linear predictor, but this should not be confused with linear predictive coding (LPC), which is described in Section 13.4.2. LPC uses the concept of linear prediction to *synthesize* speech at the receiving end of the system. In DPCM, the linear predictor is used to predict the next sample so that the *difference* between the predicted and actual values may be transmitted. On the receiving end of the DPCM system, the same linear predictor is used to reconstruct the original speech signal (see Figure 6.5). It has been found experimentally that a DPCM encoder with a predictor that uses only *one* previous sample can attain the same SNR as "standard" PCM, with 1 less bit in the DPCM quantizer. Likewise, a DPCM system with a predictor that uses *three* previous samples can match the SNR of PCM with 2 less bits in the DPCM quantizer. Normally, very little performance gain is achieved by using more than three previous samples in the predictor (Bayless et al. 1973).

Theoretically, it is possible to make the predictor adaptive in a DPCM system. However, it has been found that, for speech signals, making the predictor adaptive does not appreciably reduce the dynamic range of the quantizer input; in addition, if the quantizer is fixed, it will still have the usual problems of slope overload and granular noise (Gibson 1980). However, a DPCM system has been proposed (Jayant 1977) that has two predictors: a long-term adaptive predictor, which operates over a pitch period, and a fixed, short-term predictor, which operates over a few samples. This system has an adaptive quantizer as well, and is called pitch predictive DPCM, or PPDPCM. Since it uses two predictors that can be related to the speech signal, it is similar to adaptive predictive coding (APC), which will be described in a later section.

The DPCM quantizer for speech needs to be optimized to the difference signal obtained from the speech sample and its predicted value. Optimization techniques were discussed in Chapter 2, but what is typically more important in the quantizer is an *adaptive* capability. This adaptation can take two forms: slow-acting (over many pitch periods) or fast-acting (over a sample) (see Figure 13.1). The latter technique typically uses a one-sample memory and senses an overload or underload condition in order to increase or decrease, respectively, the interval, or step, size of the quantizer. A more elaborate method of quantizer adaptation is called the switched quantizer approach. Cohen (1973) shows that by using the two most significant bits in the previous *three* samples, a gain in SNR of 7 dB over nonadaptive DPCM can be obtained.

DELTA MODULATION (DM)

Delta modulation has been used for years for speech compression and continues to be a very powerful speech compression scheme because of its simplicity and relative immunity to transmission errors. As described in Section 6.3, delta modulation suffers from slope overload and granular noise. However, these problems are minimized by adaptive DM, and there are different ways of providing this adaptation. What is really changed by the adaptation is the imbedded *gain* in the *adaptive function* (see Figure 6.4).

In adaptive DM speech compression systems, a distinction is made between fast and slow adaptation. Fast adaptation occurs over a few samples and is called *instantaneous*. Slow adaptation occurs over one or more pitch periods, a time period that is usually comparable to a syllable, and thus it is called *syllabic*. In Section 6.3.2, we looked at the Song algorithm for adaptive delta modulation (Song 1971).* This type of adaptation is instantaneous, as is the somewhat similar adaptive delta modulator proposed by Jayant in 1970.

Another type of delta modulator in use is the so-called continuously variable slope delta modulator (CVSD) (Greefkes 1970). The CVSD works as follows: If three identical output levels occur in a row, a large increment is added to the step size; otherwise, a small increment is added. Mathematically (following Rabiner and Schafer 1978):

If output

$$c(n) = c(n - 1) = c(n - 2) \tag{13.3.2}$$

then step size

$$\Delta n = \beta \Delta(n - 1) + D_2 \tag{13.3.3}$$

Otherwise,

$$\Delta n = \beta \Delta(n - 1) + D_1 \tag{13.3.4}$$

where: $0 < \beta < 1$
$D_2 \gg D_1 > 0.$

The rate of buildup and decay of the step size is controlled by the parameter β, which makes the adaptation either syllabic or instantaneous.

A COMPARISON OF PCM, ADAPTIVE DPCM, AND ADAPTIVE DM

In the literature, when different adaptive predictive coding schemes are compared, a comparison is usually made to companded PCM. Jayant (1974) performed such a comparison (with μ-law PCM) and his results are shown in Figure 13.2. In this figure, an analog signal bandwidth of 200–3200 Hz is used. As can be seen, adaptive DPCM has a consistently higher SNR, and below approximately 50 kbps, adaptive DM is superior to log PCM (which is another name for companded PCM).

---

* A hardware version of this algorithm is produced by Delta Modulation, Inc. Albertson, NY 11507.

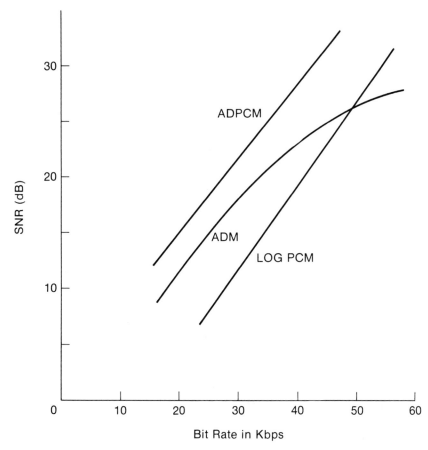

Figure 13.2 *Comparison of Log PCM, Adaptive DM, and Adaptive DPCM for a Bandwidth of 200–3200 Hz. From: Jayant, N. S. "Digital Coding of Speech Waveforms: PCM, DPCM, and DM Quantizers," Proc. of IEEE, vol. 62, no. 5, May 1974, p. 626. © 1974 IEEE.*

ADAPTIVE PREDICTIVE CODING (APC)

Adaptive predictive coding is similar to PPDPCM in general configuration but it uses two adaptive predictors: a long-term predictor based on the pitch period and a short term predictor based on the part of the signal that is due to the vocal tract. The quantizer is usually a two-level quantizer with a variable step size. Atal and Schroeder (1970) used an adaptive predictor as shown in Figure 13.3. In this figure, predictor P_1 is the long-term predictor operating on a pitch period (5–15 msec) and predictor P_2 is the short-term predictor operating over eight previous samples. (The number of previous samples used is made greater than twice the number of formants expected in the frequency range of interest—in this case three formants are usually expected.) The coeffi-

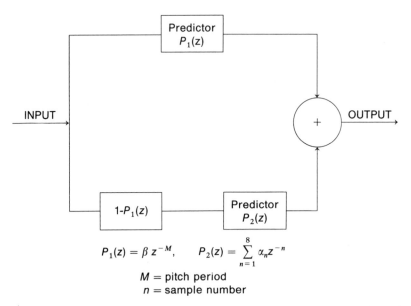

Figure 13.3 with block diagram containing Predictor $P_1(z)$, Predictor $P_2(z)$, $1-P_1(z)$, INPUT, OUTPUT, and summing junction.

$$P_1(z) = \beta z^{-M}, \qquad P_2(z) = \sum_{n=1}^{8} \alpha_n z^{-n}$$

M = pitch period
n = sample number

Figure 13.3 *Dual Adaptive Predictor for APC. From: Atal, B. S. and Schroeder, M. R. "Adaptive Predictive Coding of Speech Signals." Bell System Tech. Journal, vol. 49, Oct. 1970, p. 1978. Reprinted with permission from the Bell System Tech. Journal. Copyright 1970 AT & T.*

cients of this predictor need to be updated once every 10 to 30 msec. APC systems have been simulated that provide the same quality of 35–40 kbps PCM at 7.2 kbps (Bayless et al. 1973).

VARIABLE SPEECH CONTROL (VSC)

Another type of speech compression technique operates on the waveform but does *not* preserve it totally. The idea behind this technique is quite simple: The speech is recorded and then played back at double speed. Samples corresponding to the pitch period duration (~ 10 msec; see Figure 13.1) are taken and every other one is discarded. Then the remaining sample segments are stretched out to fill in the time gaps left by the discarded samples (see Figure 13.4). Now the speech can be played back at double the speed it was originally recorded, with little distortion and no appreciable change in pitch—giving a *time* compression.

A commercial version of this idea is marketed under the name *VSC* for "variable speech control" by the VSC Corporation of San Francisco, CA. This commercial device has been applied to teaching by tape, in which material can be presented to the student in one-half the time it took to record it. It has also been used in speeding up radio commercials. This speed-up is possible due to the redundancy inherent in the pitch periods.

Normally Recorded Sound

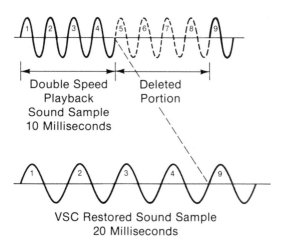

Figure 13.4 *Variable Speech Control. Reprinted with permission from the VSC Corp., San Francisco, CA.*

13.3.2 Frequency Domain Waveform Coding

In speech compression, there are two types of transform coding techniques in use: subband coding (SBC) and adaptive transform coding (ATC), Both techniques operate in the frequency domain, but not in the same way that channel VOCODERs and formant VOCODERs do (see Section 13.4.1). SBC and ATC transmit a frequency transformation of the speech signal that will eventually be reconstructed by inverse transformation at the receiving end. They are *not synthesizing* a speech signal using artificial excitation as is the case with VOCODERs.

SUBBAND CODING (SBC)

In subband coding the speech energy is divided into a fixed number of bands (typically four to eight). Each band is then shifted to zero frequency so that it can be sampled at a rate equal to twice the bandwidth (the Nyquist sampling rate). Then these samples are quantized for transmission by a non-uniform quantization technique such as the A-law and μ-law logarithmic functions described in Section 2.5 (see equations 2.5.18 and 2.5.19). At the receiving

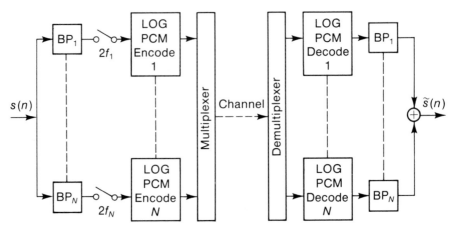

Figure 13.5 *Sub Band Coder/Decoder. From: Flanagan, J. L. et al "Speech Coding." IEEE Trans. on Comm., vol. COM-27, no. 4, April 1979, p. 721. © 1979 IEEE.*

end, these samples are modulated back to their original position in the spectrum and then summed to provide the output speech signal.

Since the speech signal is divided into separate frequency bands, the quantization steps can be tailored to the characteristics of each band in order to minimize the overall quantization noise. For example, in the lower frequency bands, a larger number of steps can be used to preserve pitch and formant structure; in the upper frequency bands, a smaller number of steps can be used since the sounds are more noiselike. A representation of subband encoding is shown in Figure 13.5 and a comparison of SBC to adaptive DPCM and adaptive DM based on listener preference is shown in Figure 13.6 (Flanagan et al. 1979). In Figure 13.6 we see that—based on listener preference—it requires an ADPCM bit rate of about 22 kbps to match the "quality" of SBC at 16 kbps.

ADAPTIVE TRANSFORM CODING (ATC)

Adaptive transform coding (ATC) is really the application of adaptive transform coding, as discussed in Chapter 5, to speech compression. Basically, we operate on time blocks of sampled input speech with a discrete linear transformation, and perform adaptive quantization on the coefficients in the transform domain. Upon reception, these quantized coefficients are inverse-transformed and the time blocks are joined to form the speech signal. A diagram of an adaptive transform coding system is shown in Figure 13.7. The interesting feature of the system is the use of "side information," that is, information about the coefficient variances for the adaptive quantization/bit assignment. It is normal practice to use a uniform quantizer with a fixed number of levels for each coefficient, with the flexibility of having *different* step sizes and a *different* number of steps for each coefficient, depending on the variance of the coefficient.

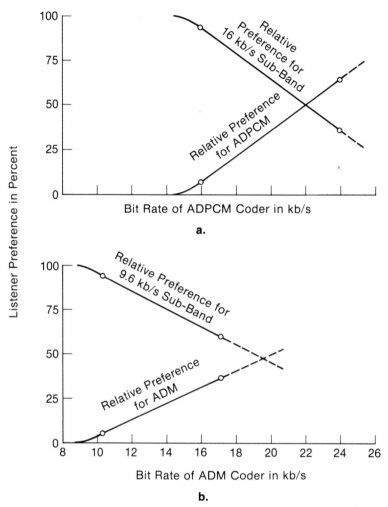

a. Relative comparison of quality of 16-kbit/s sub-band coding against ADPCM coding (based on listener preference) for different ADPCM coder bit rates. **b.** Relative comparison of quality of 9.6-kbit/s sub-band coding against ADM coding for different ADM coder bit rates.

Figure 13.6 *Comparison of SBC, ADPCM and ADM. From: Flanagan, J. L. et al "Speech Coding." IEEE Trans. on Comm., vol. COM-27, no. 4, April 1979, p. 722. © 1979 IEEE.*

Bit-assignment formulas such as equation (5.4.1) are used (Zelinski and Noll 1977) to estimate the number of bits per coefficient. The bit-assignment formula may give zero or even a negative number for some coefficients, in which case they are set to zero. Normally the total number of bits per block is fixed so that this acts as a constraint on the final bit allocation per coefficient. The

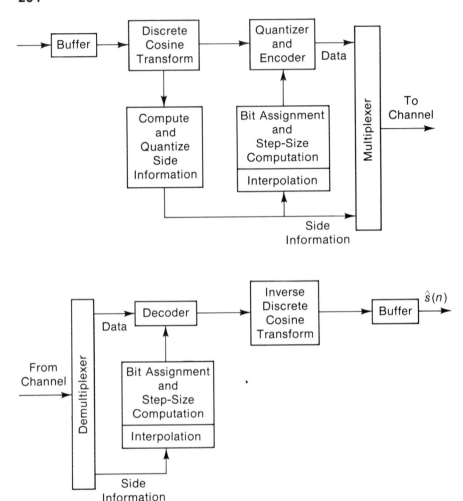

Figure 13.7 *Adaptive Transform Coding (ATC). From: Flanagan, J. L. et al "Speech Coding." IEEE Trans. on Comm., vol. COM-27, no. 4, April 1979, p. 722. © 1979 IEEE.*

step sizes are computed from a knowledge of the number of bits, the variance, and the probability distribution function (usually assumed to be Gaussian) for each coefficient.

The variances of the coefficients are not known a priori, so we must send some information about them to the receiver—the "side information." Normally, not all the coefficient variances, or levels of the power density spectrum, are sent; rather, only a subset is sent to be used to "fill in" the other values by interpolation. This interpolation method is adequate, in terms of fine structure fidelity, down to about 16 kbps. Below 16 kbps, one can weight the variances in equation (5.4.1) with a positive weighting function that is a function of the spectral envelope of the input spectrum (Flanagan et al. 1979).

The transformation used is typically the discrete cosine transform, as is shown in Figure 13.7, since, on the average, it performs almost as well as the optimum principal component transform, as described in Chapter 5.

With regard to the performance of different linear transformations for speech compression, Campanella and Robinson (1971) compared three linear transformations and found that they ranked in the following (best at the top) order for signal-to-quantizing noise improvement over log PCM. For a block length of 16 samples, the gain over log PCM was averaged over three bit rates: 14, 28, and 56 kbps and found to be:

Principal component	9 dB
Fourier	5 dB
Hadamard	3 dB

In 1977, Zelinski and Noll obtained similar results.

13.4 VOICE CODING

Voice coding techniques perform two basic operations: (1) they analyze the original signal into component parts at the sending end and (2) they synthesize a facsimile of the original signal from these components at the receiving end.

In effect, they characterize the data set or signal at the transmitting end and then, using these characteristics, *reconstruct* a close approximation to the original at the receiving end. In order to produce a compression, the component parts transmitted are typically a subset of the total set of component parts.

In the analysis and synthesis of speech signals, selection of the subset of components takes into account the way in which speech is produced in the vocal tract. This a priori information makes possible a larger compression ratio than is usually obtainable with waveform coders.

Two types of voice coding techniques are in common use for speech compression: VOCODERs and linear predictive coders. Since VOCODERs were developed first, we look at them in the next section.

13.4.1 VOCODERs

As mentioned earlier, the VOCODER, developed by Dudley in 1939, was the first speech compression system. A simplified block diagram of Dudley's VOCODER is shown in Figure 13.8. The analysis operation is simply a division

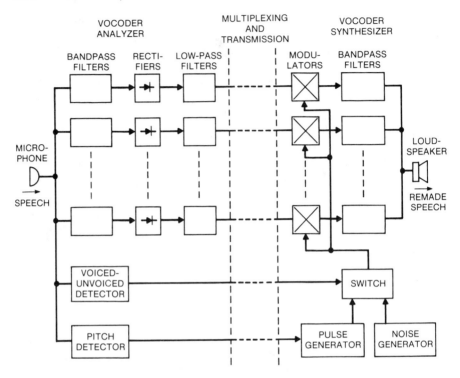

Figure 13.8 *The VOCODER Concept. From: Schroeder, M. R. "VOCODERS; Analysis and Synthesis of Speech." Proc. of IEEE, vol. 54, no. 5, May 1966, p. 724. © 1966 IEEE.*

of the speech signal into separate spectral bands by band-pass filters, followed by an envelope detector for each band consisting of a rectifier and a low-pass filter. The filter bandwidths usually increase logarithmically with increasing frequency in order to keep the amount of voice energy in each band roughly equal. A pitch detector is used to characterize the pitch of the speaker's voice. (For example, a female voice typically has a higher pitch than a male voice.)

An appropriate detector is used to indicate which of the two types of speech sounds, voiced or unvoiced (see Section 13.2), is being generated. Sometimes the pitch detector is used to trigger the voiced-unvoiced detector. In the VOCODER synthesizer, the transmitted spectral envelope samples are used to modulate the appropriate sound generator (voiced: pulse generator; unvoiced: noise generator). A similar set of band filters is used at the output of the modulators to properly shape the overall spectrum of the "remade" speech. What comes out of the VOCODER synthesizer is *synthetic* speech, but the goal is to make it sound as close to the original as possible. Sometimes, this type of VOCODER is called a channel VOCODER because it breaks up the speech into spectral bands as channels.

In recent years, much work has been done on improved methods of pitch detection, and a technique that has proven very useful is called "cepstrum" analysis. In this method, the spectral envelope is separated from the line structure due to the voiced sound (see Figure 13.1) by means of the Fourier transform of the *logarithm* of the spectrum.

Other methods of pitch detection also exist. The parallel processing method of Gold and Rabiner (1969) utilizes the peaks and valleys in the voiced speech waveform to create impulse trains from which the pitch is estimated. The average magnitude difference function (AMDF) method of Ross et al. (1974) monitors the dips or nulls in the autocorrelation function of the voiced speech signal to determine the pitch period.

In order to illustrate the compression potential of VOCODERs, consider the following analog design:

Original signal bandwidth	3000 Hz
Number of filters	15
Filter output sampling period	20 msec
VOCODER bandwidth: $(15)(\frac{1}{2})\left(\dfrac{10^3}{20}\right)$	375 Hz
Compression ratio	8:1

Other types of VOCODER have been developed since Dudley's original version. These later versions use the same general approach except that they "sample" different characteristics of the speech signal for transmission. Some of the more common VOCODER variations are as follows.

The *formant VOCODER* transmits the frequencies and the amplitudes of the major spectral resonances in the speech signal (the formants). There are typically three formants in adult speech, and these represent the resonances in the vocal tract. The formant frequency locations are transmitted, and at the receiver they are used to control the resonances of a formant synthesizer made up of tuned resonant circuits. A block diagram of the formant VOCODER is shown in Figure 13.9.

The *correlation VOCODER* is based on the fact that the Fourier transform of the power density spectrum of a signal is its autocorrelation function. So instead of analyzing and synthesizing the signal spectrum or its envelope, as we do in channel and formant VOCODERs, we can analyze and synthesize the signal's *autocorrelation* function. A block diagram of an autocorrelation VOCODER is shown in Figure 13.10. In the analyzer, a tapped delay line is used with multipliers to create the samples of the autocorrelation function, which are then transmitted. In the synthesizer, the autocorrelation samples are used to "remake" the speech signal with an excitation signal as input. This excitation signal has the appropriate dual form: quasiperiodic pulses for voiced speech and flat spectral noise for unvoiced speech. One complication with

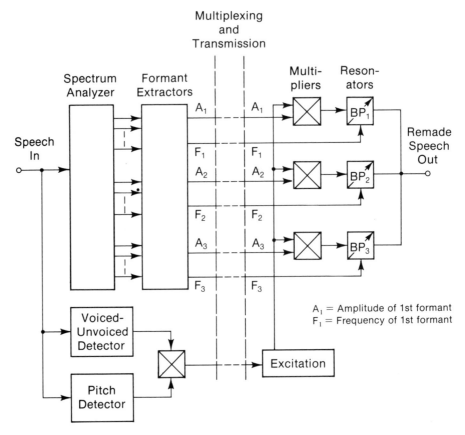

Figure 13.9 *Formant VOCODER. From: Schroeder, M. R. "VOCODERS; Analysis and Synthesis of Speech." Proc. of IEEE, vol. 54, no. 5, May 1966, p. 725. © 1966 IEEE.*

autocorrelation VOCODERs is not shown in the figure—namely, that the output spectrum is the *square* of the input spectrum. Special equalizers are required that perform a spectrum square-rooting function to correct for this. This correlation VOCODER, as compared to the channel and formant VOCODERs, requires a wider bandwidth to ensure sufficient spectral resolution at low frequencies (Flanagan et al. 1979).

The *orthogonal function VOCODER* is based on the principle that any signal can be represented by an expansion into a weighted sum of orthogonal functions that are well-suited to the speech signals.

Since it is often necessary to take a Fourier transform of the logarithm of the speech signal in order to estimate the pitch ("cepstrum" analysis), this Fourier transform can be used directly for transmission. Such systems are called *cepstral VOCODERs* or *homomorphic VOCODERs* (see Rabiner and Schafer 1978, chapter 7.)

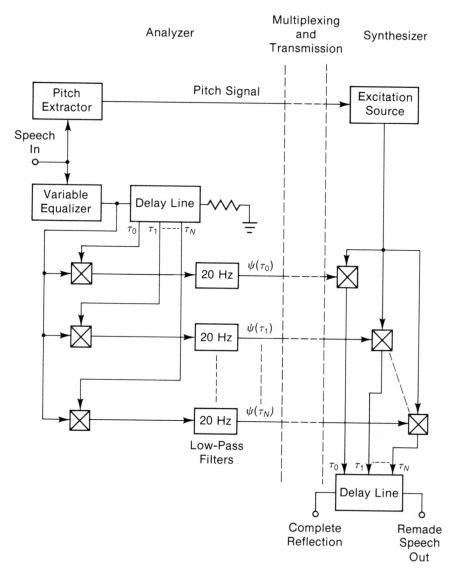

Figure 13.10 *Autocorrelation VOCODER. From: Schroeder, M. R. "VOCODERS; Analysis and Synthesis of Speech." Proc. of IEEE, vol. 54, no. 5, May 1966, p. 727. © 1966 IEEE.*

13.4.2 Linear Predictive Coders (LPC)

In the case of the VOCODERs, we synthesize speech at the receiving end of the system without actually having to transmit the entire speech signal by working in the frequency domain. In the time domain we can model the human speech production system as a discrete, time-varying linear filter. Such a filter can be realized as a recursive filter utilizing a positive feedback circuit with a linear predictor in the feedback loop, as shown in Figure 13.11. As was discussed in Section 13.2, the excitation or input to the filter is either a pulse train or noise depending on whether the speech is voiced or unvoiced at the given instant in time. With this time-domain model of the speech production process, then, we can transmit sufficient information to exercise it as a speech synthesizer at the receiving end of the system. The information to be transmitted is the following:

> Voiced or unvoiced (V/UV)
>
> Pitch
>
> RMS signal strength (or amplifier gain, G; see Figure 13.11)
>
> Linear predictor parameters

In Section 13.4.1 the first three items were discussed, so now we must examine the linear predictor parameters.

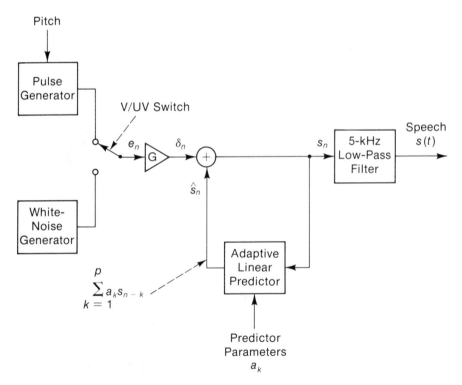

Figure 13.11 *Speech Production Model for Linear Predictive Coding (LPC). From: Atal, B. S., and Hanauer, S. L. "Speech Analysis and Synthesis by Linear Prediction of the Speech Wave." Journal of the Acoustical Soc. of America, vol. 50, no. 2 (Part 2), August 1971, p. 641. Reprinted with permission. © 1971 Acoustical Society of America.*

LPC PARAMETERS

In Figure 13.11, we can see that the output of the linear filter is s_n, given by the combination of the excitation δ_n and the output of the linear predictor $\hat{s}_n$ or,

$$s_n = \sum_{k=1}^{p} a_k s_{n-k} + \delta_n \tag{13.4.1}$$

where: p is the number of samples used for the prediction

a_k is the linear predictor coefficient

Now it remains to determine the number p and the p linear predictor coefficients. The number p is often referred to as the number of "poles" in the transfer function of the filter. This transfer function can be written from Figure 13.11 as a z-transform:

$$T(z) = \frac{1}{1 - \sum_{k=1}^{p} a_k z^{-k}} \tag{13.4.2}$$

The "poles" of $T(z)$ are those values of z (frequencies in this case) where the denominator of (13.4.2) becomes zero.

The poles, then, are like *resonances* in the vocal tract. Two poles are usually used to represent the opening between the vocal cords in the larynx (called the glottis). Additional poles are needed to model the "radiation," the voice path to the lips, which corresponds to a delay of about 1 msec. At a sampling period of 0.1 msec, this results in ten additional poles. So p should be 12. The 12 coefficients are determined by minimizing the mean-square prediction error, in a method similar to that used in Chapter 6 (see Section 6.4.2). When we add the other three items to be transmitted, we have a total of 15 numbers to transmit. The next question is: How often should these numbers be updated, and a typical rate is once every 5 or 10 msec.

In the literature, this method of analysis-synthesis has come to be known as *linear predictive coding* (LPC). Since it operates in the time domain, it does not suffer from some of the shortcomings—such as the distortion of higher pitched voices—of the frequency domain techniques (such as channel and formant VOCODERs).

To get some idea of the compression ratio one might obtain with LPC, Atal and Hanauer (1971) give the following quantization budget:

12 poles	60 bits
pitch	6 bits
level (rms)	5 bits
V/UV	1 bit
TOTAL	72 bits

If we update these parameters once every 10 msec, then we need a bit rate of 7200 bits per sec. If we compare this to a PCM speech system with 56,000 bits per sec, we see a compression ratio of 7.8:1. Obviously, if we lower the sampling rate (rate of updating) of the parameters, we get a higher compression ratio.

In the literature, this method of solving for the predictor coefficients is called the covariance method (Atal and Hanauer 1971). Another method, which is based on the use of partial correlation coefficients, is called the PARCOR method (Itakura and Saito 1968). A third method also found in the literature is based on a lattice structure. For a detailed description and analytical comparison of these methods, see Rabiner and Schafer (1978, chapter 8).

QUANTIZING THE LPC PARAMETERS

There are a number of ways of quantizing the information for the poles of an LPC system. The obvious approach of quantizing the *coefficients* a_k in (13.4.2) is usually not followed since it requires 8–10 bits per coefficient to ensure the stability of the synthesis filter. However, two other methods have been used which require, on the average, fewer bits per pole, and these are as follows:

1. Quantize the *roots of the predictor polynomial* (the denominator of equation 13.4.2):

$$A(z) = 1 - \sum_{k=1}^{p} a_k z^{-k} \tag{13.4.3}$$

   The roots correspond to the poles, and Atal and Hanauer (1971) quantized the 12 roots with a total of 60 bits, as shown above.

2. Quantize *a function of the PARCOR coefficients* (k_i) as follows:

$$f(k_i) = \log\left[\frac{1 - k_i}{1 + k_i}\right] \tag{13.4.4}$$

   In the literature, one sees other terminology for this type of quantization, namely *reflection coefficients* and *log area ratio*. They are related to the PARCOR coefficients thusly: If the vocal tract is modelled as a concatenation of lossless tubes of different areas, A_i, this will give rise to reflection, with reflection coefficients, r_i, where:

$$r_i = \frac{A_{i+1} - A_i}{A_{i+1} + A_i} \tag{13.4.5}$$

   It can be shown that the reflection coefficients are related to the PARCOR coefficients as follows:

$$r_i = -k_i \tag{13.4.6}$$

so that, from 13.4.4

$$f(k_i) = \log\left[\frac{A_{i+1}}{A_i}\right] \tag{13.4.7}$$

This is called the *log area ratio*.

In an interesting example of concatenation of compression techniques, Sambur in 1975 applied DPCM to the log area ratios, and reduced the bit rate of his LPC system to 1500 bps.

Vector quantization has been applied to LPC to reduce the bit rate to 800 bps. See Wong et al. (1982).

EFFECT OF CHANNEL ERRORS ON LPC PERFORMANCE

The effect of channel errors on LPC performance was investigated by Un and Lee (1983) and it was found that the LPC system was fairly robust to error rates of 10^{-3} or less. It was also found that the pitch signal and the first two reflection coefficients were most sensitive to the channel errors.

CONCATENATION OF WAVEFORM CODERS WITH LPC

In some speech communication networks, there may be a need to use LPC in only certain portions of the network, where there are severe bandwidth constraints, and higher data rate speech coders in the rest of the network. Such higher rate coders are typically waveform coders, and one possible tandem arrangement that has been studied involves a 2.4 kbps LPC coder and a 16 kbps waveform coder. Three waveform coders were studied: delta modulator, adaptive delta modulator, and CVSD. The conclusion of the study was that this tandem arrangement is of lower quality than either the waveform coder or LPC coder alone (see Goodman et al. 1979).

13.5 HARDWARE IMPLEMENTATION OF SPEECH COMPRESSION TECHNIQUES

In recent years, it has become feasible to implement in hardware some of the speech compression techniques described in this chapter. Two such examples are an ADM speech compressor and an LPC speech compressor.

ADM Speech Compressor A single chip ADM LSI Codec has been designed (Irie et al. 1983) that operates at 16 or 32 kbps. The adaptive quantizer uses digital step-size adaptation with a fixed multiplier. The predictor uses a double integrator. The chip uses CMOS technology and contains about 4000 MOS devices. It operates on 3.6–5.5 V and dissipates 30 mW. It is intended to be used in portable telephones and other mobile communication systems.

LPC Speech Compressor   Three chips were designed (Fette et al. 1983) to implement in CMOS an LPC speech compression system: an LPC analysis chip, a pitch extractor chip, and an LPC synthesis chip. The PARCOR algorithm was used in the LPC analysis chip and the AMDF algorithm was used in the pitch extractor chip.

The device count and power dissipation for the chips are:

CHIP	TRANSISTORS	POWER DISSIPATION
LPC analysis	28131	25 mW
Pitch extractor	43000	50 mW
LPC synthesis	11784	20 mW

These chips were combined with a general-purpose microprocessor to implement an LPC speech compressor operating at 2.4 kbps.

HIGHLIGHTS

- In a communication system involving speech, the data source is the human voice, the channel is typically a telephone system, and the receiver is the human ear and brain.

- The goal in speech compression systems is to preserve intelligibility and recognizability.

- Speech compression techniques are of two types: waveform coding and voice coding.

- The techniques used in waveform coding, in which the speech waveform is sampled and then coded, can be divided into time domain techniques, including PCM, DPCM, DM, APC, and VSC, and frequency domain techniques, including subband coding and adaptive transform coding.

- Two types of voice coding techniques, which analyze the original signal into component parts and synthesize a facsimile of the original at the receiving end, are in common use: VOCODERs and linear predictive coders.

- Some speech compression techniques have been implemented in hardware, including an ADM speech compressor and an LPC speech compressor.

SUGGESTIONS FOR FURTHER READING

The following items are suggested for further reading and study:

Abut, H., Gray, R. M., and Rebolledo, G. "Vector Quantization of Speech and Speech-Like Waveforms." *IEEE Trans. on Acoustics, Speech, and Signal Processing,* vol. ASSP-30, no. 3, June 1982, pp. 423–435.
Vector quantization for speech, which requires no explicit modelling of the source, but instead uses a long training data sequence and provides a rate of 1 or 2 bits per sample, is described.

Anderson, J. B., and Bodie, J. B. "Tree Encoding of Speech." *IEEE Trans on Info. Theory,* vol. IT-21, *July* 1975, *pp.* 379–387.
The authors show that tree coding for speech can provide SNR gains as high as 7 dB over DPCM.

Atal, B. S., and Hanauer, S. L. "Speech Analysis and Synthesis by Linear Prediction of the Speech Wave." *Journal of Acoustical Society of America,* vol. 50, no. 2 (Part 2), August 1971, pp. 637–655.
This paper introduces and describes the technique of linear predictive coding (LPC). A phonograph record with speech samples is provided.

Atal, B. S., and Schroeder, M. R. "Adaptive Predictive Coding of Speech Signals." *Bell System Tech. Journal,* October 1970, pp. 1973–1986.
A DPCM approach to speech compression, with the special predictor memory of two pitch periods is described.

Bayless, J. W., Campanella, S. J., and Goldberg, A. J. "Voice Signals: Bit-by-Bit." *IEEE Spectrum,* vol. 10, no. 10, October 1973, pp. 28–34.
An easy-to-read overview of the two groups of speech compression techniques given in this chapter: waveform coding and voice coding. A phonograph record with speech samples is provided.

Buzo, A., Gray, A. H., Gray, R. M., and Markel, J. D. "Speech Coding Based upon Vector Quantization." *IEEE Trans. on Acoustics, Speech, and Signal Processing,* vol. ASSP-28, no. 5, October 1980, pp. 562–574.
This paper describes the application of vector quantization to LPC and compares its performance to that of LPC with scalar quantization.

Campanella, S. J., and Robinson, G. S. "A Comparison of Orthogonal Transformations for Digital Speech Processing." *IEEE Trans. on Comm. Tech.,* vol. COM-19, no. 6, December 1971, pp. 1045–1050.
Three orthogonal transformations (Karhunen-Loève, Fourier, and Hadamard) are compared to PCM in terms of the bit rate required to achieve the same signal-to-quantizing noise ratio. A μ-law compander is used on all schemes.

Cohen, F. "A Switched Quantizer for Markov Sources Applied to Speech Signals." *NTZ,* vol. 26, no. 11, 1973, pp. 520–522.
An adaptive DPCM system is described in which 1 out of 64 different quantizing functions is switched into the DPCM encoder, using the two most significant bits from the three previous difference words as the selection information.

Dudley, H. "Remaking Speech." *Journal of the Acoustical Society of America,* vol. 11, no. 2, October 1939, pp. 169–177.

This paper describes the channel VOCODER, the first speech compression system.

Fette, B., Harrison, D., Olson, D., and Allen, S. P. "A Family of Special Purpose Microprogrammable Digital Signal Processor IC's in an LPC Vocoder System." *IEEE Trans on Acoustics, Speech, and Signal Processing*, vol. ASSP-31, no. 1, February 1983, pp. 273–280.

This article describes three CMOS chips designed to implement an LPC analyzer, synthesizer, and pitch extractor.

Flanagan, J. L. *Speech Analysis, Synthesis and Perception.* 2d ed. New York: Springer-Verlag, 1972.

This book has become a standard reference in speech analysis and synthesis. It covers speech production, hearing, and speech analysis/synthesis—especially from the VOCODER standpoint.

Flanagan, J. L., Coker, C. H., Rabiner, L. R., Schafer, R. W., and Umeda, N. "Synthetic Voices for Computers." *IEEE Spectrum*, vol. 7, no. 10, October 1970, pp. 22–45.

This paper describes the physiological speech production system and explains the synthesis of speech from the spectral formants. A phonograph record with speech samples is provided.

Flanagan, J. L., Schroeder, M. R., Atal, B., Crochiere, R. E., Jayant, N. S., and Tribolet, J. M. "Speech Coding." *IEEE Trans. on Comm.*, vol. COM-27, no. 4, April 1979, pp. 710–737.

This is a review paper on speech compression covering the material in this chapter.

Gersho, A., and Cuperman, V. "Vector Quantization: A Pattern-Matching Technique for Speech Coding." *IEEE Communications Magazine*, vol. 21, no. 9, December 1983, pp. 15–21.

This is a review paper on the applications of vector quantization to speech compression and, in particular, to waveform coding.

Gibson, J. D. "Adaptive Prediction in Speech Differential Encoding Systems." *Proc. of IEEE*, vol. 68, no. 4, April 1980, pp. 488–525.

A detailed treatment of adaptive prediction for DPCM and APC is given, along with an extensive bibliography.

Gold, B., and Rabiner, L. R. "Parallel Processing Techniques for Estimating Pitch Periods of Speech in the Time Domain." *J. Acoust. Soc. Am.*, vol. 46, no. 2 (Part 2), August 1969, pp. 442–448.

This paper describes a method for estimating the pitch period from the peaks and valleys in the voiced speech waveform.

Goodman, D. J., Scagliola, C., Crochiere, R. E., Rabiner, L. R., and Goodman, J. "Objective and Subjective Performance of Tandem Connections of Waveform Coders with an LPC Vocoder." *Bell Sys. Tech. Jour.*, vol. 58, no. 3, March 1979, pp. 601–629.

This paper analyzes and documents subjective tests on a waveform coder/LPC coder tandem arrangement and concludes that the tandem arrangement is of poorer quality than either coder alone.

Greefkes, J. A. "A Digitally Controlled Data Codec for Speech Transmission." *Proc. IEEE Int. Conf. on Comm.*, 1970, pp. 7–33 to 7–48.

In this paper the method of continuous adaptation in delta modulation is introduced, called continuously variable slope delta modulation (CVSD).

Irie, K., Uno, T., Uchimura, K., and Iwata, A. "A Single Chip ADM LSI Codec." *IEEE Trans. on Acoustics, Speech, and Signal Processing*, vol. ASSP-31, no. 1, February 1983, pp. 281–287.

A single CMOS chip containing over 4000 components implements an adaptive delta modulator.

Itakura, F. I., and Saito, S. "Analysis-Synthesis Telephony Based upon the Maximum Likelihood Method." *Proc. 6th Int. Congress on Acoustics*, Tokyo, 1968, pp. C17–20.

In this paper, the use of partial correlation coefficients, called PARCOR coefficients, in the solution of the linear prediction coefficients in LPC is introduced.

Jayant, N. S. "Digital Coding of Speech Waveforms: PCM, DPCM, and DM Quantizers." *Proc. of IEEE*, vol. 62, no. 5, May 1974, pp. 611–632.

This paper reviews fixed and adaptive quantization, DPCM, and delta modulation and compares their performance using theoretical results and subjective listening tests. A phonograph record of speech samples is provided.

Jayant, N. S. "Pitch-Adaptive DPCM Coding of Speech with Two-Bit Quantization and Fixed Spectrum Prediction." *BSTJ*, vol. 56, no. 3, March 1977, pp. 439–454.

An adaptive DPCM system is described utilizing two predictors: one short-term predictor and one long-term predictor based on the pitch period.

Jayant, N. S. See Chapter 6, Suggestions for Further Reading.

Linde, Y., Buzo, A., and Gray, R. M. "An Algorithm for Vector Quantizer Design." *IEEE Trans. on Comm.*, vol. COM-28, no. 1, January 1980, pp. 84–95.

In this paper, a quantization method of Lloyd is used to block code an LPC speech system, resulting in a further compression of about 4:1.

Matsuyama, Y., and Gray, R. M. "Voice Coding and Tree Encoding Speech Compression Systems Based upon Inverse Filter Matching." *IEEE Trans. on Comm.*, vol. -30, no. 4, April 1982, pp. 711–720.

In this paper two approaches to speech coding are described: a pitch-excited VOCODER and a tree coder that employs a 1 bit per sample path map.

Paez, M. D., and Glisson, T. H. "Minimum Mean Squared Error Quantization in Speech." *IEEE Trans. on Comm.*, vol. Com.-20, April 1972, pp. 225–230.

In this paper the authors found that the probability density function of the speech input was closely matched by that of a gamma distribution.

Rabiner, L. R., and Schafer, R. W. *Digital Processing of Speech Signals*. Englewood Cliffs, N.J.: Prentice-Hall, 1978.

This book covers the following areas: speech signal models; waveform coding; voice coding, including LPC; and digital speech, for man-machine communication.

Ross, M. J., Shaffer, H. L., Cohen. A., Freudberg, R. and Manley, H. J. "Average Magnitude Difference Function Pitch Extractor." *IEEE Trans on Acoust. Speech and Signal Proc.*, vol. ASSP-22, October 74, pp. 353–362.

In this paper, the method of pitch extraction stated in the title, namely AMDF, is introduced.

Sambur, M. R. "An Efficient Linear-Prediction VOCODER." *Bell System Technical Journal,* vol. 54, no. 10, December 1975, pp. 1693–1723.

In this article, DPCM was used to encode the LPC parameters to be transmitted, with a resulting bit rate of 1500 bps. Principal component analysis was used to send only the most significant eigenvalues, for a resulting bit rate of 1000 bps.

Schroeder, M. R. "VOCODERS: Analysis and Synthesis of Speech." *Proc. IEEE.,* vol. 54, no. 5, May 1966, pp. 720–734.

A good review of VOCODER techniques is given including: channel, formant, autocorrelation, and orthogonal VOCODERS.

Shannon, C. E. See Chapter 1, Suggestions for Further Reading.

Song, C. et al. See Chapter 6, Suggestions for Further Reading.

Un, C. K., and Lee, S. J. "Effect of Channel Errors on the Performance of LPC Vocoders." *IEEE Trans. on Acoustics, Speech, and Signal Processing,* vol. ASSP-31, no. 1, February 1983, pp. 234–237.

LPC vocoders were found to be robust at error rates of 10^{-3} or less, and it was found that the first two reflection coefficients were most sensitive to channel errors.

Wong, D. Y., Juang, B-H, Gray, A. H. "An 800 bit/s Vector Quantization LPC Vocoder," *IEEE Trans. on Acoustics, Speech, and Signal Processing,* vol. ASSP-30, no. 5, October 1982, pp. 770–780.

In this paper, vector quantization is applied to LPC using different codebooks for voiced and unvoiced vectors.

Zelinski, R., and Noll, P. "Adaptive Transform Coding of Speech Signals." *IEEE Trans. on Acoustics, Speech and Signal Processing,* vol. ASSP-25, no. 5, August 1977, pp. 299–309.

This paper examines adaptive transform coding and shows that a discrete cosine transformation with adaptive quantization and bit assignment is ideally suited to speech compression.

CHAPTER 14

Telemetry Compression

14.1 INTRODUCTION

The word *telemetry* means "measurement at a distance." In many situations where it is impractical, dangerous, or too costly to record data measurements at the *place* of the measurement, we use telemetry in the form of a transmission link [cable or radio frequency (rf)] to bring the measurement data to the recording site.

Historically, telemetry has been used to monitor the condition and performance of rockets and missiles, and some of the early applications of data compression were in this area. As the Space Age developed, telemetry became the essential connecting link between the spacecraft and the ground system. Two types of data flow from the spacecraft to the ground system over the telemetry link: scientific measurements and measurements of the "health" of the spacecraft. The data rates of the former have steadily increased over time, creating a growing need for on-board compression.

Seismic data is telemetered from remote sites to a central recording/processing point. As the number of remote sites increases, the data congestion increases at the input to the central site. Data compression is used to reduce this congestion by reducing the data rate from each remote site.

In recent years, there has been a growing interest in the compression of telemetered medical data, especially electrocardiographic (ECG) data.

In this chapter, we examine some of the special considerations in telemetry data compression, as well as some applications in space, seismology, and medicine.

14.2 TELEMETRY CHARACTERISTICS

A number of characteristics of telemetry systems have a direct influence on the design of the data compression system to be used in each case. These are: channel bandwidth, time dependence, multiplexing vs. packetizing, and error control.

14.2.1 Channel Bandwidth

In telemetry systems, the channel bandwidth is usually fixed, and not a parameter that is under the system designer's control. In the typical case, the bandwidth is insufficient for transmission of the raw data—hence the need for compression. The required compression ratio is easily computed:

$$\text{Required R} = \frac{\text{Raw data bandwidth}}{\text{Channel bandwidth}} \qquad (14.2.1)$$

We can compute the theoretical maximum compression ratio as given in Chapter 3:

$$\text{Maximum R} = \frac{\log_2 M}{H} \qquad [\text{equation (3.4.1)}]$$

Then the choice of either redundancy reduction or entropy reduction is made as follows:

1. If: Required R < maximum R
   Use redundancy reduction
2. If: Required R > maximum R
   Use entropy reduction

Of course, in some cases, especially for condition 2, a combination of entropy reduction and redundancy reduction can be used. An example of this is given in Section 14.3.2.

14.2.2 Time Dependence

Because telemetry is typically used to measure or monitor remotely some parameter as a function of time, the time dependence of the data is important, especially when compressed data is reconstructed. Historically, telemetry was used primarily to transmit what may be called one-dimensional data, such as voltages, temperatures, pressures, and so on, where there may or may not be a data correlation over some period of time. In recent years, telemetry systems have been used to transmit two-dimensional data, usually in the form of scanned images, where there is a *strong* correlation over a period of time corresponding to a scan line.

In Chapter 8, various methods of time coding were examined where the assumption was made that the time dependence of the original data would be preserved. Such time dependence is important in telemetry and in many cases the effect of channel errors on the time information has to be considered as treated in Chapter 10.

To repeat, this need for time dependence is created by *correlation*. In many applications, we want to correlate the received telemetry data with other telemetry data or other data. Correlation is achieved, of course, by means of the time base.

14.2.3 Multiplexing vs. Packetizing

The methods by which telemetry systems handle multiple data sources have evolved over time. Originally, most telemetry systems used some type of frequency-division multiplexing (FDM) wherein each data source was modulated onto a separate subcarrier frequency. In many cases, the data was in analog form and not generally amenable to compression. Time-division multiplexing (TDM) then became the "standard" telemetry system, with each data source digitally encoded. This type of system did lend itself to compression, but not without the "overhead" requirements of data buffering and data source identification (Lynch June 1967). A new type of telemetry system is the "packet" system, wherein the data from each source is sent in a block or packet whenever the block is ready to be sent. This type of system is actually more suitable for compression than the TDM system since the compressed data can be easily sent as a packet and reconstructed as a packet. Since buffering is an integral part of packet telemetry systems, part of this same buffer can be used to implement compression schemes that require buffering, such as the nonredundant sample coders described in Chapter 7.

14.2.4 Error Control

Telemetry channels are usually subject to noise effects, so the errors introduced by the channel have to be controlled. We normally divide channels into two categories depending on the type of errors they introduce: random errors or burst errors (see Appendix A). In the use of error-control codes, the bit-error rate (BER) is specified both "before" and "after" the error-control code. The "after" BER is normally referred to as the *undetected* BER. It is this undetected BER that we must use in trade-off analyses (Lynch September 1967), as described in Section 10.2.

14.3 SPACE DATA COMPRESSION

In space research, sounding rockets and satellites are used. The sounding rockets have a relatively short flight and obviously require that transmission of information from the rocket be optimized in the allowable time. The same is true of missiles, even though their flight times may be longer. Satellites typically have a long, active lifetime—in the order of years—and can transmit telemetry continuously. Let us look at each separately.

14.3.1 Missile/Rocket Telemetry

Missile and rocket telemetry has been compressed using redundancy-reduction techniques of the nonredundant sample (NRS) coding type (see Medlin 1963 and Gardenhire 1964). For example, the zero-order predictor has been used in multistage rocket telemetry compression quite successfully. This is true because many measurements, such as voltages, temperatures, and pressures exhibit a behavior that is correlated with the staging of the rocket (the shutdown of one stage, separation, and ignition of the next stage). During the staging phase, the various measurements show a high variability with time, and very little compression is possible. However, in the time *between* staging phases, many measurements are quiescent and lend themselves to high compression by means of algorithms such as the zero-order predictor.

14.3.2 Satellite Telemetry

In satellite telemetry, there are two kinds of data to be transmitted: scientific measurements and engineering data (sometimes called "housekeeping data"). The engineering data is typically sampled at a much lower rate than the scientific measurements, so that compression of this data is not normally required. However, the scientific data is often sampled at a rate higher than necessary (from the Nyquist standpoint) because in many cases the frequency range of the power density spectrum is not known a priori. For this reason, many scientific data sources become highly redundant and thus highly compressible. Usually the statistics of the data source are not known either and some form of adaptive compression must be used. See Rice and Plaunt (1971) for an adaptive variable-length code.

A special type of data for satellite telemetry is image data. Image data can be either scientific or engineering data. Imaging sensors that take pictures of the earth in multiple spectral bands, or sensors that look out from the earth and take multispectral pictures of the stars are certainly producing scientific information. However, sensors that take pictures of different parts of the spacecraft for monitoring purposes are producing engineering-type information.

A good example of the latter (and an unusual one too, since compression became necessary) was the real-time visual monitoring system on the Radio Astronomy Explorer-B (RAE-B) spacecraft, which was put into lunar orbit in 1973. On the RAE-B were four long (229 m) antenna booms that were used for gravity-gradient stabilization as well as for radio astronomy signal reception. These long, lightweight booms were subject to possible bending and deformation, and it was necessary to monitor their *shape* in real-time in order to take corrective action if serious deformation began to occur.

The on-board camera system that was used to take panoramic pictures of all four booms produced an output data rate of 20 kbps. It was necessary to design an on-board image compression system to reduce this rate by a factor of 32 in order to accommodate the VHF telemetry channel capacity of 625 bps. The details of the design of this image compression system are described in the paper by Miller and Lynch (1976). Following is a brief summary of its main features.

The compression system used a combination of entropy reduction (ER) and redundancy reduction (RR). Since the image was scanned, three out of four scan lines were discarded at the camera output (ER) and the remaining line in each case was adaptively run-length encoded (RR). The scan-line skipping provided a 4:1 compression ratio, and the adaptive run-length coding averaged an 8:1 compression ratio—giving the required 32:1 overall compression ratio. For image reconstruction on the ground, each transmitted scan line was reconstructed and then repeated three times. The resulting picture exhibited a fine "sawtooth" feature at boundaries because of this scan-line repetition. However, the essential shape of the booms was not changed nor were the large features on the moon in the image (see Figure 14.1).

The adaptive run-length coding on each saved scan line worked as follows. A threshold was established at a low-intensity level in order to take advantage of the relatively high probability of long, dark runs in the image. Dark runs were expected to dominate since the camera was looking at dark space most of the time in the 360° panoramic view created by a rotating mirror in front of the lens (Figure 14.1). Two different-length, run-length words were used: a 12-bit word when the level fell below the threshold and a 4-bit word when the level was above the threshold. In this way, the shorter, higher-intensity-level

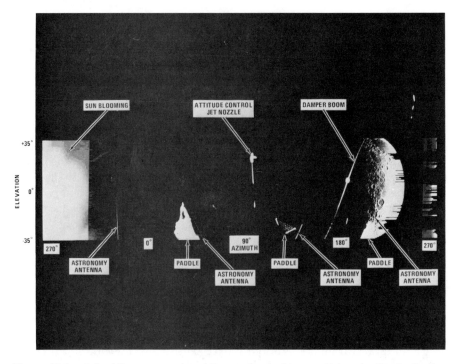

Figure 14.1   *Actual Compressed and Reconstructed Image Taken by the Radio Astronomy Explorer-B Spacecraft. From: Miller, W. H., and Lynch, T. J. "On-Board Image Compression for the RAE Lunar Mission." IEEE Trans. on Aerospace and Electronic Systems, vol. AES-12, no. 3, May 1976, p. 333. © 1976 IEEE.*

runs (due to the moon, the spacecraft booms, and other appendages) were coded with shorter run-length words, and the longer dark runs by the longer run-length words.

This on-board image compression system was implemented with C-MOS (complementary-metal oxide semiconductor) integrated circuits, occupied a volume of about 1000 cm^3, and consumed 0.4 watt. This system produced usable images on the ground of the RAE-B booms as well as of the moon for the 18-month period the spacecraft was actively operating.

14.4 SEISMIC DATA COMPRESSION

Seismic data are really measurements of the earth's vibrations due to natural or man-made causes. The natural causes are usually earthquakes, and the man-made causes are usually surface explosions created during the exploration for petroleum and natural gas.

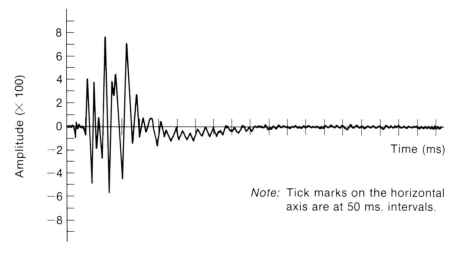

Figure 14.2 *A Seismic Trace. From: Stigall, P. D., and Panagos, P. "Data Compression in Microprocessor-Based Data Acquisition Systems." IEEE Trans. on Geoscience Electronics, vol. GE-16, no. 4, Oct. 1978, p. 325. © 1978 IEEE.*

In both the natural and man-made seismic situations, arrays of seimsmometers are used to measure and record the vibrations over a wide geographical area. The waveforms from both have some basic similarities: They are oscillatory in nature and show an amplitude decay with time (Figure 14.2)

There are two reasons for compressing these seismic signals: (1) to reduce the general storage requirement, and (2) to relieve congestion in the transmission of the raw data from the seismometers back to a central point. An interesting variation on the latter motivation has come about by virtue of the availability of microprocessors.

In a paper by Stigall and Panagos (1978) two types of compression algorithms were tried out on seismic data to see if all data gathering, processing, and storage could be performed at the remote sites using a microprocessor (based on the Intel 8080). In particular, a high compression ratio was of interest since all data was to be stored in RAM (random-access memory) chips.

The two algorithms used were: (1) the first-order predictor (FOP; see Section 7.2), and (2) DPCM with optimum source coding of the differences (see Sections 3.5 and 6.4). The FOP algorithm gave a compression rate of 2.33 and the DPCM algorithm gave a compression ratio of 3.94 for the data waveform in Figure 14.2. The FOP algorithm used a binary sequence time code (see Section 8.3.1) for the timing information, which is the most inefficient of all time codes (see Sections 8.4.1 and 8.4.2). The compression ratios are also not consistent in terms of uniform distortion. Stigall and Panagos point out that the average error per sample for the FOP algorithm is fixed and equal to the tolerance (or window) used in the algorithm. But in the DPCM case, the average error is due to the *cumulative* quantization error for the differences. This error

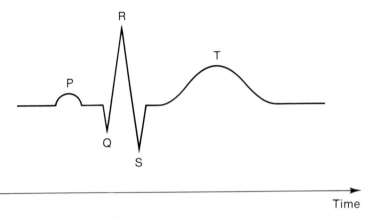

Time

Figure 14.3   *ECG Features of Interest. From: McFee, R., and Baute, G. M. "Research in Electrocardiography and Magnetocardiography." Proc. IEEE, vol. 60, no. 3, March 1972, p. 291. © 1972 IEEE.*

can become quite large and can easily exceed the tolerance error of the FOP algorithm.

An interesting combination of DPCM and LPC was used by Bordley (1983) in compressing marine seismic data. In this scheme, the predictor in the DPCM feedback loop was designed as an LPC predictor, using the correlation technique for the determination of the predictor coefficients (see Section 13.4.2). Original data of 12-bit samples was compressed to 2 bits per sample, with a resulting rms distortion that was estimated to be within 2 bits per sample of the rate distortion bound (see Section 2.5).

14.5 ELECTROCARDIOGRAM COMPRESSION

The electrocardiogram (ECG, sometimes abbreviated EKG) records the electrical activity of the heart as it acts as a cyclic pump. A typical cycle or period of an ECG is shown in Fig. 14.3. The P wave represents the activation of the atria, which are the receiving chambers of the heart. The left atrium receives oxygen-laden blood from the lungs and the right atrium receives oxygen-deficient blood from the body. The atrium activation takes about 90 msec. The next portion of the ECG is the QRS complex, which represents the activation of the ventricles, the sending chambers of the heart. The left ventricle sends oxygen-laden blood back to the body and the right ventricle sends oxygen-deficient blood back to the lungs. This activation takes about 80 msec. During the QRS complex, the atria are recovering and getting ready to repeat the cycle. During the T wave, the ventricles are recovering and getting ready for their next cycle. The heart cycle or heart *beat* is measured as the time between the R peaks of the QRS complexes. See McFee and Baule (1972) for more details.

These functions of the heart are basically what cardiologists wish to study using the ECG. Useful information is contained in the time locations, shapes, and sizes of the various features of the waveform (P, Q, R, S, and T), and this information must be preserved in any compression scheme that is used.

The need for compression of electrocardiograms is twofold. First, there is a large number of ECGs. The annual volume in the United States alone has been estimated to be in the order of 10 million. For many patients, a new ECG does not necessarily replace an "old" ECG, but instead is added to the patient's file for comparison purposes. This time-history use of the ECG adds to the storage and retrieval requirements, so compression is needed to reduce the sheer data volume. Second, there is a growing need to transmit ECGs over telephone lines for remote analysis. For this, digital encoding is preferred since analog/FM systems have some inherent distortion. The digitized ECG typically requires a bit rate as follows: The American Heart Association recommends 10 bits per sample, 500 samples per sec, and 3 "leads," which produces 15,000 bit per sec. This rate exceeds the capacity of most analog telephone lines, hence the need for compression for real-time transmission.

A number of different approaches have been tried in the compression of ECGs. In some cases, combinations of compression algorithms have been used in order to approach the required compression ratio. The following are some significant examples of what has been done in ECG compression.

Transform coding has been used, especially the principal component transform (Womble et al. 1977), the Haar transform, and the discrete cosine transform (Ahmed et al. 1975). In the case of the principal component application, the eigenvector solution (see Section 5.2.1) was performed in two successive stages: the first stage was used to reduce the effects of respiration and different patient heart orientations; and the second was used to obtain the desired principal component transform by using a one-time (same for all patients) eigenvector solution. Inherent in this approach is the subtraction of a "population mean heartbeat" from the transformed data. The compression ratio obtained was about 12:1. Both the Haar and the DCT gave a compression ratio of about 3:1, but in all these transforms the intrinsic problem existed of correctly identifying each heartbeat and its alignment.

DPCM has been used with a predictor in the feedback loop and with an interpolator in the feedback loop, followed by a Huffman encoder (Ruttimann and Pipberger 1979). It was found that the optimum predictor was second order, with the following coefficients: $a_1 = 1.91$, $a_2 = -0.93$ to be used in:

$$\hat{x}_n = \sum_{k=1}^{2} a_k x_{n-k} \tag{14.5.1}$$

The optimum interpolator was also second order, with one previous and one following sample used. The coefficients were: $a = 0.5$, $b = 0.5$ to be used in:

$$\hat{x}_n = ax_{n-1} + bx_{n+1} \tag{14.5.2}$$

It was found that the interpolator produced a smaller variance difference signal going into the quantizer than did the predictor. The original data was sampled at a rate of 500 samples per sec, but the data for the compressor was sampled at 200 samples per sec. With this further reduction, the overall compression ratio was about 9:1 for the DPCM/interpolator scheme and about 7.5 for the DPCM/predictor scheme. If we normalize the sampling rates, the compression ratios drop to 3.6:1 for the interpolator and 3:1 for the predictor. This result is comparable to the compression ratio of 2.5:1 obtained by Krishnakumar et al. (1981) using DPCM with a third-order predictor and a 5-bit quantizer (with no Huffman code) on 12-bit ECG data.

Waveform interpolators have been used directly on the ECG waveform, and the most widely used interpolator is called amplitude-zone-time-epoch coding (AZTEC), a description of which was published in 1968 by Cox et al. AZTEC converts raw ECG data into plateaus and slopes. It is capable of high compression ratios (in the order of 10:1), but it has some data distortion problems such as possible loss of the PR- and ST-segment duration and amplitude detail and a widening and attenuation of the QRS complex. A somewhat similar algorithm is the turning point (TP) algorithm (Mueller 1978). This eliminates every other sample while monitoring information on the data *trend*. In particular, it maintains peak and valley points when the slope is changing sign—the "turning point." This algorithm provides a compression ratio of only about 2:1, even though it preserves the important characteristics of the QRS complexes. The inevitable result of all these attempts has also occurred: algorithms have been combined. AZTEC and TP have been combined into one scheme that applies them *selectively* to the ECG waveform. Specifically, AZTEC is applied to the P and T regions and TP to the QRS complex (Abenstein and Tompkins 1982). This hybrid system is called the coordinate-reduction-time-encoding system (CORTES) algorithm.

HIGHLIGHTS

- Telemetry characteristics that have a direct influence on data compression systems include channel bandwidth, time dependence, multiplexing vs. packetizing, and error control.

- Missile and rocket telemetry has been compressed using NRS coding type redundancy-reduction techniques.

- In satellite telemetry there are two kinds of data to be transmitted: engineering ("housekeeping") data and scientific measurements. Compression may be necessary for both kinds, especially if imagery is to be transmitted.

- Seismic data are compressed to reduce storage requirements and relieve transmission congestion from numerous remote sites to a central processing facility.

- Electrocardiogram (ECG) data is compressed to reduce storage requirements and to meet the growing need for ECG transmission, which requires the more precise digital encoding, which must, in turn, be compressed for telephone transmission; different approaches to ECG compression have been taken because of the difficulty of compressing the variety of medical information that must be preserved.

SUGGESTIONS FOR FURTHER READING

The following items are suggested for further reading and study. They are grouped into the three telemetry application areas covered in this chapter: space data, seismic data, and electrocardiographic data.

SPACE DATA

Gardenhire, L. W. See Chapter 7, Suggestions for Further Reading.

Lynch, T. J. *Data Compression with Error-Control Coding for Space Telemetry.* NASA Technical Report: TR R-261, Washington, D.C., June 1967.

In Chapter 4 of this report the data overhead due to time-division multiplexing is included in compression ratio formulations.

Lynch, T. J. "Performance Measures for Compressed and Coded Space Telemetry Systems." *IEEE Trans. on Aerospace and Electronic systems*, vol. AES-3, no. 5, September 1967, pp. 784–795.

Two performance measures based on rate distortion theory are developed to compare systems with different combinations of source and channel coding. These measures include the effects of the compression ratio and channel errors on the overall distortion.

Medlin, J. E. See Chapter 7, Suggestions for Further Reading.

Miller, W. H., and Lynch, T. J. "On-Board Image Compression for the RAE Lunar Mission." *IEEE Trans. on Aerospace and Electronic Systems*, vol. AES-12, no. 3, May 1976, pp. 327–335.

One of the first image compression schemes ever to be flown on a spacecraft is described from initial design through successful operation. A compression ratio of 32:1 was achieved through a combination of entropy reduction and redundancy reduction.

Rice, R. F., and Plaunt, J. R. "Adaptive Variable-Length Coding for Efficient Compression of Spacecraft Television Data," *IEEE Trans. on Comm. Tech.*, vol. COM-19, no. 6, December 1971, pp. 889–897.

Three different variable-length codes are used to match the changing data source statistics in an adaptive coding design.

SEISMIC DATA

Bordley, T. E. "Linear Predictive Coding of Marine Seismic Data." *IEEE Trans. on Acoustics, Speech, and Signal Processing*, vol. ASSP-31, no. 4, August 1983, pp. 828–835.

This paper describes a DPCM/LPC system in which the predictor in the feedback loop is designed as an LPC predictor.

Stigall, P. D., and Panagos, P. "Data Compression in Microprocessor-Based Data Acquisition Systems." *IEEE Transactions on Geoscience Electronics*, vol. GE-16, no. 4, October 1978, pp. 323–332.

In this article, a first-order predictor was applied to a sample of seismic data, producing a compression ratio of 2.33:1. A DPCM/optimum encoder combination was applied to the same seismic data, producing a compression ratio of 3.94:1.

ELECTROCARDIOGRAPHIC (ECG) DATA

Abenstein, J. P., and Tompkins, W. J. "A New Data-Reduction Algorithm for Real Time ECG Analysis." *IEEE Trans. on Biomedical Engineering*, vol. BME-29, no. 1, January 1982, pp. 43–48.

An adaptive combination of AZTEC and TP is used to form CORTES (coordinate-reduction-time-encoding system).

Ahmed, N., Milne, P. J., and Harris, S. G. "Electrocardiographic Data Compression via Orthogonal Transforms." *IEEE Transactions on Biomedical Engineering*, vol. BME-22, no. 6, November 1975, pp. 484–487.

The Haar and the discrete cosine transform (DCT) are applied to electrocardiographic data.

Cox, J. R., Nolle, F. M., Fozzard, H. A., and Oliver, G. C. "AZTEC, a Preprocessing Program for Real-Time ECG Rhythm Analysis." *IEEE Trans. on Biomedical Engineering*, April 1968, pp. 128–129.

This short communication introduces the algorithm AZTEC, which stands for: amplitude-zone-time-epoch-coding. This algorithm is basically a modified zero-order interpolator, which converts raw ECG data into a sequence of plateaus and slopes.

Krishnakumar, A. S., Karpowicz, J. L., Belic, N., Singer, D. H., and Jenkins, J. M. "Microprocessor-Based Data Compression Scheme for Enhanced Digital Transmission of Holter Recordings." *IEEE Conf. on Computers in Cardiology*, 1981, pp. 435–437.

In this article, DPCM with a third-order predictor is used to compress ECG data.

McFee, R. and Baule, G. M. "Research in Electrocardiography and Magnetocardiography." *Proc. IEEE*, vol. 60, March 1972, pp. 290–321.

This invited paper on the status of research in cardiography provides a good introduction to the basic measurements and waveform features of electrocardiograms.

Mueller, W. C. "Arrhythmia Detection Program for an Ambulatory ECG Monitor." *Biomed. Sci. Instrum.*, vol. 14, 1978, pp. 81–85.

The turning point (TP) ECG compression algorithm, which eliminates every other sample while monitoring information on the data trend, is described.

Ruttimann, U. E., and Pipberger, H. V. "Compression of the ECG by Prediction or Interpolation and Entropy Encoding." *IEEE Trans. on Biomedical Engineering*, vol. BME-26, no. 11, November 1979, pp. 613–623.

This article describes how a DPCM with either a second-order predictor or interpolator in the feedback loop followed by a Huffman code is used to compress ECG data.

Womble, M. E., Halliday, J. S., Mitter, S. K., Lancaster, M. C., and Triebwasser, J. H. "Data Compression for Storing and Transmitting ECG's/VCG's." *Proc. of the IEEE*, vol. 65, no. 5, May 1977, pp. 702–706.

This paper describes the application of the principal component transformation to ECGs and VCGs (vector cardiograms). In the process of making this transformation, the same eigenvectors are used for all patients' cardiograms.

CHAPTER 15

Television Compression

15.1 INTRODUCTION

To many people, television means the broadcast television signal received by the home TV set that meets the NTSC (National Television System Committee) standards and that, therefore, cannot or should not, be compressed. So why this chapter on television compression?

Compression will potentially pay off in the two obvious classes of television—*broadcast*, and *nonbroadcast*—since they are both "going digital," so to speak. Broadcast television will still be analog as it arrives at the home receiver, but along the transmission path from the studio transmitter to the home receiver a digital link will be used, such as in a communications satellite link, and herein will be a logical place for compression. Nonbroadcast television deals with a variety of special television applications, such as teleconferencing, where, again, a digital transmission link can be compressed in a cost-beneficial way, keeping in mind the specific system requirements.

The parameter of interest for television compression would seem to be the transmission rate, which is also directly related to the bandwidth. This is true in most applications to date, but with the widespread use of video recording (which is analog now), it is possible that digital recording techniques will be utilized in the future, and these may require compression as a necessary adjunct.

In this chapter we concentrate on the video part of television, leaving the audio portion alone (see Chapter 13 for voice compression). In the literature, the techniques for television compression are all aimed at the video portion, and in many cases, at only black-and-white, or monochrome video. Color video is usually treated as a combination of the black-and-white (*luminance*) signal and the color (*chrominance*) signal. Thus, the compression techniques developed for black-and-white video can be applied directly to the luminance signal of color video.

We look first at television as an information source to be compressed and then describe compression techniques that can be applied to both black-and-white and color television in various applications, such as remotely piloted vehicles (RPV), teleconferencing, videotex/teletext, and high-definition television (HDTV).

15.2 TELEVISION AS AN INFORMATION SOURCE

Television contains different kinds of information: two-dimensional frame information; frame-to-frame motion information; intensity, or contrast, information; and color information. For the sake of simplicity, let us first look at black-and-white video as a data source. Color video is treated in Section 15.4.

The NTSC (National Television Systems Committee) standard provides for a 525-line frame and 30 frames per sec. If we convert these into a near-equivalent digital system, we get the following. A digital version of the NTSC frame is close to a 512- $\times$ -512-pixel image in resolution. At 8 bits per pixel, and 30 frames per second, this gives:

$$512 \times 512 \times 8 \times 30 = 63 \times 10^6 \text{ bits per sec}$$

This is the equivalent bit rate of only the black-and-white picture element information—the *luminance*.

Now for the luminance, what compression ratio is possible? Schreiber (1956) measured the entropy of television images on a frame basis using 6-bit raw image pixels and obtained the following results:

Zero-order entropy, $H_{(y)} = 4.4$ bits per pixel

First-order entropy, $H_{(y/x)} = 1.9$ bits per pixel

Second-order entropy, $H_{(y/x_2, x_1)} = 1.5$ bits per pixel

These results indicate that a maximum compression ratio of 6:1.5 or 4:1 is possible. However, this simple estimate does not take into account the fact that video is actually a sequence of frames in which there is both considerable redundancy from frame to frame as well as the possibility of considerable motion from frame to frame. This motion may be distorted or blurred by the compression technique that is used to reduce the redundancy between successive frames. Compression between frames is called *interframe coding*, as opposed to the compression *within* a single frame, which is called *intraframe coding*.

An important thing to remember for video compression is the fact that the receiver is the human visual system, and not a computer. For this reason, certain types of distortion can be tolerated (by the human observer) that would be unacceptable to a computer-based observing system. In video compression, then, we are typically using a combination of entropy reduction and redundancy reduction to achieve the desired compression ratio. The performance test of a given compression technique is often made by a group of human observers making subjective evaluations.

15.3 MONOCHROME VIDEO COMPRESSION

Over the last 30 years there has been a great deal of interest in the compression of black-and-white television, or as it is also called, *monochrome* video compression. Of particular interest was the challenge of the videotelephone, or PICTUREPHONE, as it was called by the Bell System. During the 1960s, work was done at Bell Laboratories to compress the PICTUREPHONE video, which had an uncompressed bandwidth of about 1 MHz. With the advent of teleconferencing, and TV transmission by satellite, further interest was generated in compressing the bandwidth (or data rate) of the video. Numerous techniques have been used for video compression, some general in nature, some specifically designed to take advantage of the peculiar characteristics of the video signal (for example, the frame repetition). In this section, we look first at the more general compression techniques (such as transform coding and DPCM) and then the more TV-unique techniques (such as the slant transform, pseudorandom coding, and slow-scan).

The extensive paper by Jain (1981) covers most of the material in this section.

15.3.1 Transform Coding Techniques

As was discussed in Chapter 5, transform coding has some inherent advantages, such as relative noise immunity and the potential for a relatively high compression ratio. The price one pays for these features is increased storage requirements and complexity. However, as the technology of microelectronics advances, the latter issues may become less important.

Transforms are applied in one, two, or three dimensions. In one- and multidimensional transforms, an optimum block quantizer is used as described in Chapter 5. The optimum transform is, of course, the principal component transform. In practice, however, the cosine and Hadamard transforms are used, as will be seen in the next two subsections on two- and three-dimensional transforms, respectively.

TWO-DIMENSIONAL TRANSFORMS

An example of a two-dimensional transformation for video is included in the VIDAP (Video Data Processor) developed by TRW (Spencer 1979). The VIDAP is a real-time video data compressor that utilizes a two-dimensional Hadamard transform. This transform function is implemented in a CCD chip in the form of a pipeline version of the fast Hadamard transform. It operates on reduced frame-rate video (7.5 frames per sec) and handles one 8- × -8 pixel block at a time. Starting with 6 bits per pixel, this compressor provides compression ratios of 3:1 and 6:1 (not without some distortion).

THREE-DIMENSIONAL TRANSFORMS

Television is a three-dimensional image data set because the frame-to-frame changes add a dimension to the two dimensions of each frame. With this data model in mind, one can use a three-dimensional transform to compress video on an intraframe and interframe basis.

An example of this is the experimental system designed by Knauer in 1976 (see Section 5.4.3). Knauer transformed a "cube" of 4 pixels × 4 lines × 4 frames by means of a Hadamard transform and obtained compression ratios of up to 6:1 (see Figure 15.1).

The compression was obtained by setting some of the resulting 64 coefficients equal to zero and using variable-length words for different coefficients. As was stated in Chapter 5, more quantization levels were used in the time-dimension coefficients for rapid movement and fewer for slower movement.

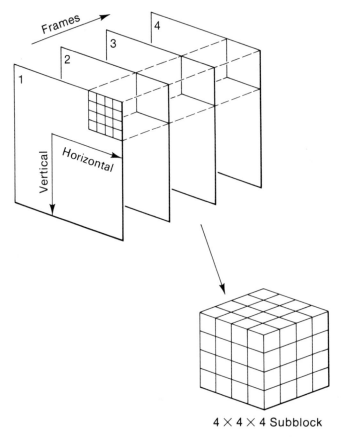

4 × 4 × 4 Subblock

Figure 15.1 *Three-Dimensional Hadamard Transform for TV. After: Knauer, S. C. "Real-Time Video Compression Algorithm for Hadamard Transformation Processing." IEEE Trans. on Electromagnetic Compatibility, vol. EMC-18, no. 1, Feb. 1976, pp. 28–36.*

15.3.2 Predictive Coding Techniques

In Part II, we treated two kinds of prediction techniques: predictive coding and nonredundant sample coding. Historically, there have not been many video applications of nonredundant sample coding. This may be due to the fact that this type of compression technique requires buffer storage and requires that timing information be sent.

In contrast, predictive coding has been applied extensively to video compression. In this section we look at four types of predictive coding that have been applied to video:

Delta modulation

DPCM

Two-dimensional DPCM

Interframe coding

DELTA MODULATION

Because video contains pixels of a certain "gray scale," simple delta modulation will not "keep up" with the slopes in the image intensity function. Adaptive delta modulation (ADM) has been used for video in which the step size is progressively varied in order to "catch up" with the intensity function. An example of this type of ADM is the Song algorithm discussed in Section 6.3.2.

A recent variation on the Song ADM for video takes advantage of the potential redundancy in the string of output pulses (bits) from the delta modulator. The modified algorithm works in two modes. When the input function has a steep slope, the algorithm works in the Song mode ADM. When the input waveform is "more constant," the encoder produces a predetermined fixed-length steady state pattern of 1s and 0s, which can repeat. This pattern is chosen so as not to be confused with a typical pattern of all 1s or all 0s during the steep slope period. Run-length coding is then applied to the output string of bits so these predetermined patterns can be recognized and their number "counted." In such a way, a higher compression ratio can be achieved (40–50% increase) than is possible with the Song algorithm. A description of this modified ADM algorithm is given in the paper by Barba et al. (1981).

DPCM

DPCM has been applied extensively to video compression. One of the earliest applications was to the PICTUREPHONE by Bell Labs. (see Millard and Maunsall 1971). Since that time, it has been applied to many forms of video including color television, remotely piloted vehicles (RPV), and teleconferencing. A comprehensive survey of DPCM in video applications is given by Musmann (1979).

DPCM was covered in Section 6.4 as a one-dimensional compression technique, a technique that matches, to some extent, standard broadcast television. The match occurs because of the practice of scan-line interlacing, which reduces the dependence between lines compared to that along the lines. However, this is not to say that there is *no* dependency in the vertical direction, since two-dimensional DPCM has also been applied, as will be discussed in the next section.

An important consideration in the application of DPCM to video is the problem of slope overload and its visual manifestations. As was discussed in Chapter 6, slope overload affects both delta modulation and DPCM, and the effect is most noticeable at a boundary between two widely spaced intensity levels. At such an "edge," there would be blurring in a still picture, but the effect in video is a randomly moving edge in the frame-to-frame pattern. This effect is called "edge busyness" and can be very objectionable to the human observer. One way of minimizing this effect is to design the DPCM quantizer for a visual error criterion instead of the classical mean-squared error criterion. This method has been reported by Candy and Bosworth (1972) and Netravali and Prasada (1977).

TWO-DIMENSIONAL DPCM

Two-dimensional DPCM was mentioned in Section 10.4.2. The second dimension is used in the prediction process, and using the simple pixel arrangement shown in Figure 10.2, we can write a general form for a typical two-dimensional predictor:

$$\hat{s} = a_1 A + a_2 C + a_3 B \tag{15.3.1}$$

Typical values used for the coefficients* are (as shown in Figure 10.2):

$$a_1 = \frac{3}{4}$$

$$a_2 = \frac{3}{4}$$

$$a_3 = -\frac{17}{32}$$

It has been found that a higher order two-dimensional predictor does not appreciably improve performance (see Habibi 1971).

INTERFRAME CODING

If the next frame of video could be predicted, then only the frame-to-frame differences would have to be transmitted. This is the aim of interframe coding, which is really interframe prediction. There are two types of interframe coders, and they are identified by these functions: frame replenishment and motion compensation.

Frame Replenishment   In this type of interframe coding, pixels are differentiated between those that change and those that do not change from frame to frame. If a

---

* These values for the coefficients normally add up to 1.0. However, when we introduce the concept of the "leak" in order to lessen the effect of error propagation, their sum should add up to a number slightly less than 1.0. In this case, the sum is 0.97. See Figure 10.2.

pixel does not change, it is repeated in the next frame at the receiving end. If a pixel does change, it is *replenished* by the amount it changes. An important trade-off exists between spatial and temporal resolution in this type of interframe coding. It has been found that the human observer can tolerate poorer spatial resolution in moving areas of a video image and poorer temporal (frame-to-frame) resolution in the nonmoving areas. Because of this fact, we can use fewer bits per pixel, or even subsample the pixels in the moving areas (also called dot interlacing) and skip frame-to-frame pixels for the nonmoving areas to keep the overall bit rate down.

Another aspect of frame replenishment is the need to send discrimination information for the changing and nonchanging pixels. One way this has been done is through cluster coding, which was described in Section 8.3.2. In cluster coding only the changes to the changing pixels are sent, and only in clusters along a scan line. The beginning and end of each cluster is all that need be sent in terms of timing information. The isolated pixels that change are ignored by this timing method. A buffer is needed when a synchronous output is required and, thus, so is buffer control, as discussed in Chapter 9. Haskell et al. (1977) has simulated a conditional replenishment interframe coder to operate at 1.5 Mbps.

Motion Compensation In this type of interframe coding, the image is regarded as a superposition of moving pixels on a stationary image. The challenge is to find ways of describing the trajectories of the moving pixels so that each moving pixel can then be propagated along its trajectory at reconstruction. Compression is obtained by skipping frames on the transmitting side and repeating frames on the receiving side. Various motion compensation methods have been proposed, and development is still going on in this area. See Netravali and Robbins (1979) for a discussion of motion compensation techniques.

15.3.3 Hybrid Coding

Hybrid coding is a combination of transform coding and DPCM. Usually, this type of combination is applied to two-dimensional data, but it can be applied to three-dimensional data also—which includes video if the frame-to-frame direction of change is considered the third dimension.

The reason for using hybrid coding is to take advantage of the favorable characteristics of both transform coding and DPCM, which are as follows:

TRANSFORM CODING

1. Relatively insensitive to data statistics
2. Relatively insensitive to transmission errors

3. Block quantization effects relatively less objectionable, in a gray-level sense, to a human observer

DPCM

1. Implementation complexity minimal
2. No need for buffering
3. Capable of operation at high data rates

For a two-dimensional, line-scanned image, the usual order is: a one-dimensional transform *along* each line and then DPCM *across* the lines (of coefficients). The first operation takes advantage of correlation along each line, and this is usually the same transform applied to each line. The second operation takes advantage of the correlation among coefficients of the same order. However, here, the quantizer in each DPCM operation will typically be different, since the variances of the coefficients will be different. Either a bank of different DPCM encoders or one DPCM encoder with switchable quantizers can be used. One should remember that the transformation of a block of pixels on a line will result in some of the transformed coefficients being set to zero.

One form of three-dimensional hybrid coding that has been proposed for video includes a two-dimensional transformation of each frame and then a bank of DPCM encoders in the temporal (frame-to-frame) domain.

Habibi (1974) has compared, both visually and by performance, various hybrid coding combinations using different transforms (Hadamard, Fourier, cosine, slant, and principal component), including the effects of a noisy channel.

15.3.4 Slant Transform

In 1971 Enomoto and Shibata published an orthogonal transform that has "slant" basis vectors and is aimed specifically at the compression of video since linearly increasing and decreasing intensity segments also occur in video frames. The 4-$\times$-4 and 8-$\times$-8 slant transform matrices look as follows:

$$S_4 = \frac{1}{\sqrt{4}} \begin{bmatrix} 1 & 1 & 1 & 1 \\ (3 & 1 & -1 & -3) \times \dfrac{1}{\sqrt{5}} \\ 1 & -1 & -1 & 1 \\ (1 & -3 & 3 & -1) \times \dfrac{1}{\sqrt{5}} \end{bmatrix} \qquad (15.3.2)$$

$$S_8 = \frac{1}{\sqrt{8}} \begin{bmatrix} 1 & 1 & 1 & 1 & 1 & 1 & 1 & 1 \\ (7 & 5 & 3 & 1 & -1 & -3 & -5 & -7) \times \frac{1}{\sqrt{21}} \\ (3 & 1 & -1 & -3 & -3 & -1 & 1 & 3) \times \frac{1}{\sqrt{5}} \\ (7 & -1 & -9 & -17 & 17 & 9 & 1 & -7) \times \frac{1}{\sqrt{5 \times 21}} \\ 1 & -1 & -1 & 1 & 1 & -1 & -1 & 1 \\ 1 & -1 & -1 & 1 & -1 & 1 & 1 & -1 \\ (1 & -3 & 3 & -1 & -1 & 3 & -3 & 1) \times \frac{1}{\sqrt{5}} \\ (1 & -3 & 3 & -1 & 1 & -3 & 3 & -1) \times \frac{1}{\sqrt{5}} \end{bmatrix}$$

$$(15.3.3)$$

These matrices are applied to blocks of data samples by means of a post-multiplication by the sample block arranged as a column matrix, as illustrated in Chapter 5.

In 1972 Pratt, Welch, and Chen developed a generalized procedure for obtaining an Nth-order slant transform matrix from the $N/2$th-order matrix. An interesting result is that some of the vectors for the slant transform are the same as those for the Hadamard transform. For example, for $N = 8$, the vectors of sequence 0, 4, and 5 are the same for slant and Hadamard (see (15.3.3) and Figure 5.4). In 1977 Ohira et al. used the slant transform for the compression of the NTSC color television signal from 8 bits per pel to 3 bits per pel and 2.25 bits per pel.

As N increases, the slant transform looks more like the Hadamard transform (see Figure 15.2).

15.3.5 Pseudorandom Techniques

Two types of video compression techniques take advantage of the limited response time of the eye-brain system in the human observer. These are pseudorandom quantization ("dithering") and pseudorandom scanning. They each achieve a compression by sending fewer bits, but in such a way as to create a distortion that is minimally noticeable to the human observer. Let's look at each type.

Sequency

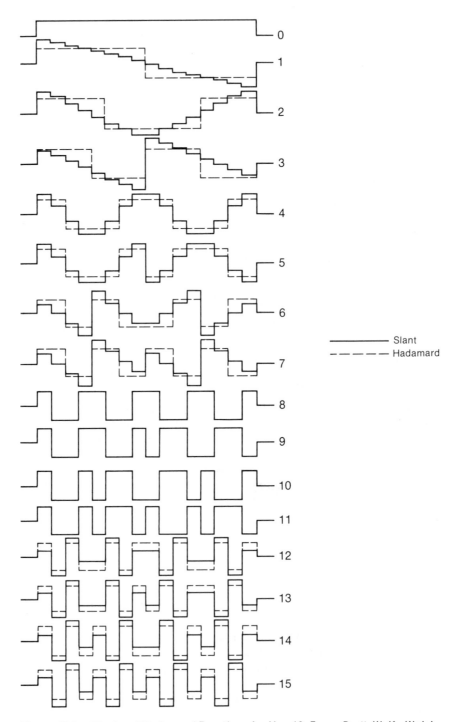

Figure 15.2 *Slant and Hadamard Functions for N = 16. From: Pratt, W. K., Welch, L. R., and Chen, W. "Slant Transforms for Image Coding." Applications of Walsh Functions Symposium Proceedings, Washington, D.C., March 1972, p. 231.*

DITHERING

The basic technique involved in dithering is to add pseudorandom noise to the analog video signal *before* quantization and then to subtract this same noise from the analog signal coming out of the digital-to-analog (D-to-A) converter at the receiving end of the system. This process has the effect of "breaking up" the sharply defined boundaries or contours in an image that has been coarsely quantized and then converted to analog form. The pseudorandom noise, when added to the original signal, causes pixels of the same intensity that would normally be quantized to the same digital level, to be randomly "flipped" between two or more digital levels. This process minimizes the contouring effect of a coarse quantizer, but at the same time maintains the same average value of the pixels that are "dithered." This idea was first suggested by Roberts in 1962 and is sometimes referred to as "Roberts coding." Roberts proposed using a 3-bit quantizer with pseudorandom noise, and in 1971 Thompson described an experimental system for 625-line monochrome television utilizing a 3-bit quantizer and pseudorandom noise.

PSEUDORANDOM SCANNING

In pseudorandom scanning, fewer pixels are actually transmitted, but the pixel elimination process is random across each scan line so as to minimize the "flicker" effect. This idea was first suggested by Deutsch in 1965 (see Deutsch 1973), and it led to the development of a system by the General Electric Company called SAMPLEDOT in 1976 (see Stone 1976). The SAMPLEDOT system is reported by Stone to be able to achieve a compression ratio of 10:1 by sending only about 3% of the picture every scan field, instead of the usual 50% with 2:1 interlaced scanning. This is achieved by gating each scan line with a row from a pseudorandom dot-sample matrix. Minimal *observable* distortion is possible because of two factors: the integrating effect of the human eye-brain system, and the correlation between adjacent pixels.

15.3.6 Slow-Scan Techniques

When the video image is stationary, as in the case of photographs, charts, and so on, the information can be sent over a narrow-band communication channel. This can also be done when the image is moving very slowly. The techniques are variously called "slow-scan" or "single-frame." Actually, a more descriptive terminology would be "slow scan of a single frame."

Typical slow-scan rates result in 1 picture per 100 sec as compared to the normal 30 pictures per sec. This rate translates into a reduction in required bandwidth from a few megahertz to 1 kHz. With the picture in a 1 kHz bandwidth, it can be sent over voice-grade telephone channels and put back into a normal raster-scan format (30 frames per sec) at the receiving end for display on a standard TV monitor.

In the case of stationary images, this scan slowdown can be done on a line-at-a-time basis, utilizing a line buffer. In the case of a slowly moving image, this will not be satisfactory and it is necessary to "freeze" the entire frame in a frame memory and then output it at the slower scan rate. This technique is sometimes referred to as "frame grabbing."

Once a frame is slow-scanned and digitized, we can compute its transmission time as follows. A 256- × -256 pixel frame at 6 bits per pixel will constitute (with overhead) about 400,000 bits and will take the following time:

At 2400 bps:	167 sec
4800 bps:	83 sec
9600 bps:	42 sec

An interesting problem with slow-scan television is that channel noise appears as a permanent image defect—it is "frozen." In normal television, channel noise is usually less noticeable since it affects different pixel locations from frame to frame. It should be remembered, though, that slow-scan video cannot resolve high resolution imagery as well as facsimile can.

Slow-scan video has a number of applications in teleconferencing, telemedicine, and business communications. There are many systems in use, and a product line of slow-scan video compression hardware is available from: Colorado Video Inc., Boulder, Colorado 80306. (See Southworth 1977).

15.4 COLOR VIDEO COMPRESSION

As was stated previously, most of the activity in TV compression has been in monochrome video compression. But there is a growing interest in compression of color video as well, both for broadcast use and for specialized uses such as teleconferencing.

In order to understand the approaches to color video compression, we have to say a few words about the color information that is transmitted along with the luminance information in a composite color television signal.* The color information is fundamentally related to the three colors used in the color CRT: red, green, and blue (RGB). These three primary colors constitute the *source* color information as well as the *final* information (namely, the individual signals for the red, green, and blue "guns" for the receiver CRT). However, these signals are not transmitted directly. Instead, a luminance signal, which is a weighted

---

* For an in-depth review of video color coding, see Limb et al. (1977).

sum of the three color components, is transmitted along with *two* component signals, which are functions of two of the three color signals. All three *color* signals can be extracted from these three transmitted signals. The two component signals are transmitted on one or two subcarrier frequencies, and the arrangement of these subcarriers and the makeup of the component signals depends on which television system we are talking about. There are three primary TV systems in use worldwide. They are:

NTSC (National Television Systems Committee): In use in the United States, Canada, Mexico, and Japan

Number of scan lines per frame: 525

Number of frames per second: 30

Luminance signal:

$$E_Y = 0.30E_R + 0.59E_G + 0.11E_B \qquad (15.4.1)$$

where E_R, E_G, and E_B are red, green, and blue signals, respectively

Component signals:

$$E_I = \left[(E_R - E_Y)\frac{\cos 33°}{1.14} \right] - \left[(E_B - E_Y)\frac{\sin 33°}{2.03} \right] \qquad (15.4.2)$$

$$E_Q = \left[(E_R - E_Y)\frac{\sin 33°}{1.14} \right] + \left[(E_B - E_Y)\frac{\cos 33°}{2.03} \right] \qquad (15.4.3)$$

Subcarrier frequency: 3.58 MHz (both component signals are modulated on it 90° out of phase)

PAL (Phase Alternation Line): In use in Great Britain, Brazil, and most of continental Europe

Number of scan lines per frame: 625

Number of frames per second: 25

Luminance signal: Same as NTSC

Component signals:

$$U = \frac{(E_B - E_Y)}{2.03} \qquad (15.4.4)$$

$$V = \frac{(E_R - E_Y)}{1.14} \qquad (15.4.5)$$

Subcarrier frequency: 4.43 MHz (both component signals transmitted 90° out of phase)

SECAM   (Sequentiel Couleur avec Memoire or Sequential Color with Memory): In use in France, the Soviet Union, and the Middle East

Number of scan lines per frame: 625/819

Number of frames per second: 25

Luminance signal: Same as NTSC

Component signals: Same as PAL

Subcarrier frequencies: 4.25 MHz for U signal
4.41 MHz for V signal

As these characteristics show, the three systems are similar in signal structure (if not in detail) by virtue of the fact that each has one luminance and two component signals. The combination of all these signals, which is actually transmitted, is called the composite signal in each case.

There are basically two approaches to compressing color information: component signal coding and composite signal coding.

In *component signal coding* we separately code, or compress, the luminance and color component signals. Both DPCM and transformation techniques have been applied to this task and some of the results are as follows (for the NTSC system):

DPCM: Luminance—12 levels

          I—6   levels

          Q—4   levels

          (See Limb et al. 1971)

Transform coding: Luminance (by principal component): 1.0 bit/pixel
Chrominance (by Hadamard): 0.75 bit/pixel
(See Pratt 1971)

In *composite signal coding*, it is important first to sample the composite signal at some multiple of the component subcarrier frequency. This is necessary to avoid intermodulation effects beween the sampling frequency and the subcarrier frequency. Having done this, the same compression technique can be applied to the digital representation of the Y, I, and Q signals. DPCM and transformation techniques have been used for this compression also.

A recent example of composite coding is the NETEC-22H television compression system made by Nippon Electric Co., Japan. This system compresses the NTSC composite color signal by first sampling at twice the subcarrier frequency and then applying DPCM on a frame-to-frame basis, followed by a block-to-variable length code for the differences. This produces a transmission rate in the range of 16 to 32 Mbps as compared to an uncompressed rate of 88 Mbps (Ishiguro et al. 1976).

Prabhu and Netravali (1983) have recently analyzed the problem of motion compensation of composite color coding and found that it is not as efficient as motion compensation in the component domain.

15.5 REMOTELY PILOTED VEHICLE (RPV) TV COMPRESSION

Remotely piloted vehicles (RPVs) use some form of television to "see" the remote terrain, processing the pictures on-board or sending them back to the control site. This transmission back to the control site requires a narrower bandwidth than broadcast television for a number of reasons, not the least of which is the need to avoid interference from "jamming."

The techniques used to compress RPV TV usually follow a cascaded approach, namely frame deletion followed by intraframe compression. In the systems developed for the U.S. Department of Defense, reported by Camana (1979), the frame rate is reduced from 30 frames per sec to 7.5 frames per sec by one of two methods: frame grabbing or frame sampling. Frame grabbing, as described in Section 15.3.6, involves storing an entire "saved" frame and then skipping some number of frames (in this case, the next three). Frame sampling, by contrast, involves taking a subset of pixels from consecutive frames and storing them to form a "saved" frame. An example of this is the GE SAMPLE-DOT system described in Section 15.3.5. The intraframe compression that is applied to the "saved" frame is usually some linear transform or predictive coding technique, namely, DPCM or delta modulation.

A variation of delta modulation (actually continuously variable slope delta modulation, or CVSDM) has been developed for RPV applications. This is called constant area quantization (CAQ) as described by Arnold and Cavenor (1981). CAQ is really a fast-acting adaptive delta modulation technique that tests the current value of the input signal against the previous value of the reconstructed signal. If the difference of these two signals lies outside a threshold of $\pm A$, then a step of amplitude $\pm A$ is added to the new reconstructed signal for comparison with the next value of the input signal. If the difference lies inside the $\pm A$ threshold, then a step of $\pm\frac{1}{2}A$ is added and the process repeated. This adaptive scheme has the advantage of being able to detect and compensate for large changes in input signal values in only one or two sample periods.

A number of U.S. companies have developed experimental compression schemes for RPV TV. For example, the system developed by RCA, as reported by Camana (1979), has the following characteristics:

Input video: 256×256 pixels

Frame sample: $\frac{1}{8}$ of a field (32×256 pixels)

Intraframe coding for each frame sample:
First: Discrete cosine transform applied to each 32-pixel line
Second: DPCM applied to DCT coefficients line to line

Bits per pixel for saved frames: 0.75–2.0 bits per pixel

15.6 TELECONFERENCING TV COMPRESSION

One of the fastest growing application areas for television is *teleconferencing*. For obvious reasons, considerable time and money can be saved through tele-conferencing by two-way television. There has been a great interest in develop-ing techniques to compress the bandwidth or, equivalently, the bit rate required to transmit teleconference video, and now some systems are in actual operation. The *AT&T* PICTUREPHONE *Meeting Service* started commercial service between New York and Washington in 1982, and this is to be expanded to about 40 cities in the United States (see London 1981). It uses the NETEC-6/3 TV processor produced by Nippon Electric Company; a description of this system follows.

The NETEC-6/3 TV processor uses interframe coding of the frame replen-ishment type, which was described in Section 15.3.2, as well as composite signal chrominance compression which was described in Section 15.4. Since the frame-to-frame differences vary in data rate and volume, they are fed into a buffer, which requires overflow control. This overflow control operates in stages, as follows:

1. When the buffer is at its lowest level, the difference quantizer is switched to the finest step size to increase the signal-to-quantization noise ratio.

2. As the buffer fills, the quantization is made coarse so as to prevent buffer overflow.

3. When buffer occupancy reaches a first predetermined level, every other field is transmitted, thus halving the buffer input rate.

4. When buffer occupancy reaches a second predetermined level, pixel subsampling takes place in which every other pixel is deleted.

5. If the buffer continues to fill and reaches its capacity, all encoding is stopped until the buffer goes down to its lowest level. Meanwhile, at the receiver, the same picture is repeated until a new frame difference is sent.

As can be seen from this control procedure, as the picture motion increases, the picture quality gradually decreases. At 6 Mbps, a teleconferencing scene with minimal motion of subjects can be handled with the quantization control of the buffer. At 3 Mbps, quantization control is used continuously, and with large motion, field repeating must be used, causing some picture jerkiness. When the TV camera is panned or when cameras are switched, subsampling and frame repetition take place, which creates more jerkiness and distortion (Kaneko and Ishiguro 1980).

The new NEC TV processor operates at 1.5 Mbps and uses motion compensation as described in Section 15.3.2. A scheme described by Ishiguro and Iinuma (1982) is said to give the same picture quality at 1.5 Mbps that the frame replenishment types give at 3 Mbps.

Other companies also manufacture TV compression systems for teleconferencing applications (Brody 1983). GEC McMichael of Stoke Poges, Slough, England, has produced interframe codecs under contract to British Telecom for eventual use in a European teleconferencing network. Compression Labs. Inc. (CLI) of San Jose, California, produces a 1.5 Mbps intraframe codec that uses transform coding (cosine transform with threshold and spatial bit allocation).

At the present time, the 1.5 Mbps codecs are easy to integrate into a communication system since they match the rate of the T1 channel. But what about the future? Will we stop at 1.5 Mbps? There are indications that the rate will go lower. CLI is developing a new codec that will combine interframe and intraframe coding to operate down to 384 kbps. NEC; Widcom Corp. of San Jose, California; and Bell Northern Research (Montreal) are all working on 56 kbps codecs.

15.7 VIDEOTEX/TELETEXT COMPRESSION

Videotex and teletext are usually cited together (as in the section title) even though they are basically different systems. The one feature they have in common is that they both provide a still picture display on a home TV receiver, which picture can be selected by the home viewer. But in each case this is done quite differently.

In the case of *videotex*, the user makes a picture selection from a numerically coded index and enters it on a keyboard or keypad; from here it is transmitted over a telephone line to a central facility. The central facility accesses the picture and sends it back to the user over the same telephone line for decoding and display on the user's TV screen.

Teletext systems store the user's request in a special decoder at the TV set, which then displays the proper frame, coded in the vertical blanking interval, on the TV screen.

Teletext usually displays black-and-white or color graphics pictures, with each picture coded into a raster-format set of digital words. Each word has two parts: the first part indicates the character and the second part indicates the attribute of the character. Typical attributes are color, size, and display mode (blinking versus constant). Videotex uses the same approach in coding graphics. In both videotex and teletext there is a need to compress this coding. In one method, which is used in Canada's TELIDON system, the characters are coded with graphics building-block shapes such as arcs and lines.

A number of videotex systems are now in place that transmit text and graphics over telephone lines to home TV receivers. In England the system is called PRESTEL; in Germany, BILDSHIRMTEXT; in France, TELETEL; in Canada, TELIDON; and in the United States, NAPLPS.*

In one version of the PRESTEL system, called PICTURE PRESTEL, a color photograph is converted to a TV image by a TV camera, and the luminance and chrominance components are compressed (by a transformation) before storage in a central data base. When a picture is requested by a receiver, the compressed picture is sent over the telephone line to a special TV decoder, which reconstructs the original luminance and chrominance components from the compressed signal and stores them in a 24K memory (16K for luminance, 4K each for the two chrominance signals). The picture is slowly formed on the TV screen, taking about 10 sec to build to full resolution.

15.8 HIGH-DEFINITION TV COMPRESSION

High-definition television (HDTV) is proposed for the future—perhaps by 1990. It will provide a color TV image on a screen that will compare closely in quality to that of a 35mm color movie.

Experimental work on HDTV in Japan (Fujio 1980) has resulted in a developmental system with 1125 scanning lines per frame, an aspect ratio of 5:3 (as compared to the NTSC standard of 4:3), a 2:1 field interlace, 30 frames per second, modified PAL color modulation, and a video bandwidth of 27 MHz.

If an HDTV system such as this is used to transmit signals over coaxial cables or fiberoptic links, then compression may not be necessary. However, if the transmission is from a ground-based antenna or from a direct-broadcast satellite, then some form of compression is required to reduce the bandwidth so that the available bandwidth may be more effectively utilized. In particular, if the HDTV transmission system is made all digital, then compression is essential since the uncompressed bit rates could be as high as 500 Mbps. A DPCM system with 4 bits for the luminance signal and 3 bits each for the chrominance signals could theoretically reduce the bit rate to about 200 Mbps (Fujio 1980).

---

* NAPLPS stands for North American Presentation Level Protocol Syntax. This system was developed by AT&T and is based on Canada's TELIDON system.

HIGHLIGHTS

- Television compression involves both interframe and intraframe coding, and some distortion is tolerable since the receiver is the human observer.
- The more general compression techniques for black-and-white, or monochrome, video compression are two- and three-dimensional transform coding and several of the predictive coding techniques.
- The more TV-unique compression techniques are slant transform, pseudorandom techniques (dithering and pseudorandom scanning), and slow-scan techniques.
- Compression of color video involves compression of luminance (monochrome) information and color information; component signal coding and composite signal coding are two approaches to color information compression.
- Applications for television compression include TV for remotely piloted vehicles (RPVs) and teleconferencing, and for transmitting text and graphics over telephone lines to home TV receivers (videotex or teletext).
- High-definition television (HDTV), which will provide a high-quality color image, may also require television compression.

SUGGESTIONS FOR FURTHER READING

The following items are suggested for further reading and study:

Arnold, J. F., and Cavenor, M. C. "Improvements to the Constant Area Quantization Bandwidth Compression Scheme." *IEEE Trans. on Comm.*, vol. COM-29, no. 12, December 1981, pp. 1818–1823.

An improved version of the adaptive delta modulator called the constant area quantizer (CAQ) is given.

Barba, J., Scheinberg, N., Schilling, D. L., Garodnick, J., and Davidovici, S. "A Modified Adaptive Delta Modulator." *IEEE Trans. on Comm.*, vol. COM-29, no. 12, December 1981, pp. 1767–1785.

This paper presents a modification to the Song algorithms for delta modulation, utilizing a recognizable code for nonchanging or slowly changing sequences.

Brody, H. "Reach Out and See Someone." *High Technology*, August 1983, pp. 53–59.

The present situation in teleconferencing technology, and a prognosis for the future is given, especially the future of video compression.

Camana, P. "Video Bandwidth Compression: A Study in Tradeoffs." *IEEE Spectrum*, June 1979, pp. 24–29.

A survey of RPV television compression techniques and actual experimental systems are given.

Candy, J. C., and Bosworth, R. H. "Methods for Designing Differential Quantizers Based on Subjective Evaluations of Edge Busyness." *Bell System Technical J.*, vol. 51, no. 7, 1972, pp. 1495–1516.

A method of relating the edge busyness to signal slope is developed.

Deutsch, S. "Visual Displays Using Pseudorandom Dot Scan." *IEEE Trans. on Comm.*, vol. COM-22, January 1973, pp. 65–72.

The concept of using a pseudorandom dot scan instead of a linear raster scan is described for the purpose of high video compression.

Enomoto, H., and Shibata, K. "Orthogonal Transform Coding System for Television Signals." *IEEE Trans. Electromag. Compat.*, vol. EMC-13, August 1971, pp. 11–17.

The slant transform is introduced and described as a transformation particularly efficient for television compression.

Fujio, T. "High Definition Wide Screen Television System for the Future." *IEEE Trans. on Broadcasting*, vol. BC-26, no. 4, December 1980, pp. 113–124.

A description of an experimental 1125-line high-definition TV system is given, along with estimates for digital compression.

Habibi, A. "Comparison of nth-Order DPCM Encoder with Linear Transformations and Block Quantization Techniques." *IEEE Trans. on Comm. Tech.*, vol. COM-19, no. 6, December 1971, pp. 948–956.

DPCM is compared to Hadamard, Fourier, and principal component in the compression of monochrome still pictures.

Habibi, A. "Hybrid Coding of Pictorial Data." *IEEE Trans. on Comm.*, vol. COM-32, no. 5, May 1974, pp. 614–624.

One- and two-dimensional combinations of a transformation (Hadamard, Fourier, cosine, slant, and principal component) and DPCM are described.

Haskell, B. G., Gorden, P. L., Schmidt, R. L., and Scattaglia, J. V. "Interframe Coding of 525-line, Monochrome Television at 1.5 M bits/s," *IEEE Trans. on Comm.*, vol. COM-25, no. 11, November 1977, pp. 1339–1348.

In this paper, a conditional replenishment interframe coder is simulated to provide a 1.5 megabits per second rate.

Haskell, B. G., Mounts, F. W., and Candy, J. C. "Interframe Coding of Videotelephone Pictures." *Proc. of the IEEE.*, vol. 60, no. 7, July 1972, pp. 792–800.

Interframe coding by the method of frame replenishment is described.

Ishiguro, T., and Iinuma, K. "Television Bandwidth Compression Transmission by Motion-Compensated Interframe Coding." *IEEE Communications Magazine*, November 1982, pp. 24–30.

A review of interframe coding, especially using motion compensation, is given.

Ishiguro, T., Iinuma, K., Iijima, Y., Koga, T., Azami, S., and Mune, T. "Composite Interframe Coding of NTSC Color Television Signals." National Telemetering Conference, 1976, pp. 6:4-1–6:4-5.

An interframe TV coder, the NETEC-22H, is described that compresses digital color TV down to the range of 16–32 Mbps.

Jain, A. K. "Image Data Compression: A Review." *Proc. of the IEEE*, vol. 69, no. 3, March 1981, pp. 349–389.

A very comprehensive survey of image compression techniques, including video, with an extensive bibiliography.

Kaneko, H., and Ishiguro, T. "Digital Television Transmission Using Bandwidth Compression Techniques." *IEEE Communications Magazine*, July 1980, pp. 14–22.
A description of the NETEC-6/3 TV interframe coder is given.

Knauer, S. C. "Real-Time Video Compression Algorithm for Hadamard Transformation Processing." *IEEE Trans. on Electromagnetic Compatibility*, vol. EMC-18, no. 1, February 1976, pp. 28–36.
A three-dimensional Hadamard transform is applied to monochrome video for compression.

Limb, J. O., Rubinstein, C. B., and Thompson, J. E. "Digital Coding of Color Video Signals—A Review." *IEEE Trans. on Comm.*, vol. COM-25, no. 11, November 1977, pp. 1349–1385.
This is a very comprehensive review of the compression of color signals in color television, with an extensive list of references.

Limb, J. O., Rubinstein, C. B., and Walsh, K. A. "Digital Coding of Color PICTUREPHONE Signals by Element-Differential Quantization." *IEEE Trans. on Comm. Tech.*, vol. COM-19, December 1971, pp. 992–1006.
In this article, DPCM with previous pixel prediction is used with a 6-level quantizer for the *I* signal and a 4-level quantizer for the *Q* signal.

London, H. S. "A Description of the A. T. & T Video Teleconferencing System." *Proc. of the National Telemetering Conference*, vol. 3, November 1981, pp. F5.4.1–F5.4.5.
A brief description of this TV teleconferencing system, which utilizes a modified NETEC-6/3 interframe TV compressor, is given.

Millard, J. B., and Maunsall, H. I. "The PICTUREPHONE System: Digital Encoding of the Video Signal." *Bell System Technical J.*, February 1971, pp. 459–479.
The DPCM system that was utilized in the prototype PICTUREPHONE System is described. It allowed transmission over a 6.312 Mbps digital channel.

Musmann, H. G. "Predictive Image Coding." In *Image Transmission Techniques*, edited by W. K. Pratt. New York: Academic Press, 1979.
A good review of predictive coding techniques (especially DPCM) with an emphasis on color TV.

Netravali, A., and Prasada, B. "Adaptive Quantization of Picture Signals Using Spatial Masking." *Proc. IEEE*, vol. 65, April 1977, pp. 536–548.
The spatial masking imposed by neighboring pixels was investigated in this article to better define the maximum allowable quantizing noise that can be tolerated by human vision.

Netravali, A. N., and Robbins, J. D. "Motion Compensated Television Coding: Part I." *Bell System Technical J.*, vol. 58, no. 3, March 1979, pp. 631–670.
Interframe coding by motion compensation is described.

Ohira, T., Hayakawa, M., and Matsumoto, K. "Orthogonal Transform Coding System for NTSC Color Television Signal." Proceedings of the I.C.C., 1977, Part 4B, pp. 3–86 to 3–90.
This paper describes the use of the slant transform to compress NTSC color TV from 8 bits per pel to 3 bits per pel and 2.25 bits per pel.

Prabhu, K. A., and Netravali, A. N. "Motion Compensated Composite Color Coding." *IEEE Trans. on Comm.*, vol. COM-31, no. 2, February 1983, pp. 216–223.

This investigation concluded that motion compensation in the composite domain is not as efficient as motion compensation in the component domain.

Pratt, W. K. "Spatial Transform Coding of Color Images." *IEEE Trans. on Comm. Tech.*, vol. COM-19, December 1971, pp. 980–992.

This article describes how Fourier, Hadamard, and principal component transformations were used to compress the luminance and chrominance signals of NTSC color television.

Pratt, W. K., Welch, L. R., and Chen, W. "Slant Transforms for Image Coding." *Applications of Walsh Functions Symposium Proceedings*, Washington, D.C., March 1972, pp. 229–234.

In this article, the original slant transform is extended to larger blocks, and a comparison is made to the Hadamard transformation.

Roberts, L. G. "Picture Coding Using Pseudo-Random Noise." *IRE Trans. on Info. Theory*, vol. IT-8, February 1962, pp. 145–154.

In this paper, the idea of adding noise before quantization and subtracting it after digital-to-analog conversion in order to reduce the effect of "contouring" is introduced.

Schreiber, W. F. "The Measurement of Third Order Probability Distributions of Television Signals." *IRE Trans. on Info. Theory*, vol. IT-2, September 1956, pp. 94–105.

This paper contains entropy measurements for a single scene or frame of television using an independent model and a first-order and second-order Markov source model.

Southworth, G. "Single Frame Digital Television Transmission." National Telemetering Conference, 1977, pp. 41:3-1–41:3-2.

The techniques of slow-scan TV compression are discussed.

Spencer, D. J. "VIDAP: A Real-Time Video Data Compressor." *SPIE*, August 1979.

A description of a hardware video compressor utilizing a Hadamard transform on a chip is given.

Stone, R. F. "A Practical Narrow-Band Television System: SAMPLEDOT." *IEEE Trans. on Broadcasting*, vol. BC-22, no. 2, June 1976, pp. 21–32.

This article describes how a compression of up to 10:1 can be achieved with this GE system, which is based on the pseudorandom dot scan technique of Deutsch (1973).

Thompson, J. E. "A 36-Mbps Television Codec Employing Pseudorandom Quantization." *IEEE Trans. on Comm. Tech.*, vol. COM-19, no. 6, December 1971, pp. 872–879.

In this article, the technique of pseudorandom quantization is applied to 625-line monochrome TV pictures using a 3-bit quantizer.

CHAPTER 16

Picture Compression

16.1 INTRODUCTION

Picture compression means many things to many people. In the literature, it is often called "picture coding," and in many cases it means the coding of still pictures as well as television pictures. In this chapter, we define a "picture" to be a *still* picture that is to be transmitted by means of a system other than television, such as facsimile. Television compression, including single-frame television compression, was covered in Chapter 15.

There are basically two types of still pictures to be compressed: *two-level* and *multilevel*. A two-level picture is often called a "black-and-white" picture or simply "graphics," whereas a multilevel picture is usually called a "gray-scale" picture. In the digital domain, there is a fundamental relationship between two-level or binary pictures and multilevel pictures. If we represent each pixel (picture element) of a multilevel picture by means by a k-bit binary code word, then we can decompose this digital picture into k-images, each having only two levels. Each two-level or 1-bit image is referred to as a *bit plane*, and one can think of an ordering of these bit-plane images from most significant (bit) to least significant (bit) plane, as shown in Figure 16.1 An obvious advantage of this decomposition is that whatever techniques are available for compressing two-level pictures can now be applied to a gray-level picture, 1 bit-plane at a time.

In the rest of this chapter we show examples of both two-level and multilevel picture compression.

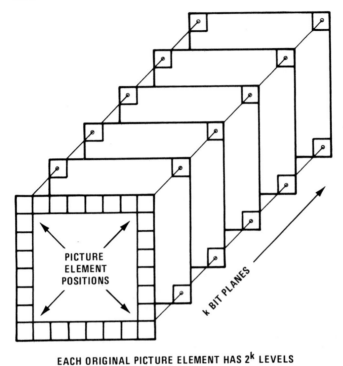

PICTURE
ELEMENT
POSITIONS

k BIT PLANES

EACH ORIGINAL PICTURE ELEMENT HAS 2^k LEVELS

Figure 16.1 *Decomposition of a Gray-Level Image Into Two-Level Bit Planes.*

16.2 TWO-LEVEL PICTURE COMPRESSION

A two-level, or binary, picture can be coded with 1s and 0s, and thus it constitutes a special source with a maximum entropy of 1 bit. But this maximum entropy is reached only when the probability of a 1 is equal to the probability of a 0 (see Section 3.3). Most two-level pictures do not have equiprobable levels, and this is why they are *compressible*. Most text, line drawings, and data plots (such as a weather chart) have a much higher probability for a white pixel than a black pixel. Because of this less than maximum entropy, a number of compression algorithms have been applied to two-level pictures, and we look at some of these, as well as at an interesting application in the publishing industry.

16.2.1 Two-Level Facsimile Compression

There has been an interest in compressing two-level facsimile for many years, from the standpoint of both transmission bandwidth *and* transmission time. At first, the approach was to compress a line at a time, and since within each line there are alternating black runs and white runs, run-length coding was used. There is a direct analogy here to the time coding problem discussed in Chapter 8. In Chapter 8, we identified two types of symbols for time coding: nonredundant and redundant. In the data model used in that chapter, each block, frame, or line contained alternating runs of nonredundant (n) and redundant (r) symbols—hence the analogy to two-level facsimile. In Chapter 8 also, three basic methods of coding the alternating n and r runs were identified:

1. Send the *n-r* sequence
2. Send the time of each n sample
3. Send the length of each n and r run

Historically, the trend in two-level facsimile coding has been along the lines of the *third* method: that is, send the length of each black and each white run. Not surprisingly, the *Huffman code* was found to be the most efficient for this purpose, as it was in Chapter 8. A practical variable-length, run-length code was developed by Musmann and Preuss in 1973.

Since facsimile images have two-dimensional redundancy, various schemes of two-dimensional coding were developed, most of these operating on *two* adjacent scan lines at a time. The simplest approach, is to encode the first line of an image and then to encode the line-to-line differences from then on (Huang 1972). In 1975 Preuss developed a two-dimensional code based on a Markov model. This code has been referred to as the TUH code in the literature since Preuss was at the Technische Universität of Hannover. In 1977 Musmann and Preuss compared six codes for the compression of two-level facsimile: three for one-dimensional and three for two-dimensional coding.

A significant development has occurred in two-level facsimile compression over time, and that is *standardization*. Facsimile was used by many different countries for many years, and as systems developed, the need for international standards became obvious if different countries were to communicate with one another. The standardization activity has been under the auspices of the International Telegraph and Telephone Consultative Committee (CCITT). All facsimile equipment now is classified by CCITT into one of three groups:

Group 1. Analog, 6-minute transmission for an A-4 size page (8.27″ × 11.69″)

Group 2. Analog, 3-minute transmission for an A-4 size page

Group 3. Digital, 1-minute transmission for an A-4 size page

The standardization for compression is for group 3, and there are now two recommended standards (Hunter and Robinson 1980) for compression:

1. One-dimensional: Modified run-length Huffman code
2. Two-dimensional: Relative element address designate (READ) code

The modified Huffman code is based on the run-length statistics of many types of documents, including typewritten pages in different languages (including Japanese), line drawings, and handwriting. There are separate Huffman codes for black runs and white runs because of their different statistics, and every run is broken up into two parts, as follows. Since each line is 1728 pixels in an A-4 size document page, the first part of the code refers to the part of the run that is a multiple of 64 pixels—it is the multiple integer. The second part of the code is the difference between the run length and the integral multiple of 64. This difference is, of course, between 0 and 63 pixels. With this segmented approach to run-length coding, measurements have shown that the code efficiency is *not* too sensitive to changes in the image statistics.

The relative element address designate (READ) code takes advantage of the two-dimensional redundancy in the facsimile image. This scheme codes the position of each changing pixel in a scan line relative to either the position of a corresponding changing pixel on the previous scan line or with respect to the preceding changing element on the same line. There is a "K factor" associated with this code that is used as follows. In order to prevent error propagation from line to line, no more than $K - 1$ successive lines are two-dimensionally coded, and the next line is one-dimensionally coded. The coding procedure for the READ code covers a number of different arrangements of black and white runs on the two adjacent lines. For a detailed description of the code, see Hunter and Robinson (1980).

The READ code is actually an outgrowth of two previous two-level facsimile two-dimensional codes—the relative address code (RAC) and the edge difference code (EDIC), both of which can be looked upon as modified versions of the predictive differential quantization (PDQ) code of Huang (1972). The RAC (Yamazaki et al. 1976) codes distances between changing pixels on two adjacent lines, and the EDIC (Yamada 1979) codes positions of changing pixels on two adjacent lines as a function of the *locations* of these changing pixels.

16.2.2 Newspaper Compression

Another type of two-level picture that is actually compressed today is the page master for a newspaper printing system. If a newspaper has a nationwide, as opposed to a local, circulation, then it may be cost-effective to do the printing and distribution from a number of regional centers throughout the country. Each printing center needs the page masters in a timely fashion in order to produce the daily edition at the optimum time for distribution. A star configuration network is needed to tie the regional centers to the central location where the page masters are made up.

This has been done, using a communications satellite, for the *Wall Street Journal*, for example. The *Wall Street Journal* system was put into operation in 1975, and uses two-level picture compression.

To begin with, the page masters contain black-and-white graphics (print, line figures, and so on) as well as half-tone images of photographs or artwork. These half-tone images are each made of a matrix of black dots on a white background, with the width of each black dot a function of the gray level of the image at that location. Half-tone images, then, even though they appear to be gray-scale pictures when viewed from a reasonably far distance, are really two-level pictures and can be compressed as such. The half-tone matrix dot density (called the screen function) is typically 120 cells per inch, and a typical sampling rate for digitizing half-tone pictures is about 1000–1200 samples per inch (Stoffel and Moreland 1981). In the case of newspaper page masters, the entire page is sampled at this rate, so that the digitized image is a set of scan lines containing white runs and black runs, as in the case of two-level facsimile. However, this sampling rate for page masters is approximately ten times the normal sampling rate for two-level facsimile. The *Wall Street Journal* system uses a form of run-length coding and achieves a compression ratio of about 5:1 over a 1.5 Mbps link (Cacciamani and Jenkins 1976).

16.3 MULTILEVEL PICTURE COMPRESSION

In many situations a multilevel (gray-scale) picture has to be stored or transmitted in digital form. Due to the bandwidth expansion effect caused by the digitization, some form of compression is usually required to allow the picture to be handled by the communications link or by the storage and retrieval system in use. Some examples of such pictures are:

Multilevel facsimile

Multilevel computer graphics

Aerial photographs

Multispectral images

Microscopic images

X-ray images

In this section we look at three of these: multispectral images, x-ray images, and multilevel facsimile.

16.3.1 Multispectral Image Compression

In studying the earth's surface and atmosphere from aircraft or satellites, instruments called radiometers are used that, in effect, create a multispectral image, usually in a raster-scan format. Each image set consists of multiple versions of the same picture, but in different spectral bands. This image is a three-dimensional data set, just as is television, where the frame rate provides the third dimension. And just as there is correlation from frame to frame in television, so there is correlation from band to band in a multispectral image, and it is this correlation that lends itself to compression.

We can apply the concept of concatenated compression, such as hybrid coding, as described in Chapter 15, to the multispectral image, as shown conceptually in Figure 16.2. In this schematic representation, the multispectral image data set is depicted as a three-dimensional box. This box has the following dimensions:

Horizontal: along-scan direction

Vertical: cross-scan direction

Into the page: spectral direction

As shown in this figure, we could start with a compression in the spectral direction, then a compression in the along-scan direction in each of the compressed spectral bands, followed by a compression in the cross-scan direction, and complete the process with block-to-variable-length coding (such as Huffman) of each compressed pixel. Starting with compression in the spectral direction has been found to be most efficient, as reported by Moik (1980) in his book on multispectral image processing. Two efficient concatenated schemes, according to Moik, are as follows:

CONCATENATION 1

Spectral: Principal component

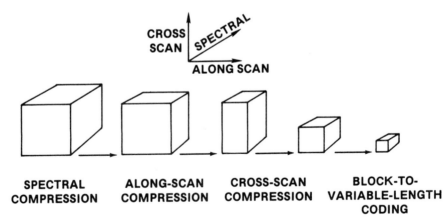

SPECTRAL COMPRESSION   **ALONG-SCAN COMPRESSION**   **CROSS-SCAN COMPRESSION**   **BLOCK-TO-VARIABLE-LENGTH CODING**

Figure 16.2 *Example of Compression in Three Dimensions: Multispectral Image Compression.*

Along-scan: Cosine

Cross-scan: DPCM

CONCATENATION 2

Spectral: Principal component

$$\left.\begin{array}{l}\text{Along-scan:}\\\text{Cross-scan:}\end{array}\right\}\text{Two-dimensional DPCM}$$

There are other techniques of compressing multispectral images besides concatenation. One of these is called *multispectral cluster coding*. To understand multispectral cluster coding we must understand the concept of clustering. Think of each pixel of the multispectral image as an n-dimensional vector. Each vector component corresponds to a spectral band and each pixel can be thought of as a point in n-dimensional space. The clustering process creates boundaries in n-dimensional space that separate "clusters" of vectors according to a predefined statistical hypothesis test. The number of clusters is usually fixed beforehand, and two quantities are developed as a result of the clustering process: the mean position or *centroid* of each cluster in n-dimensional space and the *variance* of each cluster with respect to each dimension.

Multispectral cluster coding, as described by Hilbert (1975), creates a "feature map" that is simply an image made up of labeled pixels. Each pixel is labeled according to which cluster its original n-dimensional vector fits into. Figure 16.3 is a representation of clustering in two dimensions. By means of multispectral cluster coding, the n dimensions are collapsed into one dimension and the resulting digital image has pixels with a smaller number of possible values than the original pixels. Such an image can be further compressed (by run-length coding, for example). The individual pixels do indeed lose their n-dimensional resolution; however, there are some applications in which the feature-map representation (usually in terms of the position of the centroid of each cluster in n-dimensional space) is sufficient. An example of this is multispectral image classification in which each pixel is classified into one of m classes based on its spectral components, or spectral "signature." In this particular application, the clustering operation can act as a preclassifier, which can have the effect of speeding up the classification operation.

16.3.2 X-Ray Image Compression

An x-ray image, when digitized, represents a large data set to transmit or to store. A typical 14-x-17-inch x-ray picture scanned at 250 lines per inch, with each pixel quantized to 256 levels constitutes approximately 10^8 bits. The time needed to transmit this picture (with overhead) is approximately 40 minutes at

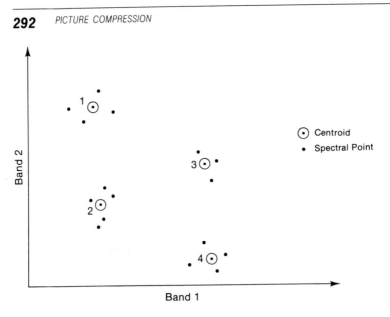

a. Centroid Location for Four Clusters

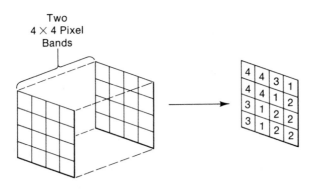

b. Two Bands Collapse to One Feature Band

Figure 16.3   *The Concept of Multispectral Clustering in Two Dimensions.*

50 kbps and 2 minutes at 1 Mbps. So there is a growing interest in compressing this type of imagery once it is digitized.

Some experiments were performed by Kunt in 1978 using four different x-ray images and three compression algorithms. Following are the compression algorithms he used and the resulting average compression ratios:

1. The *synthetic highs* technique, introduced by Schreiber et al. (1959) and further developed by Graham (1967), divides the original digitized picture into

two parts: a low-pass picture and a high-pass picture. The low-pass picture is coded with fewer bits per sample (typically 6 instead of 8) and sampled at a reduced rate (typically with a reduction factor of 8:1). The high-pass picture contains information about the significant contours or edges in the picture that is obtained by a gradient technique. (The gradient is the rate of change of pixel intensity with respect to different directions within the picture.) The contour information appears as: contour direction changes, gradient direction changes, and gradient magnitude. Each parameter is coded using a Huffman code. This method of synthetic highs produced an average compression ratio of 7:1, but it did require a large amount of computation to extract the contour information.

   2. *Block coding* was used on the bit planes of the picture and three types of blocks were coded:

     a. All zeros—coded as a "0"

     b. All ones—coded as "11"

     c. Ones and zeros—coded as "10," followed by the actual sequence of ones and zeros line by line

This coding scheme is illustrated in Figure 16.4. Kunt found that a square block with $n = 4$ yielded a compression ratio in the range of 2:1 to 3:1 with no information loss.

   3. *Run-length coding* was applied to the bit planes of the picture and an average compression ratio of 1.8:1 was obtained.

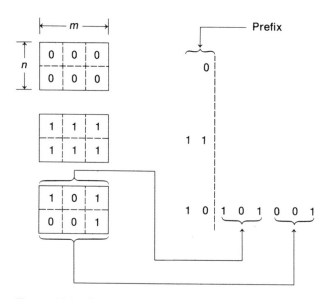

Figure 16.4   *Two-Level n × m Block Coding. From: Kunt, M. "Source Coding of X-Ray Pictures," IEEE Trans. on Biomedical Engineering vol. BME-25, no. 2, March 1978, p. 124. © 1978 IEEE.*

For both the block coding and the run-length coding, the pixels were first *Gray coded* before being broken down into bit planes. A Gray code is similar to a pure binary code except that the ones and zeros are arranged so that only *one change* (a "1" to a "0" or vice versa) takes place in moving from one code word to the next. The Gray code has the effect of making the areas of equal intensity in the bit planes *larger* than those in the pure binary code. This leads to more efficient block or run-length coding.

16.3.3 Multilevel Facsimile

Recently, a scheme has been suggested (Gharavi and Netravali 1983) for compressing a facsimile image containing both two-level and multilevel material. Instead of sampling the entire image at a high rate, as is the case in newspaper compression (see Section 16.2.2), the image is segmented into gray areas and two-level areas before coding. The gray areas are coded using DPCM, and the binary output of the DPCM quantizer is mixed in with the binary image areas to be all coded by one of the recommended CCITT codes.

HIGHLIGHTS

- Picture compression, or picture coding, generally refers to the coding of still pictures. Two basic types of still pictures are two-level (or "black-and-white" or "graphics") and multilevel (or "gray-scale").

- Two-level, pictures that are compressed include facsimile (using modified Huffman and READ codes) and newspapers (using run-length codes).

- Examples of multilevel pictures that are compressed are multispectral images (such as those created by radiometers used to study the earth's surface and atmosphere), x-ray images, and multilevel facsimile images which include two-level and multilevel material).

SUGGESTIONS FOR FURTHER READING

The following items are suggested for further reading and study:

Arps, R. B. "Bibliography on Binary Image Compression." *Proc. of the IEEE*, vol. 68, no. 7, July 1980, pp. 922–924.
    This is an update by Arps of his 1974 bibliography.

Arps, R. B. "Bibliography on Digital Graphic Image Compression and Quality." *IEEE Trans. on Info. Theory*, vol. IT-20, no. 1, January 1974, pp. 120–122.

This is a bibliography on two-level image compression.

Cacciamani, E. R., and Jenkins, G. C. "Wall Street Journal Via Satellite." *EASCON*, 1976, pp. 103.A–103.F.

This paper describes the initiation of direct broadcast of newspaper masters to remote printing centers via satellite in 1975. With the use of data compression, one page of the *Wall Street Journal* is transmitted in 1 minute.

Gharavi, H., and Netravali, A. N. "CCITT Compatible Coding of Multilevel Pictures." *BSTJ*, vol. 62, no. 9, November 1983, pp. 2765–2778.

A facsimile image is segmented into gray-level regions and two-level regions and then CCITT coded after the gray-level regions have been DPCM coded.

Graham, D. N. "Image Transmission by Two-Dimensional Contour Coding." *Proc. of the IEEE*, vol. 55, no. 3, March 1967, pp. 336–346.

Graham extended the "synthetic highs" concept to an all-digital system with two-dimensional coding of the edges derived by gradient analysis.

Hilbert, E. E. "Joint Classification and Data Compression of Multidimensional Information Sources—Application to ERTS." *International Conf. on Comm.*, vol. II, June 1975.

Hilbert describes the method of multispectral cluster coding in which individual multispectral pixels are first represented by their cluster centroids in n-dimensional space, and then the resulting "feature map" is spatially compressed.

Huang, T. S. "Run Length Coding and Its Extensions." In *Picture Bandwidth Compression*, edited by T. S. Huang and C. J. Tretiak. New York: Gordon and Breach Science Pub., 1972, pp. 231–264.

Huang introduces the concept of coding the differences between corresponding run lengths on consecutive scan lines of a two-level picture. This technique is called predictive differential quantizing (PDQ).

Hunter, R., and Robinson, A. H. "International Digital Facsimile Coding Standards." *Proc. of the IEEE*, vol. 68, no. 7, July 1980, pp. 854–867.

This paper describes in detail the one-dimensional modified Huffman code adopted by CCITT in 1977 for digital facsimile, as well as the two-dimensional relative element address designate (READ) code recommended in 1979.

Kunt, M. "Source Coding of X-Ray Pictures." *IEEE Trans. on Biomedical Engineering*, vol. BME-25, no. 2, March 1978, pp. 121–138.

In this article, three different compression techniques are applied to a selection of x-ray pictures: synthetic highs, block coding of bit planes, and run-length coding of bit planes.

Moik, J. G. *Digital Processing of Remotely Sensed Images*. NASN SP-431, National Aeronautics and Space Administration, Washington, D.C., 1980.

In this book, Moik covers the following topics as applied to multispectral images: processing, restoration, enhancement, mosaicking, analysis, classification, and compression.

Musmann, H. G., and Preuss, D. "A Redundancy Reducing Facsimile Coding Scheme." *NTZ*, 1973, pp. 91–94.

In this article, an efficient run-length code is designed for two-level facsimile using two different length runs: one for white runs and one for black runs.

Musmann, H. G., and Preuss, D. "Comparison of Redundancy Reducing Codes for Facsimile Transmission of Documents." *IEEE Trans. on Comm.* vol. COM-25, no. 11, November 1977, pp. 1425–1433.

Codes for compression of two-level facsimile are compared: three codes for one-dimensional compression and three codes for two-dimensional compression.

Netravali, A. N., and Limb, J. O. "Picture Coding: A Review." *Proc. of the IEEE*, vol. 68, no. 3, March 1980, pp. 366–406.

This is a survey paper on picture coding, with a bibliography of 210 references.

Preuss, D. "Two Dimensional Facsimile Source Encoding Based on a Markov Model." *NTZ* vol. 28, October 1975. pp. 358–363.

A two-dimensional run-length code is designed in this article based on a Markov model for a two-level source.

Schreiber, W. F., Knapp, C. F., and Kay, N. D. "Synthetic Highs—An Experimental TV Bandwidth Reduction System." *Journal of the SMPTE*, vol. 68, August 1959, pp. 525–537.

In this paper, the concept of dividing a TV picture into a low-pass analog picture and a corresponding digital picture containing edge locations and amplitudes is introduced.

Stoffel, J. C., and Moreland, J. F. "A Survey of Electronic Techniques for Pictorial Image Reproduction." *IEEE Trans. on Comm.*, vol. COM-29, no. 12, December 1981, pp. 1898–1925.

Methods of digitizing half-tone pictures are described in detail.

Yamada. T. "Edge Difference Coding—A New, Efficient Redundancy Reduction Technique for Facsimile Signals." *IEEE Trans. on Comm.*, vol. COM-27, no. 8, August 1979, pp. 1210–1217.

The technique of edge difference coding (EDIC), in which the differences in the positions of corresponding edges in two successive scan lines are coded, is introduced.

Yamazaki, Y., Wakahara, Y., and Teramura, H. "Digital Facsimile 'QUICK FAX' Using a New Redundancy Technique." *National Telemetering Conference*, 1976.

The principle of relative address coding (RAC) is described for coding pairs of adjacent scan lines in two-level facsimile.

CHAPTER 17

Data Base Compression

17.1 INTRODUCTION

As the use of digital data increases, and the demand for wider use of it grows, data bases become larger and more of them are tied into digital computer networks. In such a situation, the need for data compression is manifested in the three parameters described in Chapter 1:

Storage volume
Transmission time
Transmission bandwidth

In this chapter, we are concerned with on-line data bases as opposed to data archives. Even though the cost of on-line storage is decreasing, the per unit cost of *storage volume* for on-line storage (such as disk) is still higher than that of an archival system (such as tape). Thus, data compression can still provide a real cost saving for an on-line system.

When an external user accesses a data base, he does so typically over a communications link. The capacity of this link is usually limited, so the *access time* may be unacceptably long. Compression can shorten the access time over the original link, thereby saving the cost of a broader bandwidth link—a link that would have been needed to achieve the same result without compression.

In this chapter we look at what has to be compressed in a data base, and at the different techniques that have been developed for data base compression.

17.2 WHAT IS A DATA BASE?

Before we look at compression techniques for a data base, we have to understand what it is we need to compress in a data base. In short, where is the redundancy in a data base, and what form does it take? To answer these questions, we have to understand the structure of a data base.

A data base can be defined in a number of different ways. In the literature, there are basically two ways of looking at a data base: *logically* and *physically*. The logical view of a data base depicts the logical interrelationships of the various data files from an overall standpoint (the so-called *schema*) or from a particular user's standpoint (the so-called *subschema*). The logical representation does not give a clear picture of where redundancy can be reduced or eliminated, simply because one schema can be implemented in more than one physical arrangement, each with a different form of redundancy. So we must look at the actual physical arrangement of the data base in order to find where compression should be applied. It has become standard practice to look at a physical data base as being composed of two parts: the *data files* (the actual data), and the *index* to these data files. In the following sections, we look at each of these parts (see Martin 1977 for a description of logical and physical data base structures).

17.2.1 Data Files

The term *data files* is not special—sometimes the terms *data records* or *data base* are used to mean the same thing, namely, the actual data that is stored in the data base. This data can be stored in many different ways. The simplest, and probably the least efficient for many applications, is a sequential arrangement by file. Each data file has a unique identification called the "key." By use of the key, we can find the data file (or record) no matter what the file arrangement.

In some specific applications, a data base is often used to find more than one item at a time. In many cases, a user is interested also in data items that may be related to the one he is seeking, but he is not sure *how* they are related, let alone *where* they are located. To fill this need, data base architecture usually contains not only data items with keys but also information about the interrelationships of these items. This information is usually in the form of short data entries called "pointers." The use of pointers allows data bases to be structured in different ways depending on the predominant form of the interrelationships. Three such structures are in use today: tree (or hierarchical) structure, network (or plex) structure, and relational structure.

In a *tree* (or *hierarchical*) *structure* the elements are connected in such a way that they give the appearance of an upside-down tree with the "root" at

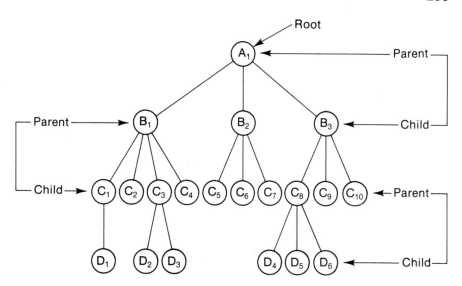

Figure 17.1 *A Data Base Tree Structure.*

the top (see Figure 17.1). Each element (the "child") can have only one connection to the level of elements (the "parents") above it.

The *network* (or *plex*) *structure* is somewhat similar to the tree structure except that a child can have more than one parent (see Figure 17.2).

In a *relational structure* all elements are arranged in tabular structure. Typically, one is working with subsets (selected columns) of the tabular

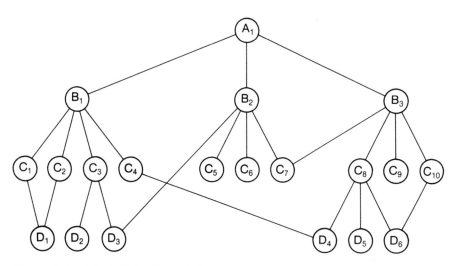

Figure 17.2 *A Data Base Network Structure.*

Employee	Name	Sex	DOB	EOD	Grade	Skill	Salary	Org. Code

— Entrance on Duty
— Date of Birth

Figure 17.3 *A Relational Data Base Structure.*

structure (see Figure 17.3). The relational structure is the newest of the three structures, and many new data base systems are using it.

17.2.2 Indices and Directories

If the data were stored in files, or records, with imbedded keys, a user would have to search through all the files or records to find the desired data item, and only if the keys were arranged sequentially could the length of a given search be predicted. Otherwise, the search could take an unpredictably long time. The use of an index relieves this problem.

An *index* is a table that takes a data record key as input (the "argument") and produces the record's physical location as output (the "function"). The procedure for finding the physical location of the record in question is called *addressing*. An index is usually searched in levels, starting with the highest level. A good analogy here is with using a card catalog found in a book library. If one is searching for a book by a certain author, one typically starts with the drawer containing the cards with the first letter of the author's last name (the highest level). Then the second, and possibly the third, letter of the author's last name are used to find the actual cards with that last name (the next-highest level). The author's first name is used at the next lower level to find all the cards of the correct author, and finally the name of the book (the lowest level) is used to find the index card of the correct book. On this index card we find the location (or address) of the book on the shelves—according to the Dewey Decimal or Library of Congress systems, for example. It is these steps through the various levels of indexing that can be compressed, as will be discussed in the next sections.

We saw in Section 17.2.1 that *pointers* imbedded in the records can be used to define the interrelationships between the various data records. This information can also be put into a separate table called a *directory*. An index can be used with a directory to provide a logical search since one can take advantage of the particular structure used. For example, in the case of a tree structure, the "child" would be reached through the "parent."

17.3 FILE COMPRESSION

File compression means the compression of the actual data in the data base, as opposed to the indices of that data. It is useful to separate actual data into two types for the purpose of data base compression: alphanumeric and nonalphanumeric. This dichotomy is useful because a large number of data bases contain alphanumeric data, and most of the work done on data base compression has focused on this kind of data. As we know from previous chapters in Part III, however, other kinds of data besides alphanumeric are candidates for on-line storage in a data base. Examples of these are digitized pictures and digitized telemetric measurements. The data base compression literature tends to ignore these other kinds of data, but let us look at them briefly before getting into the more common alphanumeric data.

17.3.1 Nonalphanumeric File Compression

In a typical nonalphanumeric data file, the data words do not represent alphanumeric characters, but instead quantized samples of some physical process (such as magnetic field measurements from a satellite) or some continuous data set (such as a natural or man-made picture). In most cases, we are dealing with slightly distorted data due to the limitations of the sampling and quantization processes.

Data associated with speech, telemetry, television, and pictures are good examples of nonalphanumeric data that might appear in a data base. Let us look at each of these areas. Why might speech be put into a data base? A possible application could be for speaker identification—identifying someone through use of the so-called *voice print* technique. Telemetric data in some cases comprise very large data bases, as in the case of scientific measurements made from a spacecraft with a multiyear lifetime. Also, medical measurements, such as ECG data, can be part of a medical data base. In videotex/teletext systems "still" pictures are stored and retrieved as required from a data base for TV display. And, finally, very large data sets resulting from high-resolution sampled-and-quantized pictures and computer graphics can be part of a data base.

All these cases involve a digitized representation of an analog data set, and in many cases this digital representation is highly redundant. Thus, for more efficient storage in the appropriate data base and/or more efficient use of a communications link compression techniques can be applied to these nonalphanumeric data sets.

An important difference exists between the user requirements for a nonalphanumeric data set as opposed to an alphanumeric data set, and that is the allowable distortion in the reconstructed data. In the case of alphanumeric data sets, absolutely *no* distortion is tolerable, but in the case of nonalphanumeric data sets, minimal distortion is sometimes tolerable, depending on the intended use of the data. This concept of an allowable distortion was discussed in Chapters 13 through 16.

17.3.2 Alphanumeric File Compression

Alphanumeric file compression must be distortion-free. There can be no errors or ambiguities in the reconstructed data records since each character is important. A single character error may produce catastrophic results, as in the case of financial transactions involving a data base.

Alphanumeric data includes text, numerical fields, computer program instructions, personnel data, stock inventories, financial accounts, and so on. In each case we are dealing with sets of alphanumeric characters, and the possibility of compression is obvious if we note that in the ASCII-8 code (American Standard Code for Information Interchange) only 95 combinations out of the possible 256 are used for noncontrol character representation.

Much of the literature that pertains to this section uses the term *text compression* and is also specifically aimed at the English language. Following are some of the methods of alphanumeric compression that have been proposed and in some cases actually tried. [See Held (1983).]

Compact Notation   Compact notation is also called "logical compression" and "minimum-bit compression." It takes advantage of the fact that in a given field each n-bit character word may *not* have meaningful values over the entire 2^n possible combinations. Thus, some characters can be coded with shorter fixed-length words, thereby providing a compression. The *date* field is usually given as an example, as follows:

Uncompressed Date: MMDDYY

where the month (M), day (D), and year (Y) are each expressed as two 8-bit characters, resulting in a 48-bit word for the date.

Compressed Date: MDY

where: M is a 4-bit word to encode 12 months

D is a 5-bit word to encode 31 days

Y is a 7-bit word to encode 100 years

resulting in a 16-bit word for the date—or a compression ratio of $3:1$. Obviously, we can shorten the Y word if we use a shorter span of years (4 bits for 10 years, for example). [See Alsberg (1975) for further examples of this kind of compression].*

Character Repeat Suppression   Character repeat suppression is a simple technique in which strings of repeating characters are replaced by what amounts to a run-length code. Usually a string is encoded with three characters: first, a special, unused character to indicate that a run-length code follows; second, the repeating character; and third, the number of times it repeats (for an 8-bit character, this can be up to 256 times). When zeros are suppressed, the technique is called null suppression. [See Ruth and Kreutzer (1972)].

Common Phrase Suppression   In many alphanumeric data files, certain patterns of characters appear very often—as words, abbreviations, or codes. Such patterns can be replaced in most cases by special single characters, thereby providing an appreciable compression ratio.

---

* Also see Young and Liu (1980) for a method of reducing the overhead required with this type of compression.

n-gram Coding   An *n*-gram is a pattern of contiguous characters (including spaces) that occurs with relatively high frequency. This is particularly true in English text, and various codes have been worked out for two characters (digram), three characters (trigram), and so on. [See Lea (1978), Rubin (1976), and Yannakoudakis et al. (1982).]

Dictionary Encoding   By using a dictionary of high-use words, one can compress text by assigning a code to each word in the dictionary. Also, by allowing for a spelling mode for the nondictionary words, one can use a relatively small (about 200 words) dictionary and share the 256 patterns of an 8-bit code between the dictionary and the characters to be used for spelling. [See Pike (1981).]

Huffman Coding   The Huffman code, which was discussed in Chapters 3 and 8, can, not surprisingly, be used efficiently to encode alphanumeric characters. This code can be used because the frequency distribution of the letters in most languages, especially English, is highly predictable. This allows an efficient Huffman code to be designed that may not have to be changed very often. [See Wells (1972) and Pechura (1982).]

An interesting data base compression software system that uses Huffman coding is:

SHRINK

Informatics, Inc.

Software Products

21050 Vanowen St.

Canoga Park, CA 91304

SHRINK is designed to run on an IBM system with IMS/VS. IMS is the IBM data base management system called Information Management System, which runs under the VS (Virtual System) operating system. SHRINK uses a Huffman code to encode each character, and the code can be changed to match the probability distribution of each file, if necessary. It achieves a compression ratio of about 2:1.

Binary Encoding   Binary coding can be applied at two levels in an alphanumeric file: at the bit level or at the character level. When the various ASCII characters are expressed as bit patterns, they often form a "low" density bit stream over a record or fraction of a record. "Low density" means a small number of 1s compared to the number of 0s. These low density or "sparse" bit patterns can be run-length encoded, as was described in Chapter 7.

Some techniques of alphanumeric file compression are basically *differential* in nature. Each succeeding record has two parts: a set of changed characters and a "bit map," which is a map of the record characters with only 1s and 0s—

the 1s showing where the changed characters belong (in order) and the 0s indicating no change from the original record.

Some theoretically based binary coding schemes have been developed in recent years (see Section 8.5) with an intended application to file compression, including computer program compression. Some examples of these techniques are: the Ziv–Lempel parsing scheme (1978), the arithmetic code of Langdon and Rissanen (1981), and the double-adaptive file compression code of Langdon and Rissanen (1983).

Storage Compaction   The arrangement of storage blocks in a data base so that all unused blocks are in a contiguous location is called *storage compaction* and the process of linking these blocks together is called *garbage collection*. If the storage medium were disk, such storage compaction would reduce the average retrieval time (see Horowitz and Sahni 1976).

17.4 INDEX COMPRESSION

In index compression, we gain not only a savings in storage volume for the index elements, but also a savings in access time. Since most indices are multi-level, it is necessary to compress at each level. There are three ways of doing this: rear-end key compression, front-end key compression, and key compression by parsing (Martin 1977).

In *rear-end key compression*, the right-hand side of the key at each level is truncated in such a way as to make an "argument" at that level a truncated version of the highest item in the corresponding "function" list at the next lower level (see Figure 17.4).

Front-end key compression reduces the redundancy in the first part (left-hand side) of the key. For example, if the key is a person's last name, an alphabetical arrangement of such keys has redundancy from key to key in the first few letters of each key. One method of reducing redundancy is to show repeated letters in successive keys by means of a number that is the count of the repeated letters. Note that front-end and rear-end compression may be used together (see Figure 17.5).

Key compression by parsing involves breaking up each key into pieces that correspond to arguments (or functions) at the various levels. One may imagine the whole key being synthesized as one goes through the various index levels (see Figure 17.6).

There may be some hesitation involved in the decision to key-compress the index to a data base since any errors or ambiguities introduced by the compression scheme could make the index useless and the data inaccessible. A fictional, and rather humorous, story based on such a catastrophe was written by Draper (1962).

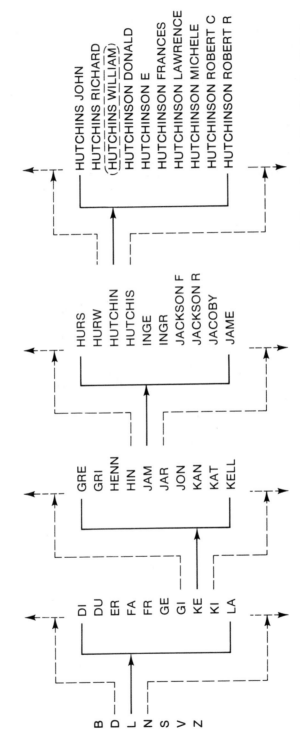

Figure 17.4 *An Example of Rear-End Key Compression. After: Martin, J. Computer Data Base Organization, Prentice-Hall, Inc., Englewood Cliffs, N.J. 1977, Second Edition.*

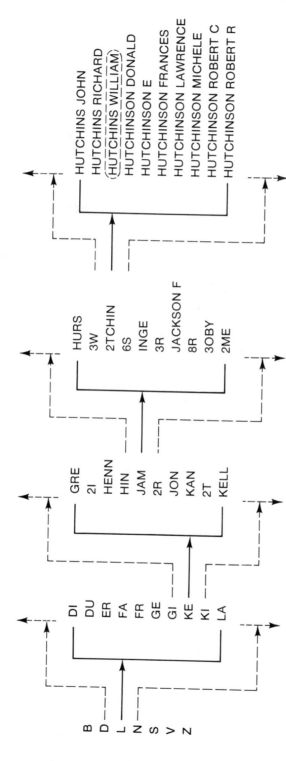

Figure 17.5 An Example of Front End/Rear End Key Compression. After: Martin, J. Computer Data Base Organization, Prentice-Hall, Inc., Englewood Cliffs, N.J. 1977, Second Edition.

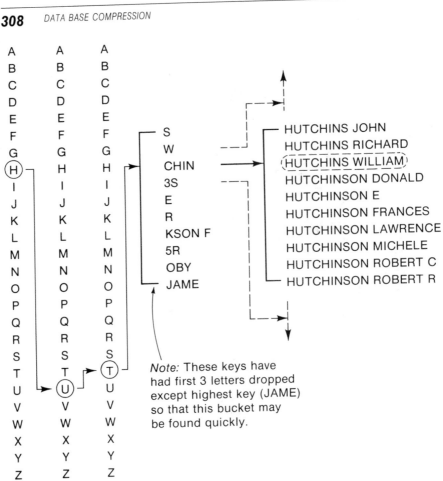

Note: These keys have had first 3 letters dropped except highest key (JAME) so that this bucket may be found quickly.

Figure 17.6 *An Example of Key Compression by Parsing. After: Martin, J. Computer Data Base Organization, Prentice-Hall, Inc., Englewood Cliffs, N.J. 1977, Second Edition.*

HIGHLIGHTS

- The growing size of, and access demand for, data bases has increased their need for data compression.
- Data base compression has advantages in lowering storage cost, shortening access time, and reducing the cost of transmission facilities.
- From a physical standpoint, a data base is composed of two parts: data files and the file index.
- Data files are identified by keys and interconnected by pointers.
- Pointers allow data bases to be structured in ways that make information searches easier and more efficient; three common structures are: the tree

(or hierarchical) structure, network (or plex) structure, and relational structure.

- File data can be divided into alphanumeric (including text, numerical fields, and so on) and nonalphanumeric (including speech, telemetric, television, and picture) data for purposes of compression.

- An index is a table that takes a data file's key as input and through the addressing process produces the file's physical location as output.

- Indices are compressed through rear-end key compression, front-end key compression, and key compression by parsing.

SUGGESTIONS FOR FURTHER READING

The following items are suggested for further reading and study:

Alsberg, P. "Space and Time Savings Through Large Data Base Compression and Dynamic Restructuring." *Proc. of IEEE*, vol. 63, no. 8, August 1975, pp. 1114–1122.

File compression is obtained by restructuring the data records, which are normally accessed together, into the same physical data file. Examples of four actual data base installations employing compression are given.

Draper, H. "MS FND IN A LBRY: or, the Day Civilization Collapsed." *Library Journal*, vol. 87, no. 5, March 1 1962, pp. 916–919.

This may well be the only science fiction story ever written about an indexing system. It describes how the original storehouse of all the world's knowledge is lost in a maze of indices when the computer-based search algorithm gets stuck in a loop.

Held, G. *Data Compression* New York: John Wiley & Sons, 1983.

This 126-page book gives descriptions and some implementation examples of alphanumeric file compression, especially for computer programs.

Horowitz, E. and Sahni, S. *Fundamentals of Data Structures*. Rockville, Md.: Computer Science Press, 1976.

This book covers the following data structure topics: arrays, stacks and queues, linked lists, trees, graphs, internal sorting, external sorting, symbol tables, and files.

Langdon, G., and Rissanen, J. "Compression of Black and White Images with Arithmetic Coding." *IEEE Trans on Comm.*, vol. COM-29, June 1981, pp. 858–867.

Arithmetic coding is applied to two-level images for the purpose of compression.

Langdon, G., and Rissanen, J. "A Double Adaptive File Compression Algorithm." *IEEE Trans. on Comm.*, vol. COM.-31, no. 11, November 1983, pp. 1253–1255.

A one-pass compression scheme is developed that assumes no statistical properties of the data source.

Lea, R. M. "Text Compression with an Associative Parallel Processor." *The Computer Journal*, vol. 21, no. 1, February 1978, pp. 45–56.

In this article, a hardware implementation of an *n*-gram coding scheme is described that utilizes an associative parallel processor, for an overall compression ratio of 2:1.

Martin, J. *Computer Data Base Organization.* 2d ed. Englewood Cliffs, N. J.: Prentice-Hall, 1977.

This book contains a comprehensive review of data base design concepts including compression. Chapter 29 covers index compression, and Chapter 32 covers file compression.

Pechura, M. "File Archival Techniques Using Data Compression." *Comm. of the ACM*, vol. 25, no. 9, September 1982, pp. 605–609.

Huffman coding of characters is used for file compression. This paper contains an annotated list of 11 references on file compression.

Pike, J. "Text Compression Using a 4-Bit Coding Scheme." *The Computer Journal*, vol. 24, no. 4, November 1981, pp. 324–330.

A combination of character encoding and common word coding is used to achieve a compression ratio of 2:1 in an 8-bit system.

Rubin, F. "Experiments in Text File Compression." *Comm. of the ACM*, vol. 19, no. 11, November 1976, pp. 617–623.

Variations on Huffman coding and n-gram coding are described for text compression, and it is explained that these techniques require a fairly high computation time.

Ruth, S., and Kreutzer, P. "Data Compression for Large Business Files." *Datamation*, vol. 18, no. 9, September 1972, pp. 62–66.

Comparisons are made of various alphanumeric file compression techniques including: null suppression, run-length coding, bit mapping, and Huffman coding. For a particular application example, Huffman coding of characters and character strings is found to be superior.

Wells, M. "File Compression Using Variable Length Encodings." *The Computer Journal*, vol. 15, no. 4, November 1972, pp. 308–313.

This paper addresses the application of Huffman coding to computer program files written in ALGOL, FORTRAN, and assembly language. It also describes a hardware-implemented tree-search algorithm for decoding a Huffman code.

Yannakoudakis, E., Goyal, P., and Huggill, J.A. "The Generation and Use of Text Fragments for Data Compression." *Info. Proc. and Mgt.*, vol. 18, no. 1, 1982, pp. 15–21.

An analysis of n-gram statistics in 31,369 bibliographic records is carried out for 2-grams to 8-grams.

Young, T., and Liu, P. "Overhead Storage Considerations and a Multilinear Method of Data File Compression." *IEEE Trans. on Software Engineering*, vol. SE-6, no. 4, July 1980, pp. 340–347.

A method of reducing the overhead imposed by the compression/decompression (C/D) table in a fixed-length minimum bit encoding scheme is described.

Ziv, J. and Lempel, A. See Chapter 8, Suggestions for Further Reading.

An Introduction to Error-Control Coding

A.1 ERROR-CONTROL CODING AND DATA COMPRESSION

In this appendix we look at error-control coding as an available method of controlling the effect of transmission errors on compressed data. These errors in data compression can be controlled in other ways—depending on the type of compression used. For example, in DPCM the *leak* is used to lessen the error propagation effect, and in delta modulation and transform coding there is an inherent "error averaging" effect. So error-control coding is incorporated when necessary and when the overall compression ratio is not seriously decreased. It has been said that data compression *removes natural redundancy*, which is of limited use for error control, and that error-control coding uses *artificial redundancy*, which is specifically designed for error control. On the surface, this would seem to be the preferred way to design almost any data system, but the two parameters of overall compression ratio and distortion, as discussed in Section 10.2, have to be examined before error-control coding is added.

This appendix is meant to serve as a very low-level introduction and topical review for readers who have little or no familiarity with error-control coding. It is not appropriate in this book to go in great detail into any of the subtopics covered here, but there are many books on the subject of error-control coding, and the reader is referred to the book by Lin (1970)* for an easy-to-read introduction to this topic.

A.2 TYPES OF ERROR-CONTROL CODES

There are basically two types of error-control codes: *block codes* and *convolutional codes*. Even though they are quite different in operation and performance, they have some common characteristics that are important from the standpoint of data compression.

Since in all error-control codes we are mapping k information digits into n code digits ($n > k$) to form an (n, k) code, there is a fundamental parameter called the code rate:

$$\text{Code rate} = \frac{k}{n} \qquad (A.2.1)$$

The code rate has obvious relevance to data compression since it acts as a multiplier of the noncoded compression ratio; thus,

$$\text{Overall compression ratio} = (R)\frac{k}{n} \qquad (A.2.2)$$

A high rate code, therefore (that is, $k/n \approx 1$) is desirable, and this then is an important factor in the choice of an error-control code for data compression.

Another characteristic of error-control codes is their error-detection and error-correction capability. Most codes can *detect* a certain number of errors but can correct only a smaller number of errors. In data compression applications, we are typically more interested in the code's error correction ability since errors in compressed data tend to propagate in the reconstructed data. A detected error still results in a propagated error region in the reconstructed data.

The number of errors a code can correct, t, is a function of the *minimum distance*, d, which is the minimum number of digits by which any two code words differ, and we have $d \geq 2t + 1$.

---

* S. Lin, *An Introduction to Error-Correcting Codes* (Englewood Cliffs, N.J.: Prentice-Hall, 1970). In this book the theory of error-control coding is outlined and the design and performance of block and convolutional codes is given.

Errors occur either in *random* digit positions or in adjacent digit positions. We call the latter *burst* errors. Different types of codes have been developed for these different types of errors. Obviously, the transmission channel determines which kind of errors exist or what mixture of the two kinds exists in a given system.

A.3 BLOCK CODES

Error-control coding has its own terminology and "famous names." The following is a brief review of block coding with enough introduction to names and terminology that the reader may approach the literature of error-control coding with some familiarity. We follow a format of numbered statements for simple reference, starting with the decoding of codes for correcting random errors:

1. *Maximum-likelihood decoding* is the basic decoding approach when all code words are equally likely. One computes the conditional probabilities of receiving the error-corrupted code word—given that each possible code word, in turn, was transmitted—and then picks the code word giving the highest probability. A knowledge of the transmission channel is necessary to perform this time-consuming operation, and one hopes that there is a faster, more reliable way—and there is, by means of something called the *syndrome*. We lead up to a definition of the syndrome in the following way.

2. The *generator matrix* G is used to generate each code word instead of using a large look-up table for code generation. If *m* is the original information word to be coded, then the code word is:

$$[v] = [m][G] \tag{A.3.1}$$

This is a matrix equation where *v* is a $n \times 1$ column matrix, *m* is a $1 \times k$ row matrix, and G is the $k \times n$ matrix. Now all we store is G and the necessary logic to implement the matrix multiplication in (A.3.1).

3. A *systematic code* is one in which each code word contains the original information word and the generated parity digits as follows:

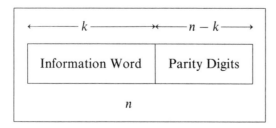

We can arrange the generator matrix for a systematic code to have the following structure:

$$[G] = [I_k P] \qquad (A.3.2)$$

where I is a $k \times k$ identity matrix (1s on the main diagonal, all other elements 0), and P is a $k \times (n - k)$ matrix. From this arrangement we obtain the parity check matrix.

4. The *parity check matrix* is defined as:

$$[H] = [P^T I_{n-k}] \qquad (A.3.3)$$

where P^T is the transpose of P in (A.3.2) and I_{n-k} is an $(n - k) \times (n - k)$ identity matrix. The parity check matrix allows us to compute the *syndrome*.

5. The *syndrome* is defined as

$$[S] = [r H^T] \qquad (A.3.4)$$

where r is the received code word equal to the sum of an error word and the original code word ($r = e + v$) and H^T is the transpose of the parity check matrix, H.

If no errors are made, the syndrome is zero, and if errors are made, we can find the location of the errors by means of the standard array method, by error trapping, or by majority-logic decoding.

6. The *standard array method* utilizes a matrix of n-tuples, arranged as shown in Figure A.1. The arrangement in this figure shows that the expected error patterns appear in the leftmost column, the so-called coset leaders. We can establish a one-to-one correspondence between the syndromes and the coset leaders, so that from the syndrome, we can find the error pattern in the word. This is basically a table look-up method, which can be replaced by a faster method called error trapping, which is particularly designed for cyclic codes.

Coset
Leader

000000	001110	010101	100011	011011	101101	110110	111000
000001	001111	010100	100010	011010	101100	110111	111001
000010	001100	010111	100001	011001	101111	110100	111010
000100	001010	010001	100111	011111	101001	110010	111100
001000	000110	011101	101011	010011	100101	111110	110000
010000	011110	000101	110011	001011	111101	100110	101000
100000	101110	110101	000011	111011	001101	010110	011000
001001	000111	011100	101010	010010	100100	111111	110001

Figure A.1 *Standard Array—for a (6, 3) code. From: Shu Lin, An Introduction to Error-Correcting Codes, © 1970, p. 50. Reprinted by permission of Prentice-Hall, Inc., Englewood Cliffs, N.J.*

7. A *cyclic code* is a code in which the digits in any code word can be end-around shifted to form another code word of the code. Cyclic codes have properties that make for efficient encoding and decoding using shift registers and simple logic circuits. An example of this is error trapping decoding.

8. *Error trapping decoding* makes use of the fact that when all the errors in an n-digit received code word are located in the $n - k$ parity bits, then the syndrome $(n - k)$-tuple equals the error $(n - k)$-tuple. This condition can be tested by using the fact that where the weight (the number of 1s) of the syndrome is equal to, or less than, t (the number of errors the code can correct) the errors are, in fact, in the $n - k$ parity check positions. When the errors are in a span of $n - k$ digits, but *not* in the parity check positions, then the syndrome weight test can be used to cyclically shift the received word until this test meets the above criterion. In the way the location of the errors can be found.

9. *Majority-logic decoding* is used for certain classes of block codes and especially for certain classes of cyclic codes. This type of coding is also referred to as *threshold decoding*, the name used by Massey (1963),[1] who unified the formulation of majority-logic decoding algorithms. In this type of decoding modulo 2 sums called parity check sums are formed (equal to 1 or 0) for each error digit, and a majority rule is used to determine whether the error digit is a 1 or a 0 (if there is a tie, the error digit is made 0).

Everything that has been mentioned so far has been for decoding of *random* errors. It is appropriate, before going on the burst-error correcting codes, to mention a few of the well-known random-error-correcting codes: the Hamming code, the Golay code, the BCH code, and the Reed-Solomon code.

10. The *Hamming code* is a *perfect* single-error-correcting code; that is, it is possible to form a standard array, as discussed in statement 6, with all possible single-error patterns as coset leaders. The Hamming family of codes is constructed as follows: For $m = n - k$, $n = 2^m - 1$.

11. The *Golay code* is the unique (23, 12) perfect code for correcting any combination of three or fewer random errors in 23 positions.

12. *BCH Codes* were developed by Hocquenghem in 1959 and independently by Bose and Chaudhuri in 1960.[2] They are very powerful, cyclic codes and are constructed as follows: To correct t errors, for a given m $(t < 2^{m-1})$, $n = 2^m - 1$ and $n - k \leq mt$. BCH codes are decoded by using the technique of representing the code digits as coefficients of a polynomial and carrying out algebraic operations with the polynomials. By such a technique, an error

---

[1] J. L. Massey, *Threshold Decoding* (Cambridge, Mass.: The M.I.T. Press, 1963).

[2] A. Hocquenghem, "Codes Correcteurs D'erreurs," *Chiffres*, vol. 2, 1959, pp. 147–156; R. C. Bose, and D. K. Ray-Chaudhuri, "On a class of Error Correcting Binary Group Codes," *Information and Control*, vol. 3, March 1960, pp. 68–79; R. C. Bose, and D. K. Ray-Chaudhuri, "Further Results on Error Correcting Binary Group Codes," *Information and Control*, vol. 3, September 1960, pp. 279–290.

location polynomial can be found, and the roots of this polynomial give the locations of the errors.

13. The *Reed-Solomon code* is a subclass of a nonbinary BCH code, more specifically, a q-ary code (q is a power of a prime number). This code is used in concatenation with other binary error-correcting codes for greater error control.

14. *Burst-error correcting codes* are special codes designed to correct bursts of errors as compared to random errors. An example of these codes are the Fire codes, which are cyclic codes. A more general technique for correcting burst errors is known as interlacing.

15. *Interlacing* is the technique of sending sequential bit planes from a block of λ code words so that burst errors will not affect adjacent digits in any one word. For example, if the number of code words interlaced, $\lambda = 3$, then we have the following transmission:

$$\text{Original block:} \begin{cases} a_1 a_2 a_3 \ldots a_n \\ b_1 b_2 b_3 \ldots b_n \\ c_1 c_2 c_3 \ldots c_n \end{cases}$$

Transmitted sequence: $a_1 b_1 c_1 a_2 b_2 c_2 a_3 b_3 c_3 \ldots a_n b_n c_n$

We can see from this simple example, that a burst error affecting three adjacent digits in the transmitted sequence will affect no more than one digit in each of the original words. Thus, if the original code can correct single errors, then in general, the interlaced code can correct bursts up to λ digits long. For an original code that can correct t random errors, the interlaced code can correct all combinations of t bursts of length λ or less. And finally, if the original code can correct brust errors of length l or less, then the interlaced code can correct any single burst of length λl or less. This allows the correction of long error bursts through the use of interlaced short-burst-error-correcting codes.

A.4 CONVOLUTIONAL CODES

Convolutional codes, discovered in 1955 by Elias,* are equal to or superior to block codes in many applications. They obtain their superior performance from the fact that the parity check digits are not functions of a short block of k information digits but rather of a longer span of information digits, called the *constraint length, K.* As a matter of fact, the concept of information words is

---

* P. Elias, "Coding for Noisy Channels," *IRE Convention Record*, Part 4, 1955, pp. 37–47.

no longer important since we are encoding a *stream* of information digits. We can illustrate the concept of a convolutional encoder by means of a simple, if not impractical, example. In this example the constraint length is short in order to simplify the illustration. In Figure A.2 a four-stage shift register allows the check bits to be computed as a function of up to four information bits (corresponding to a constraint length, K, of 4). As shown in the figure, for each information bit shifted into the encoder, three output bits are generated. This corresponds to a rate of one-third. In this particular encoder, it is noted that the first output bit is equal to the bit in the first stage of the register, whereas the other two output bits are modulo 2 sums of three or four stages of the register. The code in this example is called a *systematic code* because each information bit appears unchanged in the output bit stream. When this is not so, and each output bit is a function of more than one input bit, the code is called *nonsystematic*.

In Figure A.2 the output bit stream is shown for a 5-bit input bit stream or frame and corresponds to nine shifts through the shift register. That is, the

WHEN: $x = (1,0,1,1,0)$ (FOR L = 5)

$y = (111,\ 010,\ 100,\ 110,\ 001,\ 000,\ 011,\ 000,\ 000)$

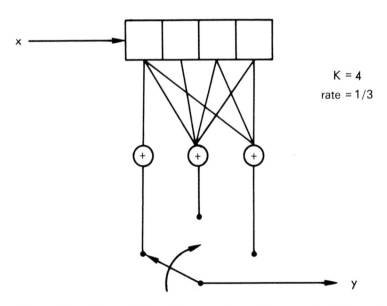

Figure A.2 *A Convolutional Encoder. From: Wozencraft, J. M., and Jacobs, I. M. Principles of Communication Engineering, p. 410. © John Wiley and Sons, Inc. 1965. Reprinted by permission of John Wiley & Sons, Inc. N.Y.*

first group of 3 output bits corresponds to the shift of the first input bit into the first stage, and the last group of 3 output bits corresponds to the shift of the last information bit out of the last stage. In this example, zeros are shifted into the shift register after the last input bit.

For a given encoder arrangement of the type shown in Figure. A.2 and a given input frame length, a *code tree* can be constructed. The code tree for the encoder shown in Figure A.2 is shown in Figure A.3. This code tree is a fundamental concept in convolutional codes, particularly in some of the decoding techniques. The tree shows the encoder output bits for each input, 1 or 0, at each tree node, corresponding to a shift through the shift register.

The code "tail" is the output bit sequence that results after the last information bit in the frame is shifted into the second, and subsequent stages of the shift register and finally out of the Kth stage. It is customary to load a sequence of zeros into the first stage of the shift register while the end of the information frame is being shifted through, although any known bit sequence may be used.

Decoding of convolutional codes usually utilizes one of two algorithms: the Fano algorithm or the Viterbi algorithm. Each is quite different from the other and each is appropriate for different applications.

The Fano[1] algorithm searches through the code tree for the path that has the best agreement in branch symbols with the received sequence of symbols. This agreement is tested by means of a *metric* that is a cumulative likelihood function computed at each branch for each symbol sequence. By means of an increasing threshold used for metric comparison, a wrong path choice can be discovered, and the process "backed up" and started on the more likely path. This very powerful feature leads to a variable computation time for the Fano algorithm, and for this reason, the Fano algorithm is not used in high data rate applications.

The Viterbi[2] algorithm computes a *likelihood function* for all paths at once and chooses the one with largest likelihood value. In order to save computation time, the Viterbi algorithm takes advantage of certain symmetries and repetitive structures in the code tree. Because of this feature, which transforms the code tree into a *code trellis*, the Viterbi algorithm can operate at higher data rates than the Fano algorithm.

---

[1] R. M. Fano, "A Heuristic Discussion of Probabilistic Decoding," *IEEE Trans. on Info. Theory*, IT-9, April 1963, pp 64–74.
[2] A. J. Viterbi, "Error Bounds for Convolutional Codes and an Asymptotically Optimum Decoding Algorithm," *IEEE Trans. on Info. Theory*, IT-13, Jan. 1967, pp. 260–269.

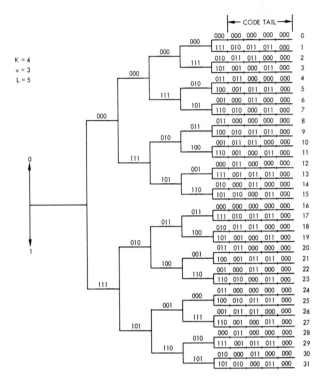

Figure A.3 *Convolutional Code Tree for the encoder in Figure A.2. From: Wozencraft, J. M., and Jacobs, I. M. Principles of Communication Engineering, p. 414. ©︎ John Wiley and Sons, Inc. 1965. Reprinted by permission of John Wiley & Sons, Inc. N.Y.*

APPENDIX B

Solutions to Problems

EXERCISE 2.1

Solution to Exercise 2.1   *Quantizing Error for Midriser Quantizer of Figure 2.4(b)*

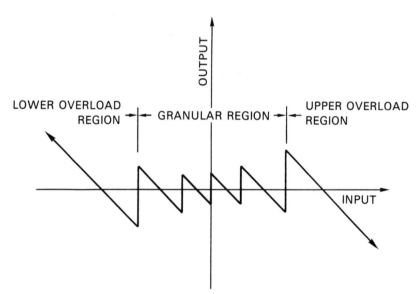

QUANTIZING ERROR FOR MIDRISER QUANTIZER

EXERCISE 3.1

a.

MESSAGE	PROBABILITY	INFORMATION
A	1/2	1 bit
B	1/4	2 bits
C	1/8	3 bits
D	1/16	4 bits
E	1/32	5 bits
F	1/64	6 bits
G	1/128	7 bits
H	1/128	7 bits

b. $H = -\sum_{i=1}^{M} P(i) \log_2 P(i)$

$= 1/2(1) + 1/4(2) + 1/8(3) + 1/16(4) + 1/32(5) + 1/64(6) + 1/128(7) + 1/128(7)$

$= 1\ 63/64$ bits

c. $P(i) = 1/8; H_{max} = \log_2 8 = 3$ bits

EXERCISE 3.2

a.

i	$P(i)$
A	1/2
B	1/4
C	1/8
D	1/8

$P(j/i)$ i \ j	A	B	C	D
A	1/2	1/2	0	0
B	1/4	1/2	1/4	0
C	1/8	1/8	1/2	1/4
D	0	1/2	0	1/2

$P(i, j)$ i \ j	A	B	C	D
A	1/4	1/4	0	0
B	1/16	1/8	1/16	0
C	1/64	1/64	1/16	1/32
D	0	1/16	0	1/16

$H(y/x) = -[1/4(-1) + 1/4(-1)$

$+ 1/16(-2) + 1/8(-1) + 1/16(-2)$

$+ 1/64(-3) + 1/64(-3) + 1/16(-1) + 1/32(-2)$

$+ 1/16(-1) + 1/16(-1)]$

$= 1\frac{7}{32}$ bits

b. For statistical independence:

$$H_{SI} = -[1/2(-1) + 1/4(-2) + 1/8(-3) + 1/8(-3)]$$
$$= 1\tfrac{3}{4} \text{ bits}$$

EXERCISE 3.3

For the source in Example 3.1:

$$\text{Redundancy} = \log_2 M - H$$

For the given Markov source:

$$\text{Redundancy} = 2 - 1\tfrac{5}{16} = \frac{11}{16}$$

For the statistically independent source:

$$\text{Redundancy} = 2 - 2 = 0$$

For the source in Exercise 3.2:

$$\text{Markov:} \quad \text{Redundancy} = 2 - 1\tfrac{7}{32} = \frac{25}{32}$$

$$\text{Statistically independent:} \quad \text{Redundancy} = 2 - 1\tfrac{3}{4} = \frac{1}{4}$$

EXERCISE 3.4

In Example 3.1:

$$\text{Markov:} \quad (H = 1\tfrac{5}{16})$$

$$R_{\max} = \frac{2}{1\tfrac{5}{16}} = \frac{32}{21} = 1.52$$

Statistically independent: $(H = 2)$

$$R_{\max} = \frac{2}{2} = 1$$

In Exercise 3.2:

$$\text{Markov:} \quad (H = 1\tfrac{7}{32})$$

$$R_{\max} = \frac{2}{1\tfrac{7}{32}} = \frac{64}{39} = 1.64$$

Statistically independent: $(H = 1\frac{3}{4})$

$$R_{\max} = \frac{2}{1\frac{3}{4}} = \frac{8}{7} = 1.14$$

EXERCISE 3.5

Shannon–Fano code

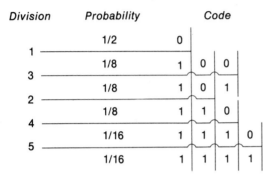

$H = -[1/2(-1) + 1/8(-3) + 1/8(-3) + 1/8(-3) + 1/16(-4) + 1/16(-4)]$
$\quad = 2\frac{1}{8}$ bits

$\bar{l} = 1/2(1) + 1/8(3) + 1/8(3) + 1/8(3) + 1/16(4) + 1/16(4)$
$\quad = 2\frac{1}{8}$ bits

Efficiency = 100%

Huffman Code

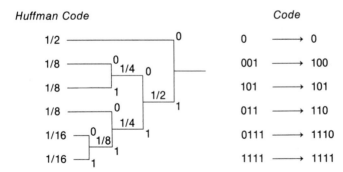

$\bar{l} = 2\frac{1}{8}$ bits

Efficiency = 100%

Glossary of Terms

Activity index A bit allocation measure used in adaptive transform coding that typically assigns more bits to those blocks with a higher activity index and vice-versa. Examples of activity indexes are the sum of squares of transformed samples and the sum of absolute values of transformed samples.

Adaptive delta modulation (ADM) A technique that minimizes the effects of slope overload and granular noise by changing the step size used to reconstruct the original signal.

Adaptive differential pulse code modulation (ADPCM) A technique that uses a combination of adaptive prediction and adaptive quantization. The latter includes: difference signal normalization, spatial masking, switched quantizers, and the reflected quantizer.

Adaptive predictive coding (APC) A speech compression technique based on an adaptive delta modulator that uses two adaptive predictors: one operating over a pitch period and one operating over several samples.

Adaptive transform coding Coding that, in general, involves the use of adaptive sampling, adaptive transformation, or adaptive quantization. When used for speech compression, adaptive transform coding is designated by its abbreviation, ATC, and specifically refers to a discrete linear transformation followed by an adaptive quantization/bit allocation scheme.

Amplitude-zone-time-epoch-coding (AZTEC) A first-order polynomial interpolator used for electrocardiogram (ECG) compression.

Average magnitude difference function (AMDF) A method of determining the pitch period of speech by monitoring the dips and nulls in the autocorrelation function of the speech signal.

BIFORE transform *Bi*nary *Fo*urier *Re*presentation; another name for the Walsh–Hadamard transform.

Binary nonconsecutive one code (BNO) A data compression time code that run-length codes the redundant samples with binary code words that do not contain consecutive ones. Discrimination words fit between these run-length codes and clusters of nonredundant samples; these words do contain consecutive ones that actually give a count of the number of nonredundant samples in the next cluster.

Binary sequence code   A code that maps a fixed-length sequence of two-valued symbols into a single binary word, with a 1 representing one value and a 0 the other value.

Binary source coding   Compression of the output of a binary source in such a way that the average code rate is less than one bit per symbol.

Bit stuffing   A procedure to prevent buffer underflow that operates by filling the buffer with dummy bits when it is about to underflow.

Block quantization   In general, the quantization of a block of samples at one time. More specifically, it is the optimization of the quantization of a block of transformed samples in transform coding so as to minimize the mean-square error between the original samples and the reconstructed samples.

Cepstral VOCODER   A speech compression technique that transmits voiced/ unvoiced signals and the Fourier transform of the logarithm of the speech signal for both pitch detection and speech synthesis.

Character repeat suppression   A database compression technique that run-length encodes repeating characters.

Chrominance signal   That part of a color television signal that contains the color information. It usually has two components, each of which is a function of one of the three color signals and the luminance signal.

Cluster coding   A scheme for compressing multispectral imagery data by collapsing the original bands into one feature band. Cluster coding also means a modified form of TNRS coding.

Codebook coding   A type of multipath search coding in which an n-sample sequence is quantized by selecting a best-matched n-sample sequence from a codebook of 2^n sequences. The selected sequence is then identified with an n-bit binary word.

Common phrase suppression   A database compression technique that codes frequently occurring patterns of words with special short codes.

Compact notation   A database compression technique that codes a given field with only enough bits to cover the range of that field.

Companding   A form of quantization in which the input data is operated on by a nonlinear function before being uniformly quantized. It is used primarily for speech signals.

Component signal coding   A method of color television compression in which the luminance and chrominance signals are compressed separately.

Composite signal coding   A method of color television compression in which the composite signal, made up of the luminance and chrominance signals together, is sampled at some multiple of the color component subcarrier frequency and then compressed.

Compression ratio: The ratio of the total number of bits in a block before compression to the total number of bits in the same block after compression.

Constant area quantization (CAQ) A variation of continuously variable slope delta modulation (CVSD) in which an increment is added to the predicted signal as follows: If the difference signal is outside $\pm A$, then $\pm A$ is added; if the difference signal is inside $\pm A$, then $\pm \frac{1}{2} A$ is added.

Continuously variable slope delta modulator (CVSD) An adaptive delta modulator that adds a large increment to the step size when three identical output levels occur sequentially, and adds a small increment if otherwise. The speed of adaptation is controlled by an attenuator in the predictor loop.

Correlation VOCODER A speech compression system that transmits voiced/unvoiced and pitch signals along with samples of the autocorrelation function of the speech signal.

Data compaction Another name for data compression.

Data compression The reduction of the amount of signal space that must be allocated to a given message or data set.

Data record key The identifying code for a given data record that is searched to find that record in a database.

Delta modulation (DM) A type of predictive coding in which the difference between the predicted sample value and the actual sample value is mapped into one of two levels, depending upon the sign of the difference.

Dictionary encoding A database compression technique in which frequently occurring words are placed in a dictionary and coded with a fixed-length code.

Differential pulse code modulation (DPCM) A type of predictive coding in which the difference between a predicted sample value and the actual sample value is quantized with a quantizer that is optimized for the difference signal.

Directory A separate table in a database that contains the pointers.

Discrete Fourier transform (DFT) A transformation that operates on a sequence of data samples with a transformation matrix composed of discrete values of sinusoidal functions.

Dithering A television compression technique in which the same pseudo-random noise is added to the analog signal before quantization at the transmitter and subtracted from the analog signal produced by the digital-to-analog converter at the receiver. This permits fewer quantizing levels to be used with little or no increase in visual distortion.

Edge busyness A type of distortion that results when DPCM is applied to television. It manifests itself as a visually noticeable jitter in those parts of the image that have high-contrast edges.

Edge difference code (EDIC) A facsimile compression technique that codes the locations of changing pixels on two successive scan lines.

Entropy The average information available from a data source.

Entropy coding Another name for optimum source encoding.

Entropy reduction Another name for irreversible data compression.

Enumerative code A source code that uniquely ranks different binary sequences.

Fan algorithm Another name for the first-order polynomial interpolator.

Fidelity-reducing coding Another name for irreversible data compression.

Formant A peak in the spectral envelope of the voiced speech signal. It is sometimes called a resonance.

Formant VOCODER A speech compression technique that transmits voiced/unvoiced and pitch signals along with the frequencies and amplitudes of the formants of the speech signal.

Frame replenishment A type of interframe coding for television in which a pixel that does not change is not transmitted but is repeated in the next frame at the receiver. A pixel that does change is replenished in the next frame at the receiver by the increment of change, which is transmitted.

Front-end key compression A method of database index compression by which the left-hand side of the key is compressed by various techniques. One common technique is to replace repeating letters from key to key by a number count of those letters.

Granular noise A type of distortion in predictive coding caused by positive and negative-level quantization of random perturbations around the zero difference region.

Gray code A type of binary code in which only one bit position changes from one code word to the next.

Haar transform A linear transformation that uses samples of the Haar orthonormal functions as elements. These functions can be thought of as rectangular waveforms of amplitudes 0, 1, -1—all multiplied by different powers of $\sqrt{2}$.

Hadamard transform A linear transformation whose elements are either 1 or -1.

Hierarchical structure Another name for a tree structure in a database.

Homomorphic VOCODER Another name for cepstral VOCODER.

Huffman code An optimum source code in the sense that it produces the minimum average code word length for a given discrete source probability distribution. When the source probabilities are negative powers of 2, the average word length equals the entropy of the source.

Hybrid coding A concatenation of transform coding and DPCM.

Index argument The higher level key at any point in an index search, which search proceeds from the higher to the lower key all along the search.

Index function The lower level key at any point in an index search, which search proceeds from the higher to the lower key all along the search. At the lowest level of the search, this index function provides the address of the item being searched.

Information Of an event, the negative logarithm of the probability of occurrence of the event.

Interframe coding The compression of television on a frame-to-frame basis.

Intraframe coding The compression of television on a single-frame basis.

Karhunen–Loève transform (KL) The continuous version of the principal component transform.

Key compression by parsing An index compression technique that breaks up each key into letters, with each successive letter representing a progressively lower level in the index search.

Leak An attenuator inserted into the predictor loop of a DPCM system to shorten the time duration effect of a transmission error on the reconstructed signal.

Linear predictive coding (LPC) A type of speech compression in which the speech production mechanism is modeled as a discrete, time-varying, linear, recursive filter. This filter is further modeled by an adaptive linear predictor in a positive feedback loop. The LPC encoder then transmits voiced/unvoiced, pitch and gain signals, along with information about the linear predictor coefficients for synthesis of the speech signal at the receiving end.

Log area ratio The logarithm of a ratio of areas of the vocal tract from a theoretical model used in LPC analysis. It can also be equated to a function of the partial correlation coefficients (PARCOR).

Logical compression Another name for compact notation in database compression.

Luminance signal That part of the color television signal that contains all three colors, as a weighted sum of their amplitudes.

Lynch–Davisson code (LD) A binary source code that codes a fixed-length binary sequence into a two-part code word: the first part is the number of 1s in the sequence; the second part is a unique ranking number that identifies the particular sequence.

Motion compensation A type of interframe coding for television in which the image is regarded as the superposition of moving pixels on a stationary background. Sufficient information is transmitted so that at the receiving end the stationary part can be repeated and the moving pixels can be projected along predicted trajectories.

Multipath search coding A type of both block and sequential quantization in which blocks or subblocks of samples are quantized by using information from previous and future samples.

n-gram coding A database compression technique in which frequently occurring patterns of contiguous characters (including spaces) are coded with special codes.

Network structure A database architecture that is similar to a tree structure, except that a given element can have more than one connection to the elements above it.

Noiseless coding Another name for reversible data compression.

Nonredundant sample A sample that cannot be predicted within a given error tolerance.

Nonredundant sample coding A compression technique that classifies samples as redundant or nonredundant according to some preselected prediction algorithm, and then transmits only the nonredundant samples with appropriate timing information.

Optimum source encoding The block-to-variable-length coding of a statistically independent source that makes the average word length approach, or equal, the source entropy.

Orthogonal function VOCODER A speech compression technique that transmits voiced/unvoiced and pitch signals along with a weighted sum of orthogonal functions of the speech signal.

Orthonormal functions Functions that belong to a set of functions that have the following property: The integral of the product of any two different functions is 0, and the integral of the square of any given function is 1.

PARCOR algorithm A method of finding the linear predictor coefficients in an LPC system by means of *par*tial *cor*relation coefficients.

Pitch period The repetition period of pulses in voiced speech.

Pitch predictive DPCM (PPDPCM) A DPCM system designed for speech compression that employs two predictors: a long-term adaptive predictor that operates typically over a pitch period, and a short-term fixed predictor that operates over a few samples.

Plex structure Another name for network structure in a database.

Pointers Short entries in a database that show the interrelationships among the elements of the database.

Polynomial interpolator A nonredundant sample coding technique that predicts the next sample to lie on an nth-order polynomial defined by $n + 1$ previous samples and with a tolerance set by a variable aperture. The most used form is the first-order interpolator, sometimes called the fan algorithm.

Polynomial predictor A nonredundant sample coding technique that predicts the next sample to lie an nth-order polynomial defined by $n + 1$ previous samples and with a tolerance set by a fixed aperture. The two most used forms are the zero-order and first-order predictors.

Predictive coding A form of sequential quantization in which the difference between the next sample and its predicted value is quantized. Predictive coding includes delta modulation and DPCM.

Predictive differential quantizer code (PDQ) A line-to-line version of DPCM for facsimile.

Prefix code A set of variable-length binary code words with bit arrangements such that no word is also the first part, or prefix, of a longer word. Prefix codes are also called instantaneously decodable codes. The Huffman code and the Shannon–Fano code are prefix codes.

Principal component transform A linear transformation whose columns are the normalized eigenvectors of the covariance matrix of the original data samples.

Pseudorandom scanning A television compression technique in which a changing random pattern is used to select pixels from each scan line for transmission. The same pattern is used at the receiver to locate the transmitted pixels, and the net result is a slower scan rate without noticeable flicker.

Quantization The representation of amplitude values from a continuous source by a finite set of levels, where each level represents all the continuous values in a related amplitude interval.

Rate distortion function The minimum average source rate, $R(D)$, in bits per sample, that guarantees that the average distortion will be no greater than the given value, D.

Rear-end key compression A method of database index compression in which the right-hand side of the key at each level is truncated in such a way as to make an index argument at that level a truncated version of the highest key in the corresponding index function list at the next lower level.

Redundancy Of an M-level source with entropy H that is binary coded with $\log_2 M$ bits is defined as: $\log_2 M - H$.

Redundancy reduction Another name for reversible data compression.

Redundant sample A sample that can be predicted within a given error tolerance.

Reflection coefficient The coefficient of reflection in a theoretical model of the vocal tract used in LPC analysis that consists of a concatenation of lossless tubes of different areas.

Relational structure A type of database architecture in which all elements are arranged in a tabular form.

Relative address code (RAC) A facsimile compression technique that codes distances between changing pixels on two adjacent scan lines.

Relative element address designate code (READ)   A two-dimensional facsimile compression technique in which the position of each changing pixel in a scan line is coded relative to either the position of a corresponding changing pixel on the previous line or the preceding changing pixel on the same line.

Roberts coding   Another name for dithering.

Run-length coding   A version of the zero-order predictor in which the timing information is sent in the form of the run lengths of the redundant samples.

SAMPLEDOT   A form of pseudorandom scanning developed by the General Electric Company.

Scalar quantization   Another name for zero-memory quantization.

Schema   The logical arrangement of a database from an overall standpoint.

Sequence time code   A time code that codes an entire sequence of time tags for nonredundant samples into a single code word.

Sequential quantization   Any method that quantizes one or more samples using stored information from previous, or previous and future, samples.

Shannon–Fano code   An optimum source code that produces an average code word length equal to the entropy when the source probabilities are negative powers of 2.

Side information   Additional information sent along with data compressed by an adaptive algorithm that indicates the mode of the adaptive algorithm.

Slant transform   A television compression technique that uses a transformation with elements that are samples of ramplike waveforms.

Slope overload   A type of distortion in predictive coding that is due to the inability of the reconstructed waveform to keep up with steep slope regions in the original waveform.

Slow scan   A method of television compression in which a single frame is slowly scanned to allow transmission over a narrowband channel.

Source coding   The information theoretic name for data compression.

Statistical predictor   A type of nonredundant sample coding technique that predicts the next sample using a function (usually linear) of a fixed number of previous samples. This function is adapted to the statistical behavior of the previous samples.

Subband coding (SBC)   A type of speech compression in the frequency domain in which the speech spectrum is first divided into a fixed number of bands, whereupon each band is shifted to zero frequency, sampled, and companded. At the receiving end, each sample is modulated back to its original spectral position to provide the output speech signal.

Subschema   The logical arrangement of a database from the standpoint of one particular application of the database.

Switched quantizer   A quantizer that provides adaptive quantization in DPCM by tracking the input waveform and appropriately switching among two or more fixed quantizers.

Syllabic adaptation   Any type of adaptive speech compression technique that operates over one or more pitch periods, which time interval usually corresponds to a syllable.

Synthetic highs   A picture compression technique that first filters the picture into a low-pass image and a high-pass image and then codes the low-pass image with fewer bits than the high-pass image.

Teletext   A one-way system for providing selected graphic displays on home TV sets. The viewer's picture selection is stored in a special decoder in the TV set, which then displays the picture when it is received and decoded from the vertical blanking interval of the TV signal.

Threshold quantization   A method of sample selection in transform coding in which those transformed samples that fall above a threshold are quantized, and those that fall below the threshold are set to zero.

Time of nonredundant sample code (TNRS)   A time code that sends the time of each nonredundant sample.

Traffic intensity   The ratio of the input rate to the output rate of a data buffer.

Transform coding   A type of block quantization in which the original correlated analog samples in a block are first decorrelated by a linear transformation and then optimally quantized.

Tree structure   A type of database architecture in which the elements are connected in a top-down fashion in such a way that a given element has only one direct connection to the elements above it.

Turning point algorithm (TP)   A waveform technique that is used for compressing electrocardiogram (ECG) signals by subsampling the digitized signal and preserving the important peaks and valleys of the ECG waveform.

Universal code   A block source code that is designed without knowledge of the source statistics but that converges in performance to a block source code designed with knowledge of the source statistics, as the block length approaches infinity.

Unvoiced sound   That portion of the speech waveform produced by air passing through constrictions in the vocal tract. This part of the speech waveform is noiselike in appearance.

Variable speech control (VSC)   A speech compression technique that deletes every other pitch period from recorded speech played back at double speed. The remaining pitch periods are then stretched to fill in the time gaps and the resulting waveform is an understandable replica of the original speech, lasting half the time of the original. A commercial version of VSC is marketed by the VSC Company, San Francisco, CA.

Vector quantization   Another name for block quantization—more specifically, another name for codebook coding.

Videotex   A two-way system for providing selected graphic displays on home TV sets. The viewer's picture selection is coded and sent over a telephone line to a central database that in turn sends back the selected picture suitably coded, over the same telephone line, to the viewer's TV set.

VOCODER   An abbreviation for *voice coder*; it includes any speech compression technique in which parameters of the speech signal, such as pitch, voiced/unvoiced, and spectral envelope descriptors are transmitted for use in synthesizing a facsimile of the original speech at the receiving end.

Voice coding   A class of speech compression techniques in which the original speech signal is analyzed into a set of preselected parameters that are then used at the receiving end to create a facsimile of the original speech signal, using a model of the speech production mechanism.

Voiced sound   That portion of the speech waveform produced by the quasi-periodic action of the vocal cords. This part of the speech waveform has a periodic appearance.

Walsh–Hadamard transform (WHT)   A linear transformation whose elements are samples of Walsh functions (with levels of $+1$ or -1), arranged by rows as a Hadamard matrix.

Waveform coding   A class of speech compression techniques in which the speech waveform in the time or frequency domains is coded so that the original speech may be reconstructed at the receiving end with minimal distortion.

Zero-memory quantization   Any method that quantizes samples independently of past and future samples, with the same quantizer for all samples.

Zonal quantization   A method of sample selection in transform coding in which those samples that fall within a specified zone in the transform domain are quantized, and those that fall outside are set to zero.

Author Index

Note: Bold face numbers indicate those pages on which the author's name appears in a citation.

Subject Index